Modern Swahili

Grammar

Modern Swahili Grammar

M. A. Mohammed

EAST AFRICAN EDUCATIONAL PUBLISHERS
Nairobi • Kampala • Dar es Salaam

Published by
East African Educational Publishers Ltd.
Brick Court, Mpaka Road/Woodvale Grove
Westlands, P.O. Box 45314, Nairobi

East African Educational Publishers Ltd.
P.O. Box 11542, Kampala

Ujuzi Educational Publishers Ltd.
P.O. Box 31647, Kijito-Nyama, Dar es Salaam

First published 2001

ISBN 9966-46-761-0
ISBN-13: 978-9966-46-761-4

Printed by Lightning Source

Contents

Foreword   *ix*

Preface   *xi*

Acknowledgements   *xii*

Introduction   *xiii*

Symbols and technical conventions   *xix*

1   Swahili Phonology   **1**
    Vowels   1
    Consonants   3
    Stress   12
    Intonation   13
    Morphophonemic changes   20

2   Word Formation in Swahili   **26**
    Inflection   26
    Derivation   29
    Morphemes   36

3   Noun Classes   **40**
    Double class membership   47

4   Nouns and Prefixes   **53**
    Adjectives prefixes   53
    Subject prefixes   58
    Object prefixes   60

5   Adjectives   **63**
    Agreement of adjectives   63
    Types of adjectives   66

**6   Verbs I: The Infinitive Form, the Imperative
and the Subjective**   **71**
    Kinds of verbs   71
    The imperative   72
    The subjective   75

7   Verbs II: Full Verbs, Auxiliary Verbs and Copular Verbs   **80**
    Full verbs   80
    Auxiliary verbs   80
    Copular verb   85

8	**Adverbs**	**93**
	Adverbs and other word classes	95
	Types of adverbs	96

9	**Prepositions and Conjunctions**	**100**
	Simple prepositions	100
	Example prepositions	100
	Complex prepositions	102
	Conjunctions	103

10	**Pronouns and Pronominalization**	**108**
	Types of pronouns	108
	Emphasis of pronouns	113
	Pronominalization	114
	Constraints in pronominalization	115

11	**Interjections**	**118**
	Terms that are essentially interjections	118
	Terms sometimes used as interjections	119

12	**Tenses I: Present Tense, the -a- Tense Marker and Simple Past Tense**	**122**
	Present verb tense	122
	The -A- tense marker	124
	Simple past tense (-LI- or -ALI-)	127

13	**Tenses II: Present Perfect Tense and Future Tense**	**131**
	Present perfect tense (-ME-)	131
	The future tense	134

14	**Tenses III: The Habitual hu- and Negative Tenses**	**137**
	The negative HU- tense	139
	Negative tenses	141
	The negative future	145
	The negative past	148
	The -JA- tense	151
	The -KI- and -SIPO- tenses	154
	The -KA- tense	159

15	**Tenses IV: NGE, NGALI and NGELI Tenses**	**165**
	NGE tense	165
	NGALI tense	166
	NGELI tense	167

16 Demonstratives of Reference   172
    Demonstrative of proximity   172
    Emphatic forms   174
    Recent findings on demostrative forms   175

17 Relatives I: Tensed Relatives   177
    Tensed relatives   177
    Amba   180
    Tenseless relatives   181
    Funtional definition of relative clauses   182
    Multiple uses of relative clauses   183
    Constraints in relative clauses   185
    Pseudo-cleft and cleft contructions   186
    The negative relative clauses   187

18 Relatives II: Relative of Time, Manner and Place   191
    Relative of time   191
    Relative of manner   191
    Syntactic position of the relative clause   192
    Relative of place   194

19 Relatives III: The Relative with the Verb
    "to be" and "to have" ("kuwa")   196
    Present negative   197
    The verb "kuwa"   198
    The relative with the verb "to have"   200
    The relative with the object   202
    "To have" in non-relative contruction   202

20 Derivative Verbs   205
    The passive verb   205
    The prepositional verb   209
    The stative   212
    The carsative form   215
    The reciprocal verb   217
    Other derivative verbs   219
    Reduplication   220

21 The Group   221
    Nominal groups   221
    Verbal groups   223
    Adverbial groups   224

22   The Clause   **227**
    Subject   227
    Predicator   228
    Complement   229
    Adjunct   230
    Kinds of clauses   231

23   The Sentence   **244**
    Simple sentences   244
    Complex sentences   245
    Subordination   245
    Compound sentences   248
    Interdependent constructions   249
    Appositional contrustions   249

References   253

Vocabulary   257

Index   267

Foreword

Modern Swahili Grammar is an important contribution to the study of Swahili grammatical structure from both pedagogical and linguistic perspectives. It studies aspects of Swahili phonology, morphology and syntax in great detail, thus shedding light on many aspects of the language structure.

Chapter 1 on Swahili phonology explores general phonological concepts and how they apply to Swahili. Effective descriptions of Swahili consonants, vowels, consonantal clusters, the syllable, and such suprasegmental features as stress, pitch, juncture and intonation are given. Morphophonemic phenomena involving consonants and vowels, including vowel harmony, are well explained. The chapter ends with practice exercises.

Chapters 2 to 4 deal with word-formation rules in Swahili. Morphological structures of the nominal and pronominal forms are described with ample illustration. Chapter 5 discusses various adjectival forms, with possessive, numerical, demonstrative and interrogative forms included. Chapter 6 describes the morphological structures of such verb forms as the infinitive, imperative and subjunctive.

Chapter 7 looks at lexical, auxiliary and copular verbs, again from a morphological viewpoint. Chapter 8 explains the use of adverbs while Chapter 9 deals with prepositions and conjunctions. Pronouns and the whole process of pronominalization are dealt with in detail in Chapter 10.

Chapter 11 looks at interjections. Chapters 12 to 15 describe the various verb tenses in Swahili and the morphological elements that indicate them. What other grammarians would treat separately as aspects, this book subsumes under tense. Demonstratives are described in Chapter 16 while the use of relatives is analyzed morphologically in Chapters 17 to 19. Chapter 20 describes verbal derivation, namely the structural and semantic functions of suffixes that form verbal extensions.

Chapters 21 and 23 deal with Swahili syntax using an earlier version of the Hallidayian system — structural grammar. The structure of groups, clauses and sentences is discussed in detail in these last chapters.

The author of *Modern Swahili Grammar* has successfully attempted to describe various aspects of the grammar of the Swahili language, covering the three descriptive levels of phonology, morphology and syntax, in one volume, something that has not been done in such detail before in a pedagogical grammar of the language. Semantic features are subsumed wherever relevant within these structural levels.

This book is an important contribution to the study of Swahili grammar, not only for pedagogical purposes, but also for purely linguistic interest. It is highly recommended as an important reference for students of linguistics.

Professor M.A.H. Abdulaziz
University of Nairobi
February, 2000.

Preface

This book covers almost all areas of Swahili grammar. These include affixes, derivation, inflection, parts of speech, relatives, tenses, demonstrative of reference, pronominalization, phrases, clauses and sentences. It can therefore be used independently as a textbook or alongside other textbooks on the same subject.

The book has been prompted by the desire to advance the works of previous grammars in light of recent findings. Strictly speaking, I have found that previous grammars have many flaws. For example, they have contended many times that the prefix *ki-* functions as a dimunitive marker. I don't dispute with this contention, but I have also argued that apart from the dimunitive function, it can also operate as an augmentative marker. In some cases, I have given examples where the prefix *ki-* gives a neutral meaning, that is, without emphasising the notions of being dimunitive or augmentative.

It is my strong view that this book will prove useful to readers in different fields. First is the student at a university or teacher training college who is past the beginning stages of his study and wishes to have a concise and general picture of the language and its setting. Second, is specialist in Swahili grammar. And third, is the area specialist such as sociologist, who would like to know basic linguistics or socio-linguistic facts about a given area.

In conclusion, I would like to welcome any criticisms from scholars and the general public. It is my hope that their constructive criticisms will improve this book qualitatively and quantitatively.

Prof. Mohamed A. Mohamed
May 2000

Acknowledgements

I would like to express my sincere thanks to Professor M.H. Abdulaziz of the University of Nairobi for reading through this book, and giving me useful suggestions. I am also indebted to Professor D. Massamba of the Institute of Kiswahili Research, University of Dar es Salaam, and Prof. A. Nchimbi of Moi University for reading some chapters of the book and giving me concrete suggestions. Finally, my thanks go to the three typists: Margaret W. Ngigi, J. Cherop and Mildred Oketch who spent long hours typing the book.

Introduction

Swahili is among the most well-known and important languages in Africa. It belongs to the vast family of Bantu languages and is spoken as a first language by approximately one million people.

Swahili has borrowed words from such sources as English, Arabic, Persian, Indian languages, Portuguese, German and even from other Bantu languages. No language can be expected to remain classically pure. As *Zawawi (1974)* explains, "No two languages came into contact without having influence upon each other. It is as a result of contact that Swahili has, in its lexicon, an extensive number of words that can be traced back to other languages."

The important thing to remember here is that when foreign words are passed into the Swahili language, they tend to become fully "Swahilized" in their phonological form and are no longer "foreign". *Perrot (1973)* accepts this view and points out that "Swahili is a Bantu language which has incorporated words from many other sources and so "Bantuized" them that even the speakers do not recognize that they are foreign words." Fundamentally, the structure of the language remains Bantu, despite this mass borrowing of words from other languages.

It was first written in Arabic characters and, more recently, in Roman. It has an abundant repertoire of poetic tradition extending back some three centuries. Poetry today is still highly esteemed by the Waswahili. Many newspapers carry poetry work contributed by Swahili speakers. In addition, Swahili poems are regularly broadcast in local radio stations in Tanzania and Kenya.

Characteristics of the Language

Like some other Bantu languages, Swahili has a derivational system, whereby suffixes can be added to the original stem in order to express an agent, state of a thing and totality. A word like **ongoza** (lead) can become **uongozi** (leadership), **kiongozi** (leader), **maongozi** (direction) and **mwongozo** (guideline).

Another method of illustrating the derivational system is by adding a suffix or suffixes in a specific order. Thus a word like **cheza** (play) has the passive form **chezwa** (be played), the causative form **chezesha**, the applicative form **chezea**, the reciprocal form **chezeana** and the stative form **chezeka**.

The language is also characterized by concordial agreement. The noun, or pronoun, is considered to govern the agreement of all other words that are associated with it syntactically. This agreement indicates person, gender and number and is signalled by concordial prefixes. For example, the following sentence shows how the concept of agreement operates in Swahili:

Mti mrefu ule umeanguka leo.
That tall tree has fallen down today.

In the above example, all the concordial prefixes are underlined. As can be seen, it is the noun which governs the selection of concordial prefixes. Each concordial prefix is determined by the class of its noun. Altogether, there are eighteen classes as illustrated later in this book.

Furthermore, as Swahili has the characteristics of a Bantu language, it possesses the complexity of the verbal system. The verbal root itself does not change. It contains various components affixed to it, and these are subject to change. This means that the Swahili verb is best characterized as agglutinative in nature. The nucleus is the root, to which a number of morphemes can be affixed. For example:

Ninawaheshimu sana.
I respect them a lot.

In this sentence, ni is the subject prefix indicating first person singular; the particle na is the tense marker for present; wa is the pronoun functioning as a direct object (in this case second person plural); and heshimu (respect) is the verb stem. As a matter of fact, the construction ninawaheshimu (I respect them) can be regarded as a complete sentence since it contains subject, verb and object.(SVO)

History of Swahili

The earliest forms of the Swahili language are unknown. *Zawawi (1974)* reveals that the first elements of the Swahili language appeared before the advent of the *Periplus* of the first century. Over the following centuries, Swahili expanded as a result of contact with Arab, Portuguese, Indian, British and German traders and colonizers (*Whitely, 1969*). According to *Polomé (1967)*, by the second half of the 15th century, Swahili had become a well-established language.

Once Swahili was well established along the trade routes, European missionaries played a prominent role in encouraging its use. Some of these missionaries attempted to produce dictionaries and grammars. Others used Swahili as a *lingua franca*. The efforts to promote Swahili by the missionaries can be further explained by the fact that the Universities Mission to Central Africa (U.M.C.A) published the first Swahili newspapers, namely, *Msimulizi* and *Habari za Mwezi*. The Lutheran Church also put emphasis on Swahili and used it as a medium of instruction in its schools.

During German rule in Tanganyika (later Tanzania mainland), Swahili was promoted both in Administration and in Education, and pressure was exerted on the missionaries to teach the language. In Administration, much of the correspondence with village headmen was conducted in Swahili; in fact, letters which were not written to the Administration in either Swahili or German were ignored (*Whiteley 1969*). In the German educational system, Swahili was used as a medium of instruction to train junior personnel and was also made a school subject in its own right. German was also taught, but without content; it was proficiency in Swahili that mattered.

Under the British rule, there was no language policy in East Africa. The British recognized Swahili as the most important language in Tanganyika, to the extent of requiring some of its officers to obtain a modest standard in it while at the same time giving them very lukewarm encouragement to learn other languages. Apart from this, the British Government treated language problems as "educational matters" and left them to the education departments. At that time it was equivalent to leaving them to the missions, as was the case in Kenya and Uganda. Consequently, there was no single policy which was pursued over any length of time in any large area.

Swahili continued to prevail in elementary education under British rule, but only as the stepchild of the educational authorities, receiving little support in the training of competent teachers and the preparation of adequate teaching materials. The establishment of the Inter-Territorial Language Committee in 1930 to standardize written Swahili improved the situation, but the prestige of Swahili compared with English remained low.

Over the years, Swahili continued to spread from the coastal areas of East Africa to the hinterland. Indeed, during the struggle for independence in Tanganyika, Swahili played a significant role in uniting people because of its egalitarian and non-tribal characteristics. All movements of national focus tried to use the language as an instrument of achieving inter-tribal solidarity and integration (*Abdulaziz, 1971*). After independence, Swahili was declared the national language of Tanganyika. Since then, tremendous efforts have been made to promote it in various institutions. For example, following the government's directive in 1967, Swahili was declared the medium of instruction for primary schools the same year. Plans are now under way to extend the use of Swahili as the medium of instruction in secondary schools and, eventually, in the national university namely, University of Dar es Salaam.

In Kenya, Swahili was used quite widely under the Colonial Administration but its status as a basic means of communication did not receive wide support. In education, it was used both as a medium of instruction and was taught as a subject, but it did not enjoy as much prestige as English. However, today the situation has drastically changed. Swahili is now the national language. It is a compulsory and examinable subject in primary and secondary schools. It is also taught in universities along with English, which is still the official language.

Swahili is also a *lingua franca* in Uganda but it has not received wide popularity because the language has often been associated with Islam, slave trade and the military. But *Maw (1985)* points out that following the downfall of the Idi Amin regime, Swahili has increasingly gained popularity in Uganda.

In addition, Swahili is spoken in the Democratic Republic of Congo, Rwanda, Burundi, Zambia and parts of Madagascar. The map on page vii shows areas where Swahili is spoken. More significant is the case of the Democratic Republic of Congo. Here, *Mushingi (1989)* points out, Swahili fulfills the function of uniting people of different tribes in the eastern parts of the country and the language is well accepted by the population. Swahili is also used in broadcasting by some of the major radio stations of the world, such as Radio Moscow, Voice of America, the British Broadcasting Corporation and All India Radio. Swahili is also taught in a number of African, American and European universities. Recently, it was adopted in the United Nations, along with English, French, Arabic, Spanish, Chinese and Russian, as a medium of communication in Security Council debates.

Groups of Swahili speakers

According to *Zawawi (1971)*, there are three groups of Swahili speakers. First, there are those who live on the coast and on islands, for whom Swahili is a "mother tongue". The islands include Zanzibar, Pemba, Mafia, the Comoros and a number of inland towns, such as Ujiji (Central Tanzania) and Tabora (West Tanzania). *Whiteley (1969)* thinks that this group does not exceed one million. Second, there are those in the interior of the East African mainland, mainly those who use Swahili outside their homes for social purposes. Finally, there are those who learn Swahili in schools and speak it as a third language, in addition to their mother tongue and English. Their first language is another Bantu language or a Nilotic language. English becomes their second language.

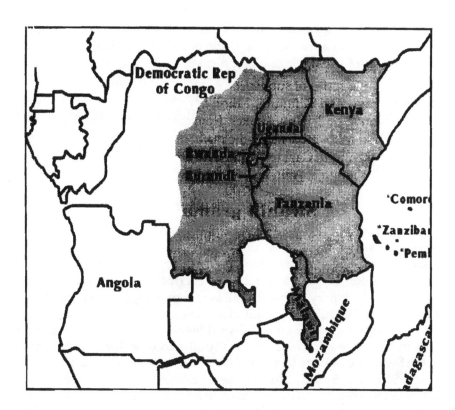

The shaded part of the map represents Swahili speaking areas.
*Also spoken in Zanzibar, Pemba and in the Comoros

Dialects of Swahili

Like English, Swahili consists of a number of dialects. Some of the dialects have died out but can be traced back through earlier writings. According to grammar books, the dialects of Swahili are Tumbatu, spoken on Tumbatu Island and in some areas of the northern part of the Zanzibar Island; Hadimu, also known as Makunduchi, spoken in the southern part of Zanzibar; Vumba, spoken on Wasini Island and Jimbo near Vanga; Mtang'ata, spoken along a twenty-kilometre stretch south of Tanga ; and Kipemba, spoken on Pemba Island, except the southern tip. The dialect of Kiunguja is the standard Swahili of Tanzania. Other dialects in the south include Mgao, spoken from south of Kilwa into northern Mozambique; Mafia, spoken on northern Mafia Island; and Mwani, which is a cluster of sub-dialects spoken on the northern coast and islands of Mozambique.

The northern dialects of Swahili include Pate, spoken on Pate Island; Amu, spoken on Lamu Island and the adjacent mainland to the south; Siu, spoken in Siu, a village along a creek on Pate Island; Kimombasa, which includes a series of subdialects spoken from Kilifi to Gazi as well as Mvita, Jomvu and Kilindini; Miini, spoken at Barawa; Bajuni, also known as Gunya or T'ik'uu, spoken from Kismayu South to just north of Tana River at Mkokotoni along the mainland and adjacent islands; and Chifunzi, spoken from Gazi to Wasini in southern Kenya. Out of all these dialects, only Kiunguja, Amu and Mvita have spread widely.

Swahili grammars

Swahili grammar books started to be published right from the time when missionaries attempted to encourage the use of the language. Krapf, a missionary for the Anglican Church Missionary Society in Mombasa, was the first person to give a linguistic description of Swahili. Later, he published a dictionary of the Swahili language. Krapf's work was the first statement of Swahili's nominal classification. Another missionary to publish Swahili materials was Edward Steere. He published a grammar book in 1934 titled *Swahili Exercises*. But the most influential publication on the Swahili language is *Ashton (1982)*, partly because of its imprimatur by the Standard Swahili Committee of East Africa. The book was first published in 1944. It is currently used in schools, universities and in other institutions for various purposes, but mainly as a reference book. More recent works in this field include over a dozen publications such as *Brain (1969)*, *Loogman (1965)*, *Wilson (1970)*, *Zawawi (1971)* and, most recently, *Maw (1985)*. Thus, a number of publications on Swahili grammar have appeared over a period of time. However, Modern Swahili Grammar advances the works of the preceding grammars in the light of recent findings. It is hoped that this book will serve the needs of universities where Swahili is taught and those of general readers who are interested in learning Swahili in the context of modern linguistic approaches.

Professor Mohamed Abdulla Mohamed
(2000)

Symbols and technical conventions

Various symbols have been used in this book. They include the following:

SPCA
These symbols refer to the elements in the clause structure .

MHQ
These symbols refer to the elements in the structure of a group.

α β ষ δ
These symbols refer to the status of the structures, i.e. whether or not the two or more structures are of equal status.

*
The asterisk indicates an unacceptable structure.

[[ ]]
The double square brackets indicate that the clause is rankshifted.

[ ]
The single brackets indicate the segmental phonetic transcription and also that a group is rankshifted.

+
The plus sign indicates a syllable boundary.

/ - /
The minus sign refers to the normal transitions between sounds within a word.

|
The vertical line is a sign for stress.

ø
This symbol indicates the absence of a class prefix on a noun.

——>
The single arrow indicates a morphophonemic, morphological or syntactic change.

V
This symbol indicates that the word is a verb.

N
This symbol indicates that the word is a noun.

1 Swahili Phonology

Phonology is a branch of linguistics which studies the sound systems of languages. There are a number of components which fall into this field of linguistics: **vowels, consonants, stress, intonation** and **rhythm.** Each of these components is discussed below in the context of Swahili language.

Vowels

Vowels can be defined in both phonetic and phonological terms. Phonetically; vowels are sounds produced without a complete closure in the mouth or a degree of narrowing which could produce an audible friction. From the phonological viewpoint; vowels are those units of sound which function between syllables. Vowels are usually voiced; that is, when they are articulated, the vocal cords tend to vibrate.

In Swahili, there are five cardinal vowels: /a/, /e/, /i/, /o/, /u/. Certain characteristics are used in phonetics to distinguish vowels from consonants although some of these characteristics may be similar to these varieties of sounds. The first characteristic is the place of articulation; in other words, where different sounds are articulated in the vocal apparatus of the human being. The following figure shows where vowels are produced in the mouth:

Front

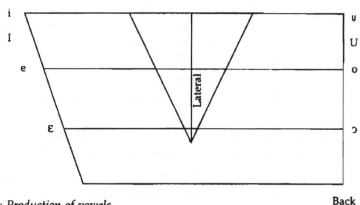

Figure 1: Production of vowels

Back

This figure shows that some vowels are produced at the front of the tongue, others at the back and some in the middle. Each vowel can be described according to the place it is produced.

1

From this figure, therefore, we can describe the places of articulation of the five cardinal vowel sounds as follows:

/a/ low front vowel.

/i/ front vowel.

/u/ back vowel.

/e/ mid vowel.

/o/ back vowel.

The occurrences of these various vowel sounds in different Swahili words is illustrated below:

/i/ occurs in **tii** (obey) and **dhii** (suffer). Vowel /i/ corresponds to the English vowel sound in words like "beat" and "feel".

/u/ occurs in **mkuu** (chief or head), **fuu,** (husk), etc.

The vowel /u/ corresponds to the English vowel sound in words like "boot" and "pool".

/e/ occurs in **pembe** (horn), **pete,** (ring), etc.

The vowel /e/ represents a vowel sound similar to the English one found in words like "bed" and "tell".

/o/ occurs in **popo** (bat), **korongo** (crane), etc.

This vowel corresponds to the English vowel sound in words like "hot" and "pot".

/a/ occurs in **baba** (father), **chama** (party), etc.

This vowel does not have an equivalent form to the English vowel sound but represents a sound between that represented by "a" in the word "hat" and that in "harder".

Apart from the five cardinal vowels, Swahili also has secondary vowels. The places of articulation of these secondary vowels are shown below:

/ɪ/ high unrounded front vowel, lower than /i/.

/ʊ/ high rounded back vowel, lower than /u/.

/ɛ/ open mid high front vowel.

/ɔ/ half open mid rounded back vowel.

Similarly, the occurrences of these vowel sounds in different Swahili words can be illustrated below:

/ɪ/ occurs in **kiti** (chair) or **hisi** (feeling), etc.

/ʊ/ occurs in **kuku** (chicken) or **buku** (a big rat), etc.

/ɛ/ occurs in **peremende** (peppermint) or **lengelenge** (blister), etc.

/ɔ/ occurs in **chombo** (utensil/vessel) or **dondoo**, (extract/quotation).

Consonants

Consonants can also be defined in terms of both phonetics and phonology. Phonetically, they are sounds made by a closure or narrowing in the vocal tract so that the air flow is either completely blocked out or restricted to produce an audible friction. From the phonological viewpoint, consonants are units which operate at the margins of syllables, either singly or in clusters.

Place of articulation

Compared with vowels, consonants in Swahili are numerous. There are 26 in total, but like vowels, they can also be described by the concept of place of articulation. The following diagram shows the different organs of speech responsible for the articulation of different sounds in Swahili.

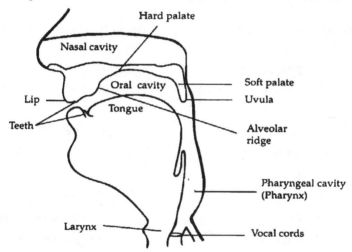

Figure 2: The organs of speech

The following is a classification of different consonants in Swahili showing their places of articulation:

/p/, /ɓ/, /m/, /w/.

These consonants are classified as bilabial. They are formed by the coming together of both lips. Since these speech sounds are produced at the same place of articulation, they are referred to as **harmorganic.**

3

/s/, /z/, /t/, /d/, /n/, /l/, /r/.

This group of consonants is known as **alveolar**. They are formed by the tip or blade of the tongue coming into contact with the alveolar ridge.

/f/, /v/.

These consonants are classified as **labiodental**. They are articulated when the lower lip comes into contact with the upper teeth.

/ө/, /ð/.

This group of consonants is known as **dental**. They are formed by the tip of the tongue against the teeth.

/k/, /g/, /ŋ/, /tʃ/, /ɬ/, /ɲ/, /x/, /ɣ/.

These consonants are referred to as **velar**. They are articulated by the back of the tongue against the soft palate.

/h/.

This consonant is known as **glottal**. It is articulated by the light narrowing of the passage between the vocal cords.

The occurrences of these various consonants in different Swahili words are illustrated below:

/p/ **paka** (cat)	/b/ **bata** (duck)
/m/ **mama** (mother)	/n/ **nazi** (coconut)
/w/ **wali** (rice)	/j/ **yai** (egg)
/s/ **samaki** (fish)	/z/ **zawadi** (present)
/t/ **tango** (cucumber)	/d/ **deni** (debt)
/l/ **laana** (curse)	/r/ **radi** (thunder)
/f/ **fimbo** (stick)	/v/ **vazi** (dress)
/ө/ **thumni** (fifty cents)	/ð/ **dharuba** (storm)
/k/ **kazi** (work)	/g/ **goti** (knee)
/ɲ/ **nyumba** (house)	/ŋ/ **ng'ombe** (cow)
/x/ **nuskha** (copy, duplicate)	/ɣ/ **ghala** (store)
/tʃ/ **chumba** (room)	/ɬ/ **jengo** (building)
/h/ **hewa** (air)	/ʃ/ **shati** (shirt)

Manner of articulation

Manner of articulation is the second characteristic in the phonetic or phonological classification of speech sounds. It refers to the kind of articulatory process used in the production of a particular sound. This property is used quite often to distinguish between consonants and vowels. Regarding consonants, several articulatory types are recognized depending on the type of closure of the vocal organs. For example, if the closure is partial, the result is a lateral sound. If there is a narrowing without complete closure, the result is a fricative sound. However, in the case of vowels, these articulatory types are not recognized. Even so, within vowels, we can have a number of auditory qualities distinguishable in the sound. For instance, we can investigate whether a particular sound is a pure vowel, a diphthong or triphthong although this may not be so common in a language like Swahili. Apart from this, we can also investigate the position of the soft palate and the type of lip position; that is, whether the lips have a rounded shape or not.

As we did in the section on place of articulation, we will now try to group the consonants along the axis of manner of articulation.

/p/, /t/, /k/, /g/, /tʃ/, /d /, /b/, /d/.

These consonants are known as **stops**. They are produced by a complete closure in the vocal tract followed by a sudden release of the air pressure which has built up behind the closure.

/s/, /z/, /f/, /v/, /q/, /ʃ/, /x/, /ɣ/, /h/.

These sounds are referred to as **fricatives**. They are produced when two organs come so close together that the air moving between them causes audible friction.

/m/, /n/, /ɲ/, /ŋ/.

These four consonants are known as **nasals**. They are nasal because when the soft palate is lowered, the air escapes through the nose.

/l/, /r/.

These are known as **laterals**. The sounds are produced when the air escapes around one or both sides of a closure in the mouth.

/w/, /j/.

The consonants above are referred to as **semivowels**. Although they are consonants, they lack the phonetic characteristics normally associated with consonants, such as friction and closure. Instead, their qualities are phonetically similar to those of vowels.

Ashton (1982) and some other Swahili grammars think that /mb/, /mv/, /nd/, /nz/, /nj/ and /ng/ are also phonemes since when combined with other letters to form words, they, like other phonemes, function as single sounds. The issue is still controversial among Swahili scholars and linguists. *Polomé (1967)*, for example, does not include the six phonemes in his list of Swahili consonants. Therefore, we have not included the six sounds in the table below. Likewise, we have not discussed in this book the aspect of long vowels in Swahili since the issue is somewhat controversial.

In short, within the classification of the manner of articulation, we can identify five categories of consonants in Swahili: stops, fricatives, nasals, laterals and semivowels. The consonants embodying the five categories are set out in the following chart:

Place of articulation	Classes according to mode of articulation					
	Stops		Fricatives	Resonants		
	Plosives	Affricates		Nasals	Laterals	Semi-vowels
Bilabial	p b			m		w
Labiodental			f v			
Dental			ð θ			
Alveolar	t d		s z	n	l r	
Palato-alveolar		tʃ ʄ	ʃ	ɲ		
Palatal		ɗ				j
Velar	k g		x ɣ	ŋ		
Glottal			h			

Table 1: *Articulatory systems of Swahili consonants*

Voiced and voiceless sounds

Earlier, we stated that all vowels are usually **voiced**. The term **voiced** refers to those sounds which produce a vibration of the vocal cords when they are articulated. Where there is an absence of such vibration, the sounds are said to be **voiceless**.

Consonants can be either voiced or voiceless. We can group them as follows:

voiceless   /p/, /t/, /k/, /tÚ/, /x/, /f/, /q/, /s/, /Ú/, /h/

voiced   /b/, /d/, /g/, /ʄ/, /ɗ/, /v/, /ɣ/, /z/, /l/, /r/, /m/, /n/, /ŋ/, /ɲ/, /w/, /j/

This voiced and voiceless dimension is another characteristic used in the phonetic classification of speech sounds. A sound which is normally voiced, but which in a particular situation is produced with less voice, or with no voice at all, is said to be **devoiced**. In Swahili, there are quite a number of instances of devoiced sounds. One example is the word **mushkil** (problem) where the /l/ sound is devoiced in fast speech.

Lax and tensed sounds

The concepts of **lax** and **tense** are also features found in the phonetic classification of speech sounds. The lax sounds are those produced with less muscular effort and movement, and which are relatively short and indistinct. Examples are the vowel sounds /u/ and /i/ in words such as **kuku** (hen) and **hisi** (feeling). On the other hand, tensed sounds have been defined both articulatorily and acoustically: they are sounds produced with a relatively strong muscular effort, involving a greater movement of the vocal tract away from the position of rest and relatively strong spread of acoustic energy. The vowels /i/ and /u/ are found in words such as **hii** (this) and **juu** (up).

Tensed sounds also occur with consonants. Examples include aspirated and long consonants. The vowel sound /r/ in **ruka** (jump) is an example of a tensed consonant.

Aspiration in consonants

Aspiration is a term used in phonetics to show the audible breath which may accompany a sound's articulation as in when plosive consonants are released. Aspiration is usually symbolized by a small raised [ʰ] following the main symbol. Thus, in examples such as **pʰaa** (deer) and **kʰaa** (crab), the aspiration may be felt by holding the back of the hand close to the mouth while saying the word. In contrast, with **paa** (scale) and **kaa** (sit down), the [p] here does not carry any aspiration and so with [k]. Hence the sounds [p] and [k] are unaspirated.

In Swahili, aspiration seems to occur along voiceless stops. However, in some languages such as Hindi, aspiration applies to both voiceless and voiced stops.

Consonant clusters

The term cluster is used in the analysis of connected speech to refer to any sequence of adjacent consonants occurring initially, medially or finally in a syllable, such as the initial [sk] of **skati** (skirt) and the medial [lh] of **alhamisi** (Thursday). Unlike English, the final cluster does not usually occur in Swahili because the morphological structure of the language

7

permits only vowels at the end of words. However, in rapid speech, there are loan words which can take final consonant clusters. Examples include words like **ratl** [tl] (pound), **milk** [lk] (possession) and *athir* (affect).

It is important to note that consonant clustering occurs less frequently in Swahili than in other languages, such as Arabic and English because of the morphological pattern of the language, namely the CVCV structure. This means that a consonant in Swahili is followed by a vowel and then again by a consonant, a vowel and so on. This pattern is also found in other Bantu languages.

In Swahili, consonant clustering is quite common at the initial position, mainly in loan words. The pattern of clustering can be a two or three way dimension. Listed below are some examples:

a. [mk] in **mkahawa** (inn).
b. [ml] in **mlango** (door).
c. [sk] in **skuli** (school).
d. [tr] in **treya** (tray).
e. [msw] in **mswaki** (toothbrush).
f. [skr] in **skrubu** (screw).

Medial clusters, although less common in Swahili, are possible. Once again, most of the words containing medial clusters are of non-Bantu origin. The following words contain medial clusters:

a. [fr] in **tafrija** (entertainment).
b. [fj] in **afya** (health).
c. [bʃ] in **rabsha** (commotion).
d. [ʃb] in **tashbiha** (simile).
e. [rb] in **tarbushi** (red cap with tassel).
f. [sk] in **askari** (soldier).

We shall now examine the constraints governing consonant clusters.

There are certain dissimilatory principles constraining consonant clusters, principles tending to juxtapose unlike contrasting sounds rather than similar sounds. For this reason, consonant sequences of voiced + voiced are less likely to be acceptable than voiceless + voiced sequences. A cluster like /fs/ as in **fsurufu** is an unlikely combination in Swahili or even in other languages like English. The reason is that /f/ and /s/ are both voiceless. In addition, both sounds are fricative. Thus, the combination of /ms/ is slightly more likely in Swahili because it introduces a contrast with respect to voicing and to the manner of articulation since /m/ is nasal and /s/ is fricative.

Arguments in respect to dissimilar sounds versus similar sounds are also applicable to other clusters like /fl/ and /sl/ as in **hafla** (banquet) and **sleti** (slate) respectively, versus /vl/ and /zl/. The first two clusters have dissimilar consonants and these are more likely to be accepted than the second pairs of voiced + voiced sequences. The second category of clusters is not acceptable as exemplified in words like **kivlu** and **zluti**. However, the dissimilatory principle governing words that have clusters of voiced and voiced sequences does not always apply. For instance, grammatical forms like **tarbushi** (red cap with tassel) and **mdudu** (insect) do exist. The former has a combination of consonantal sequences of /rb/ while the latter has the /md/ combination. Both combinations have a pattern of voiced + voiced sequences. Apart from voice, however, another feature must also be taken into consideration. This is **place of articulation**. A non-alveolar and alveolar sequence, for example, is more likely to occur than an alveolar and alveolar one.

Similarly in words of Bantu origin, two types of consonant clustering are likely to occur:

1. nasal + consonant; and

2. consonant + /j/ or /w/. For example:
    a. [mts] or [mcᵛ] in **mchungwa** (orange tree).
    b. [ns] in **nsi** (fish).
    c. [vy] in **vyema** (fine, well).
    d. [nw] in **banwa** (squeezed).

Lastly, certain phonotactic rules exist for the sequence of some sounds in Swahili:

a. Only consonants /d/, /g/, /z/, /ɟ/, /n/, /t/, /tʃ/ and /s/ can occur after /n/.

For example:
(i)   **ndugu** (brother).
(ii)   **ngoma** (drum).
(iii) **nzige** (locust).

b. Similarly, consonant /n/ before a stem beginning with /b/, /v/ and /w/ take the form of /m/:
(i)   **mbegu** (seed)
(ii)   **mvua** (rain)
(iii) **mwewe** (hawk)

9

    c. Likewise, /n/ changes to /ɲ/ before the initial vowel of a stem:

       (i) **nyonga** (hip)'

       (ii) **nyumba** (house)

    d. Consonant /w/ does not occur after /f/, /h/ or /d/, except if /d/ is preceded by /n/. For example:

       mpendwa (beloved, favourite).

    e. /j/ does not occur after /b/, /d/, /g/,/ɟ/ nor after any other non-bilabial or non-labiodental consonant.

The phoneme

The phoneme has been described by linguists as the minimal contrastive linguistic unit which can bring a change in meaning. We can, for example, make a rough list of phonemes in Swahili by collecting sets of contrasts as shown below:

    raba (rubber), **baba** (father), **kaba** (squeeze), **zaba** (beat), **haba** (scarce).

There are five contrasting sound-units in the above words. These are /r/, /b/, /k/, /z/ and /h/. The sound units produce a change of meaning in each word. Thus, each of them is called a **phoneme**.

    Vowels can also produce a change of meaning. For example:

    toka (come out), **tika** (shake), **teka** (fetch), **taka** (want), **tuka** (happen unexpectedly).

The sound-units /o/, /i/, /e/, /a/ and /u/ are vowels. Each of them is also a phoneme since each produces a change of meaning in the given examples. Thus, all the vowels and consonants which have been examined are phonemes.

The allophone

The allophone is a subclass of sounds which is in complementary distribution with another, such that the two together constitute a single phoneme. In other words, the various variants of a phoneme are called **allophones.**

    To cite a few cases of allophones in Swahili, consider the following examples:

    a. [pʰaka] (cat).

    b. [mpapai] (pawpaw).

In example (a), there is a puff of air when /p/ is pronounced. Thus, the [pʰ] is aspirated here. In contrast, the [p] in example (b) is unaspirated because it is not pronounced with a lot of breath. Furthermore, in the former, the aspirated [pʰ] occurs in the initial position whereas in the latter, the unaspirated [p] occurs in the medial position. This means that the two variants of the phoneme /p/ are allophones. They occur in different environments and are thus said to be in **complementary distribution**. Further examples of allophones in Swahili are shown below:

    a. [kʰapa] (zero).

    b. [mkate] (bread).

The [kʰ] is aspirated in example (a) whereas in (b), it is unaspirated. The two variants of /k/ which constitute a single phoneme are allophones.

The syllable

The syllable is a unit of pronunciation which is typically larger than a single sound and smaller than a word. Although it is difficult to set up syllable boundaries objectively, we can, however, establish some guidelines for the structure of a syllable in Swahili.

    First, as a rule, each vowel counts as a syllable in Swahili. Thus, in these examples below, there are two syllables for each word:

    a. u + a (flower).

    b. o + a (marry).

Secondly, where a preconsonantal nasal functions as a syllabic peak, a syllable is counted.

    a. m̩ + tu (person).

    b. n̩ + chi (country).

The small mark inserted under each consonantal nasal shows that the sound-unit carries one syllable. It is called a **syllabic consonant**.

    Thirdly, in Swahili, like in English, a syllable is formed by a combination of two sounds: vowel and consonant. For example:

    a. pa + ka (cat).

    b. me + za (table).

Here, there are two syllables in each word.

    Fourthly, a cluster of two consonants together with a vowel can also form a syllable:

    a. mwe + zi (month).

    b. twa + nga (pound).

Fifthly, a segment of clusters of three with a vowel can form a syllable:

    a. ti + mbwa (booted).

    b. ngwe + na (crocodile).

Finally, according to *Polomé (1967)*, the syllable boundary in loan words usually lies after the first of the two consonants:

    a. bus + tani (garden).

    b. lab + da (probably).

Suprasegmentals

Suprasegmental is a term used in phonetics and phonology to refer to a vocal effect which extends over more than one sound segment in an utterance such as stress, pitch, intonation and juncture. We will now discuss each of these suprasegmental features as they may apply to Swahili language.

Stress

Stress refers to the degree of force used in producing a syllable. The normal distinction is between stressed and unstressed syllables. The former is more prominent than the latter and in transcription, it is marked with a raised vertical line [']. The prominence is generally due to the increase in loudness of the stressed syllable. Increases in pitch and length can also contribute to the overall impression of prominence. In popular usage, stress is usually associated with the notion of "emphasis" or "strength".

In Swahili, stress occurs, as a rule, on the penultimate syllable, that is, on the second last syllable. Nevertheless, in some loan words, mainly from Arabic and Persian, it is possible to put a stress on the first syllable of the word, e.g. **'dhambi** (sins), **'takriban** (almost) and **'ghafula** (suddenly). Also, in some loan words, stress becomes a stylistic feature because of the free variation in the stress pattern. For example, **ta'fadhali** or **tafa'dhali** (please), **'ahadi** or **a'hadi** (promise) and **ho'tuba** or **'hotuba** (speech).

The use of stress in Swahili can be seen at two levels: word and sentence. For example, at word level, we can state that words and word sequence can be distinguished using stress variation:

    a. **ba'rabara** (exactly)

    b. **bara'bara** (highway)

    c. **'ala** (instrument, tool or sheath)

    d. **a'la** (an exclamation indicating surprise, fear, etc.)

    e. **wa'lakini** (defect, weakness)

    f. **wala'kini** (but, nevertheless)

Words with this pattern are called **homographs**. Although they have an identical spelling, they are pronounced differently and their meanings are also different.

At sentence level, the stress is used to distinguish degrees of emphasis or contrast as shown in this pattern:

    a. **wataka 'kazi** (those who are looking for jobs)

    b. **wa'taka kazi** (you want work)

    c. **wacheza 'mpira** (those who play football)

    d. **wa'cheza mpira** (you play football)

    e. **waenda 'kasi** (those who go fast)

    f. **wa'enda kasi** (you are going fast)

In some situations, double stress occurs for emphasis in reduplicated verbs:

    'sema'sema (talk continuously)

    'cheza'cheza (play continuously)

    'piga'piga (hit continuously)

Pitch

Pitch refers to the normal melodic height of an individual's speech. This term does not apply to voiceless sounds nor to whispered speech.

Pitch variation is common in all languages but its function differs from one language to another. Generally, when the pitch is higher in languages such as English and Swahili, it is associated with anger or strain.

Intonation

The regular sequences of pitch difference operating over a whole sentence or part of it are called **intonation** or **intonation tunes**.

Most grammarians argue that there are three contrastive levels of pitch in Swahili: high, mid and low. These three tone patterns can be illustrated as follows:

Tone pattern I

This tone pattern is characterized by the descending on the penultimate syllable of the last word in a sentence. The pattern occurs in plain statements, commands, questions with an interrogative particle and in answers to questions. For example:

a. **Kijana anaumwa kidogo.** (statement).
   (The youth is a bit unwell.)

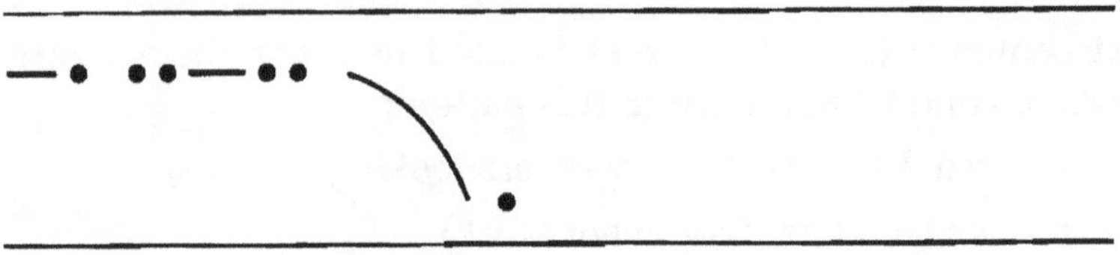

b. **Pika chakula.** (command).
   (Cook the food.)

c. **Otieno amekwenda wapi?** (question with an interrogative particle)
   (Where has Otieno gone to?)

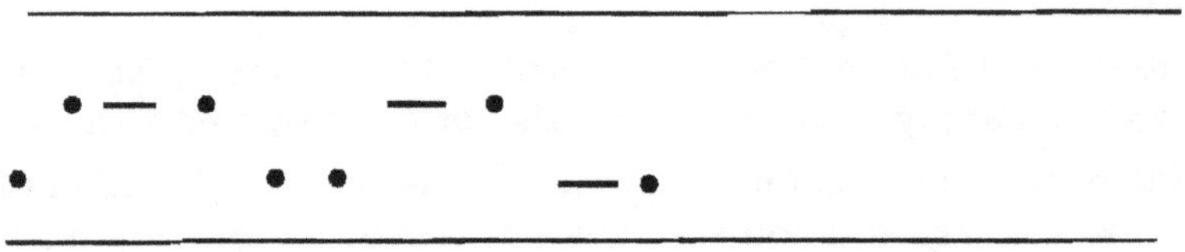

d. **Sina hakika.** (response).
   (I am not sure.)

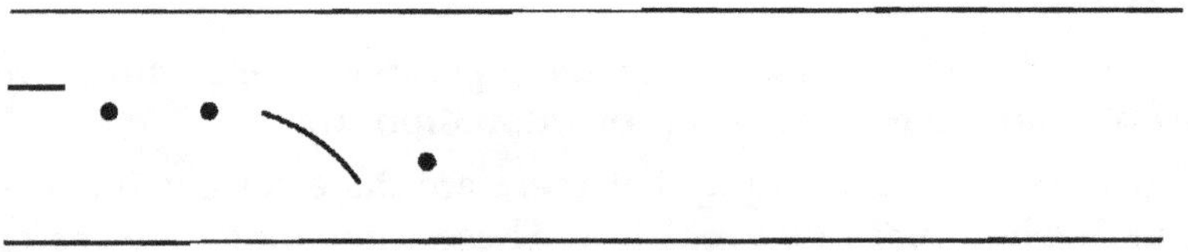

Figure 2

Tone pattern II

This pattern is only associated with questions, generally without an interrogative particle. The pitch pattern begins at a mid level syllable and rises high at the stressed penultimate syllable of the last word in a sentence.

a.   **Utavichukua viti vyote?**
      (Will you take all the chairs?)

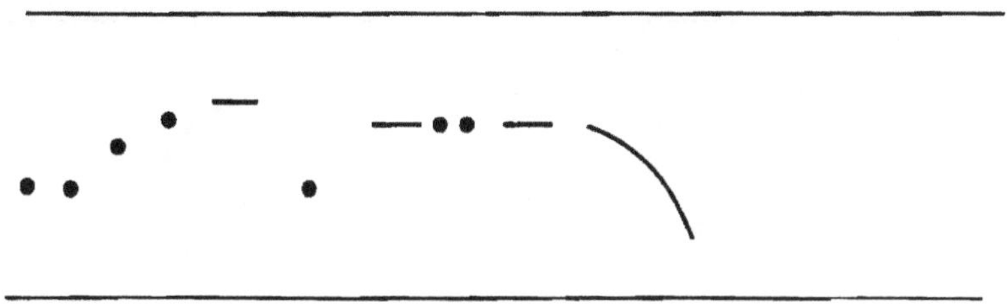

b.   **Unalala mapema?**
      (Are you sleeping early?)

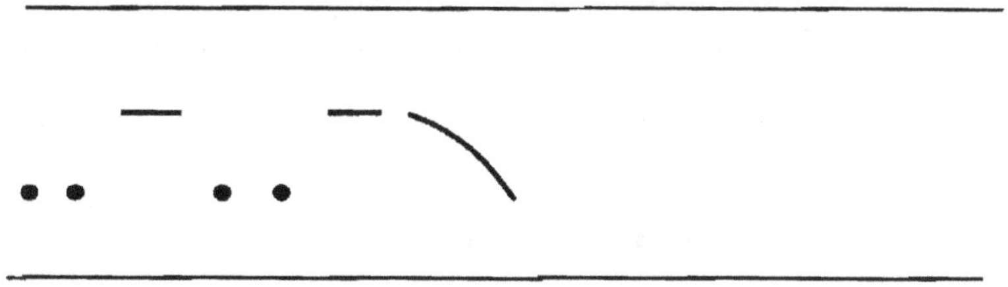

Figure 3

Tone pattern III

The tone pattern of this nature is used to mention lists of things and actions. It is also used in relative clauses, conditional clauses, initial adverbs and in adverbial subjects. The pitch in this tone pattern rises slightly higher and then falls on the penultimate syllable of the last word.

a.   **Chukua kunde, ndizi, muhogo na mananasi.**
      (Take beans, bananas, cassava and pineapples.)

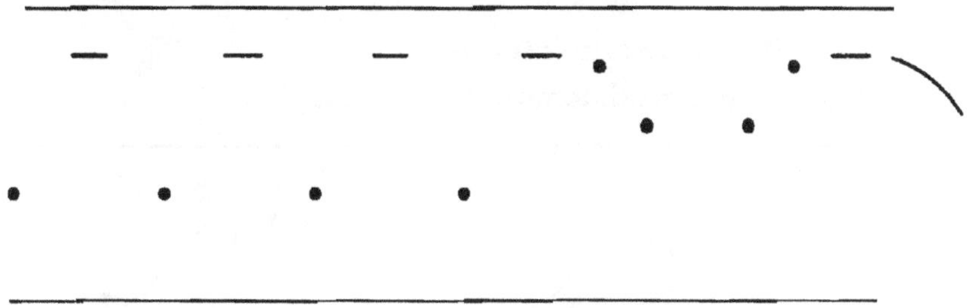

b. **Tuliamka, tukaenda, tukasita ... ndani ya gari.**
(We woke up, went, and hesitated ... inside the car.)

c. **Kijana aliyefika leo anaumwa.**
(The youth who arrived today is unwell.)

d. **Ukipika wali niarifu.**
(If you cook rice, inform me.)

e. **Leo nitasoma, kesho nitacheza.**
(Today I will read, tomorrow I will play.)

f. **Huko msikitini, watu wanasali.**
    (In the mosque, people are praying.)

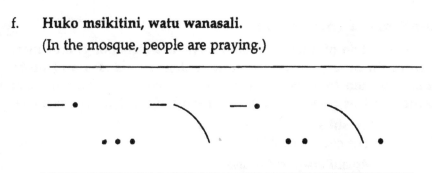

Figure 4

Tone pattern IV

This tone pattern has the characteristic of giving a stressed penultimate syllable on a high or falling tone followed by a final stressed syllable on a low rising or low level tone. The pattern is used to draw attention to a particular word in a sentence.

a. **Ule mbaya, ule mzuri.**
    (That one is bad, that one is good.)

b. **Somo lilipokwisha, wanafunzi wakaondoka.**
    (When the lesson ended, the students went away.)

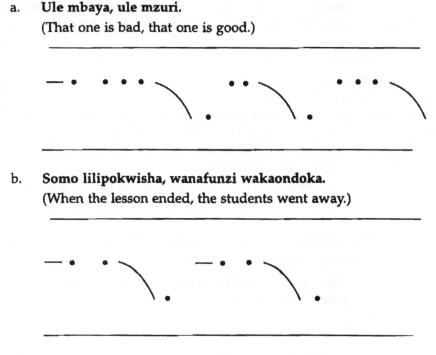

Figure 5

Functions of intonation

The first function of intonation is to serve as a signal of grammatical structure; in other words, to mark sentences, clauses and other boundaries, and to show the contrast between some grammatical structures such as questions, statements and exclamations. For example:

a. **Mpishi anapika.** (statement)
(The cook is cooking.)

b. **Mpishi anapika?** (question).
(Is the cook cooking?)

c. **Mpishi anapika!** (exclamation).
(The cook is cooking!)

In example a., we use a falling intonation contour to show that the sentence is a statement. In example b., we use a rising intonation contour to indicate that the sentence is a question. And in example c., we try to employ a strong emotion to indicate that the sentence is an exclamation.

The other function of intonation is to communicate the personal attitude of a speaker, for example, satisfaction, sarcasm, anger, puzzlement and so on. All these traits can be signalled by contrasts in pitch, along with other prosodic and paralinguistic features. For example:

a. **Huyu ni 'mjinga.**
This one is a 'fool.

b. **'Huyu ni mjinga.**
'This one is a fool.

In example a., the speaker wishes to draw attention to the concept of **mjinga** (fool). This sentence is said to be neutral or unmarked. In b., the attention is, however, given to **huyu** (this one) as opposed to **yule** (that one). The sentence is said to be marked.

This function of intonation of communicating the personal attitude of a speaker can further be illustrated by the following four identical sentences:

a. **Mwalimu mkuu amefika.** (unmarked sentence).
(The headmaster has arrived.)

b. **Mwalimu mkuu amefika.** (sentence describing happiness on the part of the speaker).

c. **Mwalimu mkuu amefika.** (sentence describing sorrow on the part of the speaker).

d. **Mwalimu mkuu amefika.** (sentence describing fear on the part of the speaker).

It is difficult to know the attitude of the speaker simply by looking at the surface structure of these four identical sentences. Only by using pitch, along with prosodic and paralinguistic features, would we be able to distinguish the difference in the attitude of the speaker in each sentence.

Junctures

Juncture is a term used in phonology to refer to phonetic boundary features which may divide grammatical units such as morphemes, words or clauses. The most common junctural feature is silence.

There have been several attempts to establish a typology of junctures. A commonly used distinction is between 'open' or 'plus' juncture <+> and 'close' or 'minus' juncture <->. These distinctions of open and close junctures can effectively be illustrated in the Swahili language. For example, the concept of vowel length in certain Swahili words should be considered as an issue of junctures as shown below:

a. [a] in **kuja** (to come) versus [a:] in **kujaa** (to get full).

b. [u] in **kuku** (hen) versus [u:] in **kuukuu** (old).

This distinction of vowel length is referred to by linguists as the **phonemic status of quality**.

Linguists have also discussed the concept of consonant length on the basis of a few minimal pairs. Here are a few examples:

a. **uma** (bite) : u + mma (nation).

b. **ala** (sheath) : a + llah (Allah; God).

These minimal contrasts apply to words of Arabic origin with double consonant featuring alongside Bantu words consisting of the same segmental phonemes.

Regarding the "close" or "minus" juncture, we can illustrate this form of syllable boundary by using the following words:

a. /**mbuni**/ [mbu:ni] (ostrich) : /**m-buni**/ [mbu:ni] (coffee plant)

b. /**mbit si**/ [mbi:t si] (raw): /**m-bit si**/ [m'bitsi] (green)

c. /**mbo:no**/ [mbo:no] (physic-nut seeds): /**m-bono**/ [m'bono] (physic-nut plant)

The contrasts in the above examples can be explained by the fact that the words on the left are dissyllabic while those on the right are trisyllabic. It can be argued that the minus sign /–/ is used to refer to the normal transitions between sounds within a word. However, *Polomé (1967)* states that the sign mainly marks the hiatus between vowels and refers to it as an **internal juncture**.

Morphophonemic changes

Morphophonemic changes are those changes which affect the appearance of morphemes or phonemes. In Swahili, morphophonemic changes can affect both vowels and consonants. We will first describe the morphophonemic changes affecting vowels.

Vowels

As shown by other linguists, morphophonemic changes involving vowel phonemes can occur on contact or at a distance. The most common change in contact is **contraction**. This concept of contraction can be defined as a fusing of a sequence of forms so that they appear like a single form.

The following examples illustrate the notion of contraction in Swahili:

a. /a/ + /a/ ————> (wa + ana = **wana** [sons])
b. /a/ + /e/ ————> (wa + enzi = **wenzi** [friends])
c. /a/ + /o/ ————> (wa + ote = **wote** [all])
d. /a/ + /i/ ————> (ma + ingi = **mengi** [many])
e. /u/ + /u/ ————> (mu + ume = **mume** [husband])
f. /i/ + /i/ ————> (vi + ingi = **vingi** [many])

Other instances of contraction in Swahili can be seen in these words:

(wa) + (vi) ————> **wevi** (thieves).
(ma) + (ino) ————> **meno** (teeth).
(ma) + (iko) ————> **meko** (fire-places, kitchens).

Here, we can see that the resultant vowel sound is different from the other two containing class prefixes and roots.

Contraction of /a/ + /e/ and /a/ + /i/ in adjectival concord is restricted to class prefixes "**wa**" and "**ma**", e.g., **watoto wengi** (many children) and **maji mengi** (much water).

With infinitives, the class prefix [ku] remains a syllable boundary marker separating it from the verbal stem beginning with a consonant, e.g., **kupika** (to cook) and **kucheza** (to play). This class prefix [ku] also remains a boundary marker for verbal stems beginning with a vowel, e.g., **kuimba** (to sing), **kuanza** (to start), **kuokota** (to collect), **kueleza** (to explain) and **kuumba** (to create). But a few verbs undergo a morphophonemic change of /ku/ to /kw/ before a vowel, e.g., **kwenda** (to go) and **kwisha** (to finish).

The class prefix /kw/ appears again when an infinitive form of a verb occurs with an adjectival concord, e.g., **kupika kwao** (their cooking) and **kufika kwake** (his coming).

Another feature of morphophonemic change that can be observed is in the subject prefix of the first person plural, that is, /tu/. The /tu/ particle changes to /tw/ before the tense marker /a/, e.g., **twauliza** (we ask). When functioning as an object prefix, the /tu/ particle is usually used although the /tw/ form can still be utilised. *Polomé (1967)* regards the choice between /tu/ and /tw/ as a stylistic feature.

The class prefix [ki] becomes [tʃ] before nominal stems beginning with a vowel, e.g., **charahani** (sewing machine), **cheti** (note, ticket), **chokochoko** (discord) and **chungu** (cooking pot). But the class prefix [ki] is retained where the vowel stem begins with /i/, and sometimes /o/, e.g., **kiini** (kernel, yolk) and **kiongozi** (leader).

With adjectival concords, the class prefix [ki] is reflected by its allomorphs: /ts/ appears before /a/, /e/ and /o/, e.g., **kitabu changu** (my book), **kikombe chenu** (your cup) and **kiti chote** (the whole chair); /ki/ appears before /u/, e.g., **kijana kiume** (young man) and /k/ before /i/, e.g., **kiti kingine** (another chair).

Similarly, the class prefix [vi] can be treated in a parallel way for plural forms. The allomorph /vj/ occurs before some of the vowel stems, e.g., **vyandalua** (mosquito nets), **vyeti** (tickets), **vyombo** (utensils) and **vyuma** (irons). But the allomorph /vi/ occurs before the vowel stem beginning with /i/, e.g., **viini** (kernels, yolks).

With adjectival concords, the allomorph /vj/ again appears before most of the vowel stems, e.g., **vikombe vyangu** (my cups), **vitu vyepesi** (light objects) and **vitabu vyote** (all books). The /vi/, however, appears before the vowel stems beginning with /i/, e.g., **vitabu vingi** (many books) and **vijana viume** (young men).

In the case of the class prefix [mi], the devocalization of /i/ does not take place before the first vowel of the following noun, e.g., **miale** (rays), **miezi** (months), **mioyo** (hearts), **miili** (bodies) and **miundu** (billhooks). However, devocalization appears in adjectival concords before /e/ and /o/, e.g., **miti myembamba** (thin trees) and **mikate myororo** (soft loaves).

We will now discuss the scope of the class prefix [m]. When referring to persons of various occupations and personalities, we would normally use /mw/ before a vowel stem, e.g., **mwalimu** (teacher), **mwezekaji** (thatcher), **Mwitalia** (Italian), **mwokozi** (saviour) and **mwundi** (carpenter, joiner). There are a few exceptions, such as **Muumba** (creator) and **muumikaji** (professional cupper), where the allomorph /mu/ is used.

The allomorph /mu/ also occurs before the initial /h/ in the names of plants and other references of a closed set, e.g., **muhogo** (cassava), **muhindi** (maize), **muhula** (season) and **muhuri** (seal).

Apart from references to occupations and nationalities, the allomorph /mw/ is also used before /a/, /e/ and /i/ to refer to inanimate objects, e.g., **mwavuli** (umbrella), **mwendo** (journey) and **mwitu** (forest). In contrast, we have **moto** (fire) and **mundu** (billhook) before /o/ and /u/ respectively.

In association with adjectival concords, the allomorph /mw/ appears before /a/, /e/, /i/ and /o/, e.g., **mwalimu mwangalifu** (a prudent teacher), **mtu mwembamba** (a thin person), **miti mingi** (many trees) and **kijana mwongo** (a deceitful youth). However, the allomorph /mu/ tends to occur before /u/, e.g., **mtu muungwana** (a civilized person).

Finally, we will now examine the contraction of the subject prefix [ni] of the first person singular before the tense marker [na], i.e., [ni] + [na] = /n /. For example, **naja** (I come) and **napika** (I cook). We can call this **ellipsis** of the subject prefix [ni]. There is no difference in meaning between the two forms of constructions. For example, the construction **ninakaa** and **nakaa** convey the same meaning (I am sitting down). The choice of one form and the rejection of the other is a stylistic feature often determined by euphony or the cadence of a sentence.

Morphophonemic change is also realised in Swahili by the principles of vowel harmony. This means that the vowel in the verbal root or stem will affect the suffix containing the vowel. Thus, the high vowel will occur when the verbal root contains /a/, /i/ or /u/. For example:

za (bear) ———>	**zalia** (to bear)
	zaliwa (be born)
	zalisha (cause to bear)
chimba (dig) ———>	**chimbia** (dig for)
	chimbiwa (be dug for)
	chimbisha (cause to dig)
fuma (weave) ———>	**fumia** (weave for)
	fumiwa (be weaved for)
	fumisha (cause to weave)

Likewise, when the verb root or stem contains /e/ or /o/, the mid vowel will be found. For example:

tenda (do)	————>	tendea (do for)
		tendewa (be done for)
		tendesha (cause to do)
choma (cauterize)	————>	chomea (cauterize for)
		chomewa (be cauterized for)
		chomesha (cause to cauterize)

For verbs of non-Bantu origin, the front vowel also occurs, except in the verbal root containing a stem with /e/:

kirimu (entertain)	————>	kirimia (entertain for)
		kirimiwa (be entertained)
		kirimisha (cause to entertain)
sujudu (worship)	————>	sujudia (worship for)
		sujudiwa (be worshipped)
		sujudisha (cause to worship)
samehe (forgive)	————>	samehea (forgive for)
		samehewa (be forgiven)
		samehesha (cause to forgive)

Lastly, with monosyllabic verbs, both the high and mid vowels occur in the suffix containing the verb stem:

la (eat)	————>	lia (eat for)
		liwa (be eaten)
		lisha (cause to eat)
cha (fear)	————>	chea (fear for)
		chewa (be feared)
		chesha (cause to fear)

Consonants

Morphophonemic changes affecting consonants in Swahili occur in the following situations:

1. In contact with the class prefix [n], the following changes occur at the initial position:

   a. /n/ + /l/ ————> /nd/, e.g., **ndimi**, [plural of **ulimi**, (tongue)].

or

/n/ + /r/ ———> /nd/, e.g., **ndefu** [from **refu**, (tall)].

or

/n/ + /o/ ————> /nd/, e.g., **ndoto** [(dream), from ku-ota (to dream)].

  b. /n/ + /w/ before a vowel ————> /mb/, e.g., **mbinja** [(whistlings) from **ubinja** (whistling)]

        or

/n/ + /w/ before a vowel ————> /mb/, e.g., **mbili** [(two) from the numeral **wili** (two)]

  c. /n/ ————> /j/ before a noun or an adjective with a vowel stem, e.g., **nyani** (ape), **nyegere** (ratel, honey-badger), **nyoka** (snake), **nyumba** (house), **nyembamba** (thin) and **nyingi** (much, many). These are all applicable to nouns of the N class.

2. Morphophonemic changes affect consonants preceding the derivational suffixes /i/ or /j/:

  a. For stops, they produce a series of fricatives by means of palatalization as shown below:

/p/ as in **ogopa** (fear) ————> [ja] e.g. **ogofya** (frighten)

/b/ as in **iba** (steal) ————> [vi] [zi] e.g. **mwivi, mwizi** (thief)

/t/ as in **takata** (be clean) ————> [sa] e.g. **takasa** (cleanse)

/d/ as in **panda** (plant) ————> [zi] e.g. **mpanzi** (planter)

/k/ as in **waka** (burn) ————> [a] e.g. **washa** (cause to burn, light)

/g/ as in **loga** (bewitch) ————> [zi] e.g. **mlozi** (witch)

  b. For nasals, morphophonemic changes occur before [ja], but not before [w]. For example:

/n/ + /j/ ———> /ny/ e.g. **kanya** (forbid) from **kana** (deny)

/ɲ/ + /j/ ———> /nz/ e.g. **fanza** (cause to make) from **fanya** (do)

  c. For the semi vowel /w/, morphophonemic changes also occur before [ja]. For example:

/w/ + /j/ ———> /vja/, e.g., **navya** (cause to wash hands or

24

face) from **nawa** (wash hands or face). This morphophonemic change also extends to words like **mjuvi** (impudent, know-all) or **mjuzi** (expert) from **jua** (know).

3. Other morphophonemic changes affecting consonants /p/ and /k/ before /u/ in the final position also occur, e.g., **upungufu** (shortage) from **punguka** (diminish). Similarly /l/ also undergoes a morphophonemic change /v/ before /u/ in the final position, e.g., **ulegevu** (slackness) from **legea** (be slack). These suffixes -fu and -vu are, however, inconsistent since, in other situations, we observe a pattern of free variation between **fu** and **vu**, e.g., **mchofu** or **mchovu** (a tiresome person) from **choka** (be tired). In Arabic loan words, the suffixes are expanded to -ivu and -ifu, e.g., **msahaulifu** or **msahaulivu** (a forgetful person) from **sahau** (forget).

Exercise 1

1. Describe the differences between a phoneme and an allophone. Give three examples in each case.

2. Describe the distinctive features of the following sounds:

   a. [i]   b. [o]
   c. [g]   d. [z]
   e. [w]   f. [k]
   g. [b]   h. [j]
   i. [p]   j. [u]

3. What is intonation? Describe the different patterns of intonation that exist in Swahili.

4. What do you understand by morphophonemic changes? Explain how they affect vowels in Swahili.

2 Word Formation in Swahili

Generally, word formation refers to the whole process of morphological variation in the constitution of words. The term includes the two main divisions of inflection and derivation. However, word formation refers largely to the latter. Both types of word formation will be discussed.

Inflection

Within the grammatical category of inflection, there are particles known as **inflectional affixes**. These particles only signal grammatical relationships such as number and possession. They do not change the grammatical class of the stems to which they are attached. In Swahili, inflection is characterized by the Bantu class-prefix system operating largely at three levels: nominal, pronominal and verbal.

Nominal forms

Nominal forms in Swahili include nouns and adjectives. They are made up of a class-prefix together with a nominal stem which can be either a root, such as **toto** in **mtoto** (child), or a deverbative, such as **chokozi** from the verbal root **chokoza** (tease). Below is an illustration of the concept of inflection involving nominal forms:

Class	Singular	Plural
1 – 2	*m*jane (widow)	*wa*jane (widows)
	*m*walimu (teacher)	*wa*limu (teachers)
3 – 4	*m*tungi (pot)	*mi*tungi (pots)
	*m*kono (arm)	*mi*kono (arms)
5 – 6	ø chungwa (orange)	*ma*chungwa (oranges)
	jina (name)	*ma*jina (names)
7 – 8	*ki*kombe (cup)	*vi*kombe (cups)
9 – 10	ø kengele (bell)	kengele (bells)
	ø sabuni (soap)	sabuni (soaps)
11 – 14	ukuta (wall)	kuta (walls)
	uma (fork)	nyuma (forks)

ø   This symbol indicates the absence of a class prefix on a noun.

As we can see from these examples, the class-prefixes of the singular nouns are quite different from those of the plural forms. Yet this difference

26

does not result in a change in the grammatical class of those words. All the words on the right are still nouns even though they have been pluralized. This is, therefore, one instance of inflection operating in Swahili. It is worth noting that in the case of classes 9-10, the contrast between singular and plural forms is not marked in the noun-prefix. This contrast is only marked in pronominal and verbal concords. For example:

    a. **Kengele yetu imeanguka chini.**
        Our bell has fallen down.
    b. **Kengele zetu zimeanguka chini.**
        Our bells have fallen down.

Pronominal forms

The pronominal forms also exhibit the concept of inflection since they do not change the grammatical class of a word. In Swahili, the pronominal forms include personal pronouns, demonstratives, possessives, interrogatives and indefinite markers.

Note that noun classes 15, 16, 17, and 18 have not been illustrated above because they do not have plural forms.

Personal pronouns. Personal pronouns are discussed later. Whether in bound or free forms, they certainly exhibit the concept of indefinite markers.

    a. nami ————>nasi
    b. naye ————>nao
    c. mimi————>sisi
    d. yeye ————>wao

Pronouns (a) and (b) are instances of bound forms since the associative particle na, (and, with) has been attached to a segment of a free form. But (c) and (d) are pronouns which are free forms since they have not been attached to any morpheme.

Demonstratives. Like personal pronouns, demonstratives also give the notion of inflection since they do not affect the grammatical class of each form of the demonstrative when the process of pluralization is effected. The following examples illustrate this:

    a. hiki ————> hivi
    b. hilo ————> hayo
    c. kile ————> vile
    d. lile ————> yale

Possessives. The possessives are other instances exhibiting the concept of inflection. In Swahili, the possessive stems are:

	Singular		Plural
a.	**-angu** (my)	———>	**-etu** (our)
b.	**-ako** (your)	———>	**-enu** (your) (pl)
c.	**-ake** (his, hers)	———>	**-ao** (their)

Each of the above stems take an appropriate prefix in agreement with the class-prefix of the noun occurring with it.

Interrogatives. The interrogative stem **pi** is the only enclitic that takes a pronominal concord. This concord agrees with the class of the noun co-occurring with it. Like other kinds of pronominal forms, the interrogative stem **pi** also exhibits inflection. Here are some examples:

	Singular		Plural
a.	**mtu yupi?**	———>	**watu wepi?**
	(which person?)		(which persons?)
b.	**kiti kipi?**	———>	**viti vipi?**
	(which chair?)		(which chairs?)

Indefinite markers. Indefinite markers are other examples of grammatical forms describing the notion of inflection. The two indefinite markers in Swahili are **-ote** and **-o -ote**. The former indicates wholeness or totality while the latter assumes the meaning of "whatsoever" or "whosoever". Their examples are shown below:

	Singular		Plural
a.	**mti wote**	———>	**miti yote**
	(the whole tree)		(all the trees)
b.	**chakula chote**	———>	**vyakula vyote**
	(all the food)		(all the foods)
c.	**nyumba yoyote**	———>	**nyumba zozote**
	(any house)		(any houses)
d.	**utambi wowote**	———>	**tambi zozote**
	(any wick)		(any wicks)

Verbal stems

Finally, we come to verbal stems. These, too, exhibit inflection because they do not effect any change in the grammatical class when they are affixed.

A verbal stem is normally comprised of the root, with or without a suffix or suffixes, together with the final particle -a. Following are few examples of verbal stems and their affixes:

	Singular	Plural
a.	*Ni*tacheza kesho	*Tu*tacheza kesho
	(*I* will play tomorrow)	(*We* will play tomorrow)
b.	*A*lianguka chini	*Wa*lianguka chini
	(*He* fell down)	(*They* fell down)
c.	*Ha*taki chochote	*Hawa*taki chochote
	(*He* does not want anything)	(*They* do not want anything)
d.	Mwalimu ali*ni*pa zawadi	Walimu wali*tu*pa zawadi
	(The teacher gave *me* a prize)	(The teachers gave *us* prizes)

Derivation

Unlike inflection, derivation generally effects a grammatical change in the class of a word in Swahili. This derivation can take place at nominal and verbal levels.

Nominal derivation

Words derived from verbs are called *deverbatives*. Noun deverbatives carry a prefix and a suffix. The prefixes concerned are the class-prefixes while the suffixes are **-I, -JI, -U, -O, -E**, and **-A**. Each of these suffixes has a semantic significance as explained in the following section.

Suffix -I. Some grammars describe suffix -I as an agentive suffix because it indicates the person or thing performing an action expressed by the verb. The nouns that are derived from it, therefore, belong to **M-WA class** which consists of human beings, although a few of the nouns can also belong to KI- class. For instance:

Verb	M-WA class
pika (cook)	mpish*i* (cook)
gomba (quarrel)	mgomv*i* (brawler)
zaa (beget)	mzaz*i* (parent)
tumika (serve)	mtumish*i* (servant)
ongoza (lead)	kiongoz*i* (leader)
nyoa (shave)	kinyoz*i* (barber)

Deverbatives with the suffix -I can also express the whole process by which an action is performed. The class-prefix, however, is either **ma-**, which gives the sense of totality, or **u-**, which gives the abstract concept of the action that is expressed by the verb. For example:

Verb	JI-MA Class
lala (sleep)	malazi (accommodation)
ongea (converse)	maongezi (conversation)
ongoza (lead)	uongozi (leadership)
tumika (serve)	utumishi (service)

Suffix -JI. The suffix -JI expresses habituality or repetition. It corresponds to the noun suffix of the verb suffix -GA which is used in many Bantu languages to express an action that is repetitive. The -JI suffix generally occurs in nouns that belong to M-WA class. For example:

Verb	M-WA class
soma (read)	msomaji (reader)
imba (sing)	mwimbaji (singer)
cheza (play)	mchezaji (player)

The -JI suffix can also express an abstract concept of a habitual action when the class-prefix U is used. For example:

Verb	U-U class
omba (beg)	uombaji (begging)
goma (strike)	ugomaji (striking)
winda (hunt)	uwindaji (hunting)

Occasionally, the -JI suffix is used with other class-prefixes to refer to a non-human agent:

nywa (drink)	kinywaji (a drink)
tambaa (creep)	mtambaaji (a creeper plant)

Suffix -U. Words with suffix -U express the possessor of a state when used with M-WA prefixes and the state itself when used with the prefix -U:

potea (lose)	—>	mpotevu (a wasteful person)	—>	upotevu (wasting)
tukuka (be exalted)	—>	mtukufu (an exalted person)	—>	utukufu (exaltation)
tulia (be quiet)	—>	mtulivu (a quiet person)	—>	utulivu (calmness)

It is important to remember the phonetic change brought by the suffix -U. As a rule, when there is a verb ending with two vowels, the noun ending is -VU. But when the verb ends with -KA, the noun ending is -FU. The table below illustrates this phonetic change:

Verb suffix	Noun suffix	Verb	Noun
Two vowels	-VU	**legea** (slack)	**ulegevu** (slackness)
-KA	-FU	**kunjuka** (be unfolded)	**ukunjufu** (cheerfulness)

Table 2: Suffix phonetic change

However, even with the above rule governing the phonetic change, there are still some inconsistencies which create suffixes **-VU** and **-FU** on the basis of free variation for some words. For example:

okoa (save) ———> **woko*vu*** or **woko*fu*** (salvation)
choka (be tired) ———> **mcho*vu*** or **mcho*fu*** (one who is tired)

Verbs borrowed from Arabic give secondary suffixes -IVU or -IFU:

haribu (destroy) ———> **uharibi*fu*** (destruction).
sahau (forget) ———> **msahauli*fu*** or **msahauli*vu*** (a forgetful person).

Many nouns with suffix -U are formed from intransitive verbs and, quite commonly with stative forms. Those with suffix -I are mainly derived from transitive verbs.

Some transitive verbs produce two forms of nouns. One has an -U suffix which stresses state and the other an -I which indicates activity. Table 3 illustrates this formation of nouns.

Suffix -O. This suffix essentially has a dual function. First, it indicates the instrument which performs the action of the verb and secondly, it indicates verbal action of the ultimate result of the action.

Verb	-U of state	-I of activity
sikia (hear)	msiki*vu* (obedient person)	msiki*zi* (a hearer)
kosa (err)	mkose*vu* (a careless person)	mkosa*ji* (one who makes mistakes)
angalia (take care)	mwangali*vu*/mwangali*fu* (a careful, attentive person)	mwangali*zi* (a caretaker)

Table 3: Formation of nouns

In the first function, it occurs frequently with the class-prefix **KI** for objects, although other class-prefixes, such as **U, M, MA** and **NY** can occasionally be used with the -O suffix as the following examples show.

Verb		Noun formation
		KI-VI class
funika (cover)	————>	kifuniko (lid)
ziba (stop up)	————>	kizibo (stopper)
vuka (cross)	————>	kivuko (ford)
		U-U class
fungua (unfasten)	————>	ufunguo (key)
fagia (sweep)	————>	ufagio (brush)
		M-M class
tega (entrap)	————>	mtego (trap)
cheza (play)	————>	mchezo (play)
		JI-MA class
lisha (feed livestock)	————>	malisho (pasture)
		N-N class
unda (construct)	————>	nyundo (hammer)

In the second function, that is, with names of non-concrete nature, the -O suffix indicates verbal action or its ultimate results. Generally, words of this nature are found in M-MI and JI-MA classes. In the former, the words refer to the action as a whole. A number of these words have no plural forms. In the latter, the words frequently refer to actions which can occur singly but in a more collective sense. Here are some examples:

Verb		Noun formation
		M-MI class
shona (sew)	———>	mshono (seam)
sema (say)	———>	msemo (saying)
		JI-MA class
patana (agree)	———>	mapatano (agreement)
onja (taste)	———>	maonjo (taste)

A few words can have class prefixes U and N:

Verb		Noun formation
		U-U class
imba (sing)	———>	**wimbo** (song)
apa (swear)	———>	**uapo** (oath)
		N-N class
ota (dream)	———>	**ndoto** (dream)
nguruma (thunder)	———>	**ngurumo** (thunder)

In some cases, certain words can refer to both forms, that is, concrete and non-concrete:

Verb		Noun formation
ponya (treat)	———>	**maponyo** (drugs, medicines, treatment, rescue, e.t.c.)
tokea (come out)	———>	**tokeo** (outlet, pore, act of giving out)

Suffix -E. -E as a suffix is used to form deverbatives expressing passivity or the performer of an action. The nominal derivations show the person or object experiencing the action and are used with a wide range of class-prefixes. For example:

Verb		Noun formation
		M-WA class
teua (choose)	———>	**mteule** (one who has been chosen)
shinda (conquer)	———>	**mshinde** (one who conquers)
zembea (be idle)	———>	**mzembe** (an idle person)
buga (cadge)	———>	**mbuge** (cadger)
bemba (coax)	———>	**mbembe** (a persuasive person)
		M-MI class
kata (cut)	———>	**mkate** (bread)
vuka (give fumes)	———>	**mvuke** (steam)
tuma (send)	———>	**mtume** (messenger, apostle)
angaa (shine)	———>	**mwenge** (torch)
songa (twist)	———>	**msonge** (a twisted thing)

Suffix -A. Some deverbatives carry the suffix -A and these operate for all noun classes. The nouns formed carry no distinctive meaning:

Verb		Noun formation
		M-WA class
ogopa (fear)	——————>	mwoga (coward)
ganga (cure)	——————>	mganga (doctor)
		JI-MA class
zoea (get used to)	——————>	mazoea (familiarity)
kosa (err)	——————>	makosa (mistakes)
		KI-VI class
chana (separate)	——————>	chanuo (comb)
nywa (drink)	——————>	kinywa (mouth)
		U-U class
ogopa (fear)	——————>	woga (fear)
lumba (quarrel)	——————>	ulumbaji (quarrelling)
		M-MI class
zinga (go round)	——————>	mzinga (anything of cylindrical shape)
		N-N class
oa (marry)	——————>	ndoa (marriage)

Some deverbatives of the M-WA and KI-VI classes indicate the agent or the doer of the action. A few nouns in the KI-VI class, however, indicate the instrument or the process denoted by the verbal stem, in other words, impersonal agencies. All these deverbatives carry a suffix -A and are followed by a qualifier, noun, used to particularize the meaning. Following are some examples:

Verb		Noun formation
panda (mount)	——————>	mpandafarasi (a horse man)
fuma (weave)	——————>	mfumanguo (a weaver)

Examples of nouns expressing impersonal agency are:

kifunguamimba (the first born)
kipamkono (a wedding fee)

In some grammars, the above words are referred to as **compound nouns**. This process of compounding words that function independently in other circumstances is called **composition**.

A similar kind of nominal compound contains the particle **ana** (son, daughter) as the first immediate constituent of the compound. The second element does not take a class-prefix if it is a noun but shows an adjectival concord if it is an adjective. To illustrate this, here are some examples:

mwanafunzi (student) ———> **wanafunzi** (students)
mwanachama (member) ———> **wanachama** (members)

In the first example, the word **funzi** is a deverbative from the verb **funza** (teach), and in the second example, the noun **chama** means "association".

Verbal derivation

The last kind of derivation in Swahili is a verbal one. Verbal derivation subsumes six major grammatical categories: passive, stative, causative, prepositional, conversive and reciprocal.

In examining the concept of verbal derivation in Swahili, we will see that it operates according to the principles of vowel harmony, as explained in the previous chapter. This means that the vowel in the verbal root or stem will affect the suffix containing the vowel. Thus, the high vowel will occur when the verbal root contains /a/, /i/ or /u/, as the following examples indicate:

za (bear) ———> **zalia** (bear to)
zawa (born)
zalisha (cause to bear)

piga (beat) ———> **pigia** (beat for)
pigwa (beaten)
pigisha (cause to beat)

chuma (pluck) ———> **chumia** (pluck for)
chumwa (plucked)
chumisha (cause to pluck)

Similarly, when the verb root or stem contains /e/ or /o/, the mid-vowel is found:

cheza (play) ———> **chezea** (play for)
chezwa (played)
chezesha (cause to play)

35

soma (read) —————> som*e*a (read for)
somwa (read)
som*e*sha (cause to read)

In verbs of non-Bantu origin, the front vowel also occurs, except in the verbal root containing a stem with /e/. For example:

jibu (answer) —————> jib*i*a (answer for)
jib*i*wa (be answered)
jib*i*sha (cause to answer)

rudi (return) —————> rud*i*a (return to)
rud*i*wa (be returned)
rud*i*sha (give back)

samehe (forgive)—————> sameh*e*a (forgive for)
sameh*e*wa (forgiven)
sameh*e*sha (cause to forgive)

Finally, with monosyllabic verbs, both the high and mid vowels occur in the suffix containing the verb stem:

la (eat) —————> lia (eat for)
liwa (eaten)
lisha (cause to eat)

cha (fear) —————> chea (fear for)
chewa (feared)
chesha (cause to fear)

Morphemes

A *morpheme* can be described as the *smallest meaningful unit of grammar in the structure of a language. Smallest meaningful unit* means a unit which cannot be divided without destroying or drastically altering the meaning. For example /daftari/ as in **daftari** (book) is a morpheme; as a whole, it conveys a complete meaning. If we divide this morpheme, we obtain fragments such as /daf/ or /tari/ which have no meaning or which are not significantly related to that of /daftari/. Any division of /daftari/ will definitely destroy or drastically alter the meaning. Therefore, /daftari/ qualifies our earlier description of a morpheme as the smallest meaningful unit of grammar in the structure of a language.

A morpheme is not synonymous with a *syllable*. The morpheme **la** (eat) happens to be a syllable also, but /daftari/ is a single morpheme containing three syllables. In short, morphemes in Swahili may consist of one syllable or several whole syllables or parts of syllables.

It can also be argued that a morpheme may only consist of a single phoneme, for example, the initial /a/ in **aja** (he comes). Here, the /a/ is a phoneme and can also be called a morpheme in the construction of **aja**. But both the phoneme /a/ and the morpheme are by no means the same thing. The phoneme can occur in many contexts where it has got nothing to do with this morpheme. Examples are **aria** /aria/ (section) and **ami** / ami/ (father's brother). Both these examples contain /a/ but have no common meaning with the initial /a/ in **aja.**

Bound and free morphemes

Morphemes which can occur freely on their own are said to be free For example:

    a.   **baba** (father)
    b.   **samaki** (fish)

A word consisting of a single free morpheme is a *monomorphemic* word. Free morphemes are also referred to as *lexical units* because of the complete meaning they have. In contrast, there are morphemes which occur only as affixes. These morphemes are said to be *bound*. For example:

    a.   **dukani** (in the shop)
    b.   **kisanduku** (a small box)

In these examples, the locative **NI** and the prefix **KI** are bound morphemes because they cannot exist as single free words. Furthermore, bound morphemes are said to have a grammatical function. In the case of **NI**, it is a marker of location for common nouns while the particle **KI** functions as a marker of prefixation for singular nouns belonging to the **KI** class.

Allomorphs

An *allomorph* is a variant of a morpheme which occurs in certain environments. A morpheme is a group of one or more allomorphs which conform to certain definable criteria of distribution and meaning. Thus, that the past tense markers /-li-/ and /-ku-/ are allomorphs of the single morpheme, namely, **Past**. Further examples of allomorphs in Swahili are given in the next page.

The passive verb symbolized by the morpheme [W] has these allomorphs: **-w, -liw, -iw** and **-ew**. Similarly, the causative verb symbolized by the morpheme [SH] has the following allomorphs: **-sh, -esh, -sh, -z, -ez** and **-z**.

VOCABULARY

linda	guard	**pagaa**	carry
mchukuzi	porter	**hama**	emigrate
tibu	cure	**bomoa**	break down
mwashi	mason	**tafuna**	bite
teketeza	destroy	**chungua**	investigate
mvua	rain	**mshtakiwa**	accused
rufani	appeal	**chukua**	match
konde	field	**palilia**	cultivate

Exercise 2

1. Construct two forms of nouns from the following verbs:

    a. linda
    b. soma
    c. tibu
    d. la
    e. teketeza
    f. shona
    g. pagaa
    h. bomoa
    i. chungua
    j. tuma

2. Find suitable verbs in the brackets, combine them with the affixes and fill in the blank spaces of the following sentences:

    Example:
    Kijana alini . . . . sana kwa maelezo yake.
    (sikitisha, sikitika).
    Kijana alinisikitisha sana kwa maelezo yake.
    The youth disappointed me a lot by his explanation.

    a. Mchukuzi atai .... mizigo hii kesho.
       (bebwa; beba)
    b. Wazee wali .... katika vijiji vyengine.
       (hamia; hama)
    c. Njia hii ina ....
       (pitwa; pitika)
    d. Waashi wana .... nyumba kwa matufali.
       (jenga; jengeka)

e. Hamisi ameni .... barua hii.
   (andika; andikia)
f. Mvua ime .... punde hivi.
   (nyamaa; nyamaza)
g. Mbwa mkali alim .... mtoto mdogo.
   (tafunwa; tafuna)
h. Kijana yule anapenda kuni .... masihara.
   (fanyia; fanyiana)
i. Mshtakiwa ali .... rufani hivi majuzi.
   (kata; katia)
j. Mtalii ame .... na kifuko chake cha pesa.
   (potea; potelewa)
k. Ukivaa nguo hizi, kwa kweli zinaku .... vizuri.
   (chukua; chukulia)
l. Kwa nini hutaki kuni .... mizigo yangu?
   (chukuliwa; chukulia)
m. Kamba ile ime .... katikati.
   (katiana; katika)
n. Mkulima huyu amewahi ku .... konde yake leo.
   (paliliwa; palilia)
o. Mimi nimem .... mtu yule pesa nyingi sana.
   (kopwa; kopesha)

3. Show the main difference between derivation and inflection. Give five examples of each in Swahili.

4. What do you understand by composition in the field of morphology? Give five examples in Swahili.

3 Noun Classes

Traditionally, nouns in Swahili have been classified according to their initial prefix. Thus, in traditional grammar (the grammar of contemporary periods of *Loogman, Ashton,* etc., which also existed before the advent of modern linguistics of *Halliday, Chomsky* and others), there are eight classes of nouns.

The following is a breakdown of these noun classes:

M-WA class

Almost all nouns referring to people belong to this class. This class is generally considered as the **Living Class** since it contains names of human beings. In the singular form, the prefix of a noun belonging to this class is either **M-** or **MW-**. In the plural, it is **WA-**.

Singular	Plural
*m*tu (a person)	*wa*tu (persons)
*mw*alimu (a teacher)	*wa*limu (teachers)

A few nouns which do not refer to human beings and which belong to this class are shown below·

Singular	Plural
*m*dudu (an insect)	*wa*dudu (insects)
*m*nyama (an animal)	*wa*nyama (animals)

Some compound words which refer to human entities also belong to this class:

Singular	Plural
*mw*anahewa (an airman)	*wa*nahewa (airmen)
*mw*anamapinduzi (a revolutionist)	*wa*namapinduzi (revolutionists)

M-MI class

Traditional grammar states that names of non-human living things, such as trees, plants, etc., belong to this class. There are also other nouns belonging to this class but which do not appear to have any general classification or distinct features. In the singular, the class prefix for these nouns in **M-** or **MW-** and in the plural, is **MI-**:

40

Singular	Plural
*m*nazi (a coconut tree)	*m*inazi (coconut trees)
*m*wembe (a mango tree)	*m*iembe (mango trees)
*m*lango (a door)	*m*ilango (doors)
*m*oyo (a heart)	*m*ioyo (hearts)

JI-MA class

This class is called JI-MA because a small number of nouns belonging to it can take the prefix JI- in the singular and MA- in the plural. The remaining nouns have no prefix in the singular but take the concord MA- in the plural.

Nouns belonging to JI-MA class can be categorized in the following ways:

a. Nouns whose singular take the prefix JI- and whose plural take MA-:

Singular	Plural
*ji*we (a stone)	*ma*we (stones)
*ji*ko (a kitchen, a stove)	*me*ko (kitchens, stoves)

b. Nouns whose singular take the letter J- and whose plural take the prefix MA-:

Singular	Plural
*j*ani (a leaf)	*ma*jani (leaves)
*j*ambo (a matter)	*ma*mbo (matters)

c. Nouns which have no prefix in the singular and take the concord MA- in the plural:

Singular	Plural
ø daraja (a bridge)	*ma*daraja (bridges)
ø gari (a car)	*ma*gari (cars)

d. Most of the nouns depicting fruits or produce of plants:

Singular	Plural
ø chungwa (an orange)	*ma*chungwa (oranges)
ø ua (a flower)	*ma*ua (flowers)

e. Nouns depicting relationships, occupation or status:

Singular	Plural
ø shangazi (aunt)	*ma*shangazi (aunts)
ø dereva (driver)	*ma*dereva (drivers)
ø rais (president)	*ma*rais (presidents)

41

f. Nouns which are "mass" or uncountable and are used only in the plural form:

   maji (water)
   mafuta (oil)

g. Nouns used as augmentatives, that is, stressing the size or importance of objects:

Singular	Plural
jitu (giant)	*ma*jitu (giants)
jumba (a building)	*ma*jumba (buildings)

Recent research has, however, shown that, apart from JI- and MA-prefixes, other prefixes can also be used as markers of augmentatives. For example, *Zawawi (1974)* shows that the little known prefix **ba-** can also be used as a marker of augmentatives, thus:

Singular	Plural
sanduku (box)	*ba*sanduku (a big box)
simba (lion)	*ba*simba (a big lion)

KI-VI class

Many of the nouns in this class are names of inanimate things, as opposed to animate sentient creatures. The prefix for nouns in this class is **KI-** for the singular form and **VI-** for the plural. For example:

Singular	Plural
kidonda (sore)	*vi*dónda (sores)
kilima (hill)	*vi*lima (hills)

Nouns with vowel stems take the prefix **CH-** for the singular and **VY-** for the plural. For example:

Singular	Plural
*ch*eti (note)	*vy*eti (notes)
*ch*umba (room)	*vy*umba (rooms)

Apart from these nouns referring to inanimate things, a few nouns referring to animals and people can also be found in this case. For example:

Singular	Plural
*ki*faru (rhinoceros)	*vi*faru (rhinoceroses)
*ki*boko (hippo)	*vi*boko (hippos)

*ki*jana (youth)	*vi*jana (youths)
*ki*ziwi (deaf person)	*vi*ziwi (deaf persons)

Many grammars have in the past described the prefix **ki-** as being a diminutive marker. For example:

a. **kimeza** (a small table) from **meza** (table).
b. **kitoto** (a small child) from **mtoto** (child).

This diminutive function of the prefix **ki-** has now taken a new dimension as a result of recent researches. It has also been found recently that, apart from the diminutive function, the prefix **ki-** can, in some instances, serve as an augmentative and emphatic marker when an accentuated stress is put on the penultimate syllable of a word. For example:

a. **Nilikiona kijua njiani.**
   I experienced an excessive burning sun during the journey.
b. **Alitokwa na kijasho.**
   He sweated excessively.

In these two examples, the prefix **ki-** in the words **kijua** (scorching sun) and **kijasho** (excessive sweat) does not have a diminutive role. Instead, it operates as an augmentative marker of the lexical items **jua** (sun) and **jasho** (sweat).

In a few cases, the use of the prefix **KI-** preceding a stem neither functions as a diminutive nor as an augmentative marker. For example:

a. Walimpiga **kipigo** kizuri
   They dealt him a big blow.

b. Anapata **kipato** kidogo.
   He gets a low income.

Here, the use of **Ki-** in **kipigo (blow)** and **kipato** (income) conveys the same meaning as in **pigo** (blow) and **pato** (income) if at all these words were used in the same sentences. In other words, the use of **Ki-** in the above two sentences conveys neutral meanings to their sentences, that is without emphasising the notions of diminutiveness or augmentative.

N-N class

Grammar books agree that this is the largest of all the noun classes in the language. Many words borrowed from other languages like Arabic and English are incorporated into this class. Words of Bantu origin placed in this class are quite few. Examples of words of foreign origin include:

Singular	Plural
sabuni (soap)	**sabuni** (soaps)
saa (watch)	**saa** (watches)
motokaa (motor car)	**motokaa** (motor cars)

Apart from borrowed words, a majority of individual species of animals, birds and insects fall in this class.

Singular	Plural
paka (cat)	**paka** (cats)
panzi (grasshopper)	**panzi** (grasshoppers)
kunguru (crow)	**kunguru** (crows)

Some words of Bantu origin whose singular and plural forms are the same, are grouped into this class.

Singular	Plural
kengele (bell)	**keŋgele** (bells)
taa (lamp)	**taa** (lamps)

Other words beginning with **N-** and occurring before the letters **d, g, j** and **z** in disyllabic and polysyllabic stems are placed in this class.

Singular	Plural
*n*dugu (brother)	*n*dugu (brothers)
*n*jia (road)	*n*jia (roads)
*n*gazi (ladder)	*n*gazi (ladders)
*n*zio (water jar, pitcher)	*n*zio (water jars, pitchers)

Similarly, some words beginning with **M-** and occurring before the labial consonants **v** and **b** are placed in this class.

Singular	Plural
*m*vi (grey hair)	*m*vi (grey hairs)
*m*binu (strategy)	*m*binu (strategies)

Lastly, some words beginning with the consonant cluster **ny** that precedes a vowel stem are also placed in this class.

Singular	Plural
*ny*umba (house)	*ny*umba (houses)
*ny*undo (hammer)	*ny*undo (hammers)

·U-U class

Traditional grammars argue that all nouns in this class have the prefix U- in the singular. The U- becomes W- when the stem starts with a vowel.

Singular	Plural
ukuta (wall)	kuta (walls)
wakati (period)	nyakati (periods)

Some nouns in the U- class do not have plural forms, yet they belong to this class because in the singular form, they take the prefix U- or W-.

Singular	Plural
umoja (unity)	–
wino (ink)	–

The nouns in the U- class can be divided into the following groups:

1. Nouns of various types (both concrete and abstract) which have singular and plural forms.

Singular	Plural
ukurasa (page)	kurasa (pages)
uma (fork)	nyuma (forks)
upepo (wind)	pepo (winds)
waraka (a document)	nyaraka (documents)

2. Nouns of abstract nature made up of adjectival or noun stems from other classes and, sometimes, from certain verb stems. These nouns do not have a plural form although there is a tendency by some speakers to pluralize a few abstract ones:

Singular	Plural
uhuru (freedom)	–
uwezo (ability)	–
urefu (length)	–
uchaguzi (election)	chaguzi (elections)
utafiti (research)	tafiti (researches)

3. Nouns which are "mass" or uncountable. They also do not have a plural form.

Singular	Plural
uji (gruel)	–
wali (cooked rice)	–

4. Nouns which indicate names of countries. Again, these nouns do not have a plural form.

Singular	Plural
Ufaransa (France)	–
Ureno (Portugal)	–

KU- class

This class is made up of verbs which begin with the prefix **KU-** but are used as nouns and are thus referred to as **verbal nouns** or **gerunds**. They can be modified by adjectives and can also appear in positions where nominal elements are typically present. The nouns in this class are also referred to as **infinitives** because they correspond to the English form of the infinitive. Since these nouns express the act of doing, of becoming or the state of being, there are no singular and plural forms. The following examples illustrate the use of nouns belonging to this class:

1. *Kusoma* kwangu kutawafurahisha.
    My reading will please them.

2. *Kusaidia* wagonjwa ni jambo zuri.
    To help the sick is a good thing.

Nouns in this class can also be used in the negative form by inserting the grammatical particle "to" as an infix between the infinitive **KU-** and the verb stem:

1. **Ku*to*kuja kwake hapa kulituudhi sana.**
    His failure to come here displeased us.

2. **Ku*to*elewa kwangu katika somo la darasani kulimchukiza mwalimu.**
    My problem of not understanding the lesson in the class displeased the teacher.

Monosyllabic verbs do not drop the infinitive **KU-**. This means that two infinitive markers remain in the verb stem:

Positive	Negative
kula (eat)	**kutokula** (not to eat)
kunywa (drink)	**kutokunywa** (not to drink)

PA- class

This class inherently contains one noun only. The noun is **mahali** (place), signifying location. But unlike English, location in Swahili is described by traditional grammars in three ways:

    a.   PA- (Definite place of position).
    b.   KU- (Indefinite place of direction).
    c.   MU- (Area, "alongness", "withinness").

Double class membership

In her doctoral dissertation, *Zawawi (1974)* points out that certain Swahili nouns belong to more than one class. A word like **shangazi** (aunt), for example, can be placed under N- class, JI-MA class and even M-WA class. Similarly, the nouns **zulia** (carpet) and **taji** (crown) can be placed under N- class and JI-MA class. Such nouns belonging to more than one class, therefore, fluctuate in their concordial agreements. The choice of a particular concordial prefix is determined by the class of the noun under examination. For example:

    a.   **shangazi langu** (my aunt): JI-MA class
    b.   **shangazi yangu** (my aunt): N- class
    c.   **shangazi wangu** (my aunt): M-WA class

To summarize, it is clear that traditional analysis of Swahili nouns uses the form of a word as a basis for classification. This method, however, poses a number of problems. For instance, nouns such as **kijana** (youth) and **kiziwi** (a deaf person) are placed in KI-VI class although their concordial markers are similar to those nouns belonging to M-WA class. Yet nouns which are inanimate such as **kitabu** (book) and **kiti** (chair) are also placed in the KI-VI class although their concordial markers are different from the human nouns such as **kijana** and **kiziwi**. Similarly, words such as **mtume** (prophet) and **mungu** (god) are placed in M-MI class although their concordial markers are different from inanimate nouns such as **mkoba** (basket) and **mtego** (trap).

    This problem of inconsistency in analysing Swahili nouns is also reflected in the U class. If traditional grammars use "form" as a basis for their classification, it is logical then that words such as **magonjwa** (diseases) and **maovu** (evils) should belong to the JI-MA class. But these two nouns are placed in the U class merely because their singular forms contain the prefix U-.

    If we base our judgement on the singular form of a word, then this practice should be consistent. Yet, we find that it is not, especially when we examine other types of nouns, such as "mass", or uncountable ones like **maji** (water) and **mafuta** (oil). These two nouns are placed in the JI-MA class simply because their concordial markers always operate in the plural form, using the concord **ma** like other nouns which are not "mass" or uncountable such as **machungwa** (oranges) and **mayai** (eggs).

Because of these inconsistencies, modern grammars such as *Kapinga (1983)* have presented a new method of analysing nouns. This means that nouns in Swahili are no longer analysed by looking at the "form", but rather at the "function". In other words, the tendency now is to analyse nouns by looking at the varieties of the grammatical markers, technically known as **subject prefixes**. Thus, instead of having eight classes of Swahili nouns, modern grammars would now have eighteen, as shown in the following sections.

A-WA (1-2)

These classes take the concordial marker **a** for all their nouns in the singular form and **wa-** for the plural. This means that all living (animate) things are placed in these classes. Thus, nouns which were originally placed in KI-VI class by traditional grammars, such as **kijana** (youth) and **kipofu** (a blind person), are now positioned in these classes. Also included in these classes are nouns such as **askari** (policeman) and **malaika** (angel), all of which were traditionally placed in the JI-MA class. Similarly, nouns such as **mtume** (prophet) and **mungu** (god) which were originally positioned in the M-MI class are now found in the A-WA classes.

In brief, almost all living creatures (with a few exceptions) are now placed in classes A-WA, that is, 1 and 2. The class prefix for nouns in these classes is **M-** or **MW-** for the singular and **WA-** for plural.

Singular	Plural
*m*zee (an old person)	*wa*zee (old people)
*m*vulana (boy)	*wa*vulana (boys)
*m*walimu (teacher)	*wa*limu (teachers)

U-I (3-4)

The concordial marker for nouns in these classes is **U-** for the singular form and **I-** for the plural. Like in traditional grammars, names of plants, trees and so on are placed in these classes. But unlike in traditional grammars, nouns such as **mtume** (prophet) and **mungu** (god) are no longer categorized in these classes. As we have already mentioned, these nouns are now placed in A-WA classes, that is, classes 1 and 2. The class prefix for nouns in U-I classes is **M-** or **MW-** for the singular form and **MI-** for the plural.

Singular	Plural
*m*kuki (spear)	*mi*kuki (spears)
*m*waka (year)	*mi*aka (years)
*mo*to (fire)	*mi*oto (fires)

LI-YA (5-6)

All inanimate nouns which were traditionally placed in the JI-MA group can also be found in LI-YA classes. Animate nouns are no longer in these classes but are placed in A-WA classes. The class prefix for nouns in LI-YA classes are **JI-, J-** or **ø** (zero morpheme) for the singular form and **MA-** for the plural.

Singular	Plural
jiti (big stick)	*ma*jiti (big sticks)
jembe (hoe)	*ma*jembe (hoes)
nanasi (pineapple)	*ma*nanasi (pineapples)

KI-VI (7-8)

Nouns in these classes are all inanimate. This means that nouns like **kiziwi** (a deaf person) and **kiongozi** (a leader) are no longer placed in these classes, as was the case with traditional grammars. The class prefix for the nouns in these classes is **KI-** for the singular forms and **VI-** for the plural. Where there is a vowel stem, the prefix becomes **CH-** for the singular form and **VY-** for the plural.

Singular	Plural
*ki*kombe (cup)	*vi*kombe (cups)
*ki*dole (finger)	*vi*dole (fingers)
*ch*umba (room)	*vy*umba (rooms)

I-ZI (9-10)

Many of the words borrowed from other languages belong to this class. The nouns have a zero morpheme for both the singular and plural forms. Thus, it is only from looking at the context in which a word is used that one can tell whether it is in the singular or plural form. In the case of the former, the subject prefix is **I-** and for the latter, it is **ZI-**.

Singular	Plural
meza (table)	**meza** (tables)
sahani (plate)	**sahani** (plates)
barua (letter)	**barua** (letters)

U-ZI (11-14)

The nouns in these classes take a subject prefix **U-** for the singular and **ZI-** for the plural. The class prefixes of these nouns are **U-** or **W-** for the singular and **M-, N-, Ny-** or a zero morpheme for the plural. In traditional grammars, the nouns belonging to U-ZI classes were all placed under U-class.

Singular	Plural
*u*so (face)	*ny*uso (faces)
*u*koo (clan)	koo (clans)
*u*bao (plank)	*m*bao (planks)
*u*devu (beard)	*n*devu (beards)
*w*embe (razor)	*ny*embe (razors)

Abstract nouns are also included in U-ZI classes. Like in traditional grammars, these nouns do not have a plural form. For example:

Singular	Plural
utoto (childhood)	–
upendo (love)	–

U-YA (11-14)

The nouns in these classes are quite few. In the singular, they take a subject prefix **U-** and **YA-** for the plural. Their class prefix is **U-** for the singular and **MA-** for the plural. In traditional grammars, the nouns in U-YA classes were placed under the U- class. Here are some examples:

Singular	Plural
*u*ovu (evil)	*ma*ovu (evils)
*u*gonjwa (disease)	*ma*gonjwa (diseases)
*u*gomvi (quarrel)	*ma*gomvi (quarrels)

KU- (15)

The words belonging to this class are referred to as **verbal nouns** or **gerunds**. These words take a prefix **KU-** and, as analysed in traditional grammars, they have no singular and plural forms.

PA- KU- MU- (16-18)

These classes indicate location. The morpheme **PA-** implies definiteness; **KU-** indefiniteness and **MU-** "withinness". Location in Swahili is indicated by many words, such as **mahali**, **mwahali** and **pahali**. Apart from these three words, location is also signalled by attaching the locative **-ni** to common nouns. For example:

a.	mti	+	ni	=	**mtini** (on the tree)
b.	jiko	+	ni	=	**jikoni** (in the kitchen)
c.	soko	+	ni	=	**sokoni** (to the market)
d.	shule	+	ni	=	**shuleni** (to school)

Other words that indicate location in Swahili are free morphemes. Some of them are names of places while others indicate directions. For example:

a. **Mashariki** (East)
b. **Unguja** (Zanzibar)
c. **Magharibi** (West)
d. **Ulaya** (Europe)

In comparison, classification of Swahili nouns by modern grammars is more constructive than that done by traditional grammars. Nouns are now classified not according to "form", but to "function". This method has worked well because it has simplified the process of grouping nouns. For instance, all human nouns are now classified in the same group instead of being dispersed into different groups as was the case with traditional grammars. Also, all nouns are now properly grouped. In traditional grammars, nouns like **maovu** (evil) and **magonjwa** (diseases) were placed under U- class even though they do not bear the prefix U- in the plural form. It is evident that classification of Swahili nouns by modern grammars seems to overcome a lot of shortcomings that were experienced in the past.

VOCABULARY

mtihani	examination	**wazalendo**	nationalists
bohari	godown	**nyumbu**	mules
chandarua	mosquito net	**nyota**	stars
twiga	giraffe	**sanduku**	box
Myunani	Greek	**mzinga**	cannon
zulia	carpet	**tango**	cucumber
mwanasiasa	politician	**mwiko**	large spoon

ajali	accident	**kilemba**	turban
bawabu	doorkeeper	**chungu**	cooking pot
ukuti	coconut leaf	**karatasi**	papers
bomba	pipe	**malkia**	queen
mshahara	salary		

Exercise 3

1. Write the plurals of the following nouns:

a.	mtihani	f.	twiga	k.	ajali	p.	bawabu
b.	bohari	g.	nyumbani	l.	tango	q.	ukuti
c.	jahazi	h.	mzinga	m.	moto	r.	kilemba
d.	sanduku	i.	zulia	n.	mwiko	s.	bomba
e.	baiskeli	j.	mwanasiasa	o.	shangazi	t.	chungu

2. Write the singular of the following nouns:

a.	wazalendo	f.	pundamilia	k.	zawadi	p.	miavuli
b.	wanasiasa	g.	Wadachi	l.	viongozi	q.	malkia
c.	karatasi	h.	mavumbi	m.	mianzo	r.	wanajeshi
d.	vyuma	i.	dini	n.	meno	s.	kondoo
e.	majengo	j.	mifumo	o.	nyumbu	t.	miji

3. Translate the following words:

a.	hills	f.	a bead	k.	crows	p.	matchboxes
b.	coconut trees	g.	axes	l.	old man	q.	a tooth
c.	a mountain	h.	a star	m.	salaries	r.	presidents
d.	a pillow	i.	weeks	n.	parties	s.	periods
e.	songs	j.	a moon	o.	a pineapple	t.	bodies

4. Translate the following words:

a.	wasichana	f.	misumeno	k.	kuta	p.	Wafaransa
b.	viatu	g.	ndevu	l.	harakati	q.	mambo
c.	mbuzi	h.	mbinu	m.	umoja	r.	viziwi
d.	mafuta	i.	vikapu	n.	vyarahani	s.	ufanisi
e.	viongozi	j.	nyaraka	o.	panzi	t.	bakuli

4 Nouns and Prefixes

In the previous chapter, we examined the class prefixes of various kinds of nouns. It is important now to examine the prefixes of other words which co-occur with nouns. In Swahili, many studies have shown that the noun determines the choice of a prefix for all the words associated with it, mainly adjectives and verbs. In order to show the various kinds of prefixes, we will first of all start with adjectives and compare them with the classes of various nouns. In other words, we will be examining the concept of agreement, which means that the noun has to "agree" with all the words associated with it, simply by adopting the same prefix.

Here are some illustrations of the various noun classes:

M-WA class

Singular	Plural
*m*tu mzuri	*wa*tu *wa*zuri
(a good person)	(good people)

Vowel stem adjectives

Adjectives with a vowel stem use the following linguistic guideline for all the noun classes:

M	plus	a vowel	=	MW
A	plus	A	=	A
I	plus	I	=	I
A	plus	E	=	E
A	plus	I	=	E

Using the above guideline, we thus get:

Singular
Mwalimu m+ema ———> **Mwalimu mwema** (a good teacher).

Plural
Walimu wa+ema ———> **Walimu wema** (good teachers).

However, borrowed words, notably from Arabic, do not normally follow the concept of agreement. Thus, we get the following constructions:

Singular
Mwalimu tajiri (a rich teacher).

Plural
Walimu tajiri (rich teachers).

M-MI class

Singular
Mti *m*kubwa (a big tree).

Plural
*Miti mi*kubwa (big trees).

Vowel stem adjectives

By using the already mentioned linguistic guidelines, the vowel stem adjectives are handled in the following way:

Singular
Mkoba m+ekundu ————————> **mkoba mwekundu** (a red purse).

Plural
Mikoba mi+ekundu ————————> **mikoba myekundu** (red purses).

As shown above, the **mi-** prefix becomes **my-** for the adjective **ekundu** (red).

KI-VI class

Singular
Kiti kikubwa (a big chair)

Plural
Viti vikubwa (big chairs)

Vowel stem adjectives

With adjective-stems, the trend is as follows:

Singular
kiatu ki+eusi ————————> **kiatu cheusi** (a black shoe).

Plural
viatu vi+eusi ————————> **viatu vyeusi** (black shoes).

Here, the **ki-** prefix changes into **ch-** and **vi-** into **vy-** in the case of the vowel-stem adjectives for the singular and plural forms respectively.

Yet, when the adjective-stem has the vowel **i**, the **ki-** prefix is maintained for the singular and **vi-** for the plural:

> **Singular**
> **kiatu kingine** (another shoe).
>
> **Plural**
> **viatu vingine** (other shoes).

Furthermore, even if a vowel-stem noun bears a **ch-** prefix, the adjective with a consonant stem will take the **ki-** prefix:

> **Singular**
> **chumba kizuri** (a good room).
>
> **Plural**
> **vyumba vizuri** (good rooms).

JI-MA class

Unlike the three previous noun classes, consonant-stem adjectives for JI-MA class nouns do not take any concord. Thus, we get the following strings:

> **shamba dogo** (a small garden)
> **sanduku zuri** (a good box)
> **nanasi tamu** (a sweet pineapple)

However, with monosyllabic adjective stems, the singular concord is **JI-**:

> **duka jipya** (a new shop)
> **jembe jipya** (a new hoe)

In the plural form, all consonant-stem adjectives take the prefix **ma-**:

> **maduka mazuri** (good shops)
> **majani makubwa** (big leaves)
> **machungwa matamu** (sweet oranges)
> **makaburi madogo** (small graves)

Mass nouns also take the prefix **ma-**:

> **maziwa machafu** (dirty milk)
> **mafuta mazuri** (good oil)

Vowel stem adjectives

Adjectives beginning with a vowel take the concord **J-** or **JI-** for singular nouns:

jicho jekundu (a red eye)
shauri jema (good advice)
jiwe jeupe (a white stone)

An exception exists in the adjective (referred to in this book as **quasi-adjectives**) **-ingine**, (another).

dafu lingine (another coconut)
shauri lingine (another piece of advice)

However, some speakers still use the concord **J-** or **JI-** in the quasi-adjectives **-ingine**:

dafu jingine (another coconut)
shauri jingine (another piece of advice)

In the plural, the **ma-** concord undergoes a morphophonemic change:

ma + eusi —————>meusi
ma + ingi —————>mingi
ma + eupe —————>meupe

Thus, we have the following constructions:

magari meusi (black cars)
majumba mengi (many buildings)
mawe meupe (white stones)

N-N class

Adjectival agreements for nouns in this class take place along the following lines:

1. The n- concord, which is a basic grammatical marker for some nouns of the N-N class for both singular and plural forms, is placed before consonant-adjectives beginning with **d**, **g** and **z**:

    ndoo ndogo (a small bucket)
    kazi ngumu (a difficult job)
    nyumba nzuri (a good house)

2. Consonant-adjectives beginning with **b**, **v** and **p** (if **pya** is a monosyllabic stem) change from m to n, thus undergoing a morphophonemic change:

    kazi mbaya (bad work)
    mtoto mvivu (a lazy child)
    kalamu mpya (a new pen)

3.   Other consonant-adjectives do not take any concord:

> **sabuni chache** (few bars of soap)
> **nguzo fupi** (short pillars)
> **lozi tamu** (sweet almonds)
> **embe kali** (sour mangoes)
> **saa ngapi?** (how many watches?)

Plural

Since almost all nouns of N-N class are morphologically the same for singular and plural forms, exemplification of further plural forms is, therefore, not necessary.

Vowel stem adjectives

Adjectives beginning with a vowel-stem take the concord **ny**:

> **kahawa nyeusi** (black coffee)
> **mali nyingi** (much property)

With irregular adjectives, the above morphophonemic rule takes a different shape:

> **-ema** —————>**njema**
> **habari njema** (good news)
>
> **-refu** —————>**ndefu**
> **njia ndefu** (a long road or long roads)
>
> **-wili** —————>**mbili**
> **nyumba mbili** (two houses)

U-U class

In the singular, consonant-stem adjectives follow the concordial agreement of the M-Mi class pattern, that is, by prefixing **mi-**:

> **ufunguo mdogo** (a small key)
> **uso mbaya** (a bad face)
> **wimbo mzuri** (a good song)

In the plural, consonant-stem adjectives follow the concordial agreement of the N- class pattern:

> **funguo ndogo** (small keys)
> **nyimbo nzuri** (good songs)
> **pepo kali** (violent winds)

However, a few nouns that have been classified by traditional grammars as U-class nouns take the concord **ma-**. For example:

> **magonjwa makubwa** (serious diseases)
> **magomvi madogo** (petty quarrels)

Vowel stem adjectives

Vowel-stem adjectives follow the M-Mi pattern by prefixing **mw-** for the singular form:

> **uso mwekundu** (a red face)
> **uzi mweusi** (a black string)
> **ukuta mweupe** (a white wall)

In the plural, adjectives beginning with a vowel take the concord **my** as in the N- class:

> **nyuso nyekundu** (red faces)
> **nyuzi nyeusi** (black strings)
> **kuta nyeupe** (white walls)

Subject prefixes

The subject prefix is assigned to the affix which occurs in the initial position in the verb stem in a sentence. The prefix relates to the noun which is described as the **subject** of the verb in the sentence.

The subject prefix performs multiple functions. First of all, it indicates the class of the noun which the prefix relates to the verb. Secondly, it indicates the marker of the noun being related. Thirdly, it may also be said to signal particular grammatical roles. Further, it should be noted here that in almost all constructions, the presence of the subject prefix is always obligatory.

Since the subject prefix conveys almost all the information relating to the noun, including the class, the number and, in the case of M-WA class nouns, the person, the prefix can, therefore, function as the pronoun. This is the case in instances where the subject noun has been deleted. The shape of the prefixes will vary according to the class, person, number and role, as shown in Table 3 below.

Noun class	Class prefix	Subject prefix
M-WA (1)	m-	a-
M-WA (2)	wa-	wa-
M-MI (3)	m- or mw-	u-
M-MI (4)	mi-	i-
JI-MA (5)	ji- or j-	li-
JI-MA (6)	ma-	ya-
KI-VI (7)	ki- or ch-	ki-
KI-VI (8)	vi- or vy-	vi-
N-N (9)	n- or	i-
N-N (10)	n- or	zi-
U-U (11-14)	u- or w-	u-
U-U (11-14)	ny- or	zi-
U-U (11-14)	u-	u-
KU (15)	ku-	ku-
PA (16)	pa-	pa-
KU (17)	ku-	ku-
MU (18)	mu-	mu-

Table 4: Swahili class and subject prefixes

The following examples illustrate the use of subject prefixes at syntactic level:

a. **Walimu wawili wanasafiri leo.**
   Two teachers are travelling today.

b. **Vikombe vimeanguka chini.**
   The cups have fallen down.

c. **Umalaya umeenea nchini.**
   Prostitution has spread in the country.

In some situations, subject prefixes merely operate as dummy elements. They are semantically empty. In some grammars, they are referred to as **dummy subjects**. For example:

a. **Inanyesha sana leo.**
   It is raining heavily today.

b. **Yawezekana kwamba Mary anaumwa siku hizi.**
   It is possible that Mary is sick these days.

59

Object prefixes

The object prefix is defined as a non-initial pronominal prefix immediately preceding the stem of a verb. Swahili grammars contend that the object prefix is used to indicate that the object of a sentence has definite reference. Grammars have also argued that object markers become mandatory when an object is animate, and that for inanimate nouns, object markers are less used.

Some scholars make a delicate distinction of object prefixes along the two traditional dimensions: **direct object prefix** and **indirect object prefix**. *Khamis (1972)*, for example, makes this distinction, explaining that where a verb is followed by a noun and the noun is related to the verb by the prefix, the prefix is termed as the direct object prefix. For example:

a. **Mwanamke ali*i*piga ngoma.**
The woman beat *the drum.*

b. **Mwizi ali*vi*iba vikapu vyangu.**
A thief stole my *baskets.*

In these examples, the object prefixes **i** and **vi** refer to **ngoma** (drum) and **vikapu** (baskets) respectively.

Khamis (1972) shows that sometimes, a verb may occur with a second object which, as the direct object, may be related to the verb by the appropriate prefix. For example:

a. **Waziri ame*m*pa mwanafunzi zawadi.**
The Minister has given *the student* a prize.

b. **Mfanyakazi ame*wa*onyesha wageni maonyesho ya kila mwaka.**
The worker has shown *the visitors* the annual exhibitions.

Here, the object markers **m** and **wa** are termed as **indirect object prefixes**, referring to **mwanafunzi** (student) and **wageni** (visitors) respectively.

The indirect object prefix is optional in the sense that it is potentially present only in verbs which allow the occurrence of the indirect object. It is also significant to note that in Swahili, the direct and indirect object prefixes cannot occur simultaneously in a verb. A complete list of all the object prefixes is presented in Table 5 below. As the table shows, object prefixes are identical phonologically to subject prefixes, except for the third person singular marker.

Noun class	Class prefix	Object prefix
M-WA (1)	m-	-m-, -mw-, -mu-
M-WA (2)	wa-	wa-
M-MI (3)	m-, mw-	u-
M-MI (4)	mi-	i-
JI-MA (5)	ji-, j-	li-
JI-MA (6)	ma-	ya-
KI-VI (7)	ki-, ch-	ki-
KI-VI (8)	vi-, vy-	vi-
N-N (9)	n-,	i-
N-N (10)	n-,	zi-
U-U (11-14)	u-, w-	u-
U-U (11-14)	ny-,	zi-
KU (15)	ku-	
PA (16)	pa-	po-
KU (17)	ku-	ko-
MU (18)	mu-	mo-

Table 5: Swahili class and object prefixes

VOCABULARY

fagio	broom	pembe	horn
dini	religion	upande	side
msiba	misfortune	mboga	vegetable
mtaalamu	scholar	-kuukuu	old
mwanaanga	spaceman	jarida	newspaper
ishara	signal	-sikivu	obedient
mgogoro	deadlock, dispute	jabali	rock
zilizala	earthquake	bashashi	humorous
fidia	compensation	mgodi	mine

Exercise 4

1. Translate the following clauses:

   a. sweet oranges
   b. a white umbrella
   c. heavy keys
   d. small brooms
   e. long journeys
   f. a red flag
   k. much rain
   l. another page
   m. all sides
   n. a white rock
   o. white soaps
   p. few friends

g. a fierce dog
h. many religions
i. beautiful cars
j. light loads

q. great misfortunes
r. bad vegetables
s. big vessels
t. a cunning farmer

2. Translate the following:

a. mkutano mfupi
b. majengo makubwa
c. fidia ndogo
d. njia nyembamba
e. miiba mirefu
f. nyembe kali
g. chumba kipana
h. wanaanga hodari
i. majarida makuukuu
j. almasi nyingi

k. kijana madhubuti
l. kuta mbovu
m. mwanafunzi msikivu
n. migodi mikubwa
o. zilizala ndogo
p. ishara mbaya
q. wachukuzi wazembe
r. mvua kubwa
s. mtaalamu bashashi
t. mgogoro mkubwa

3. Show the main difference between subject and object prefixes in Swahili.

5 Adjectives

Grammars have often described an adjective as a word that qualifies a noun or tells us something about its quality. For example:

a. **mkulima** *mnene.*
a fat farmer.
b. **kikombe** *kidogo.*
a small cup.

The words **mnene** (fat) and **kidogo** (small) are adjectives because they describe the nouns **mkulima** (farmer) and **kikombe** (cup) in examples (a) and (b) above.

Agreement of adjectives

Essentially, agreement is a surface structure phenomenon. As explained in the previous chapter, agreement is the process by which some morphemes or words determine the occurrence or non-occurrence of other morphemes. The concept of agreement is common in a number of languages. For instance, in French, German, Italian and Arabic, nouns and adjectives have to agree in gender, number and, sometimes, person. Similarly, Swahili follows the pattern of agreement. This concept is found in two types of adjectives: adjectives with a consonant stem and those with a vowel stem.

Consonant stem adjectives

Consonant stem adjectives are many. The prefixes they carry must always be identical to the concord on the noun they describe. Let us examine these consonant stem adjectives.

a. *m*vulana *m*refu
a tall youth
b. *m*kuki *m*dogo
a small spear
c. *vi*kombe *vi*chafu
dirty cups

In the above examples, the prefixes of the adjectives **refu** (tall), **dogo** (small) and **chafu** (dirty) agree with those of their nouns. However, exceptions can be found when dealing with certain humans and animals:

a. **kijana mvivu**
a lazy youth

   b. **simba mkali**
      a fierce lion

Concordial agreement does not exist in the case of the above examples. The two nouns **kijana** (youth) and **simba** (lion) have a common semantic feature, namely, **animate**. Thus, the rules of grammar allow the qualifying words of the two nouns to acquire a prefix in agreement with the class of the object qualified, in this case M-WA prefix.

Vowel stem adjectives

Adjectives with a vowel stem are few. They also follow the system of agreement. With a few minor exceptions, some rules exist for these adjectives as shown below:

M-	before any vowel often gives			MW-
WA-	plus	A	becomes	WA-
WA-	plus	E or I	becomes	WE-
MI-	before	E	becomes	MY-
MI-	plus	I	becomes	MI-
KI-	before	A, E or O	becomes	CH-
VI-	before	A, E, or O	becomes	VY-
VI-	plus	I	becomes	VI-

These rules lead to the following constructions:

M-WA class

Singular
a. Mzee m-embamba – **mwembamba** (a thin old man)
b. Mtu m-ingine – **mwingine** (another person)

Plural
a. Wazee wa-embamba – **wembamba** (thin old men)
b. Watu wa-ingine – **wengine** (other people)

M-MI class

Singular
a. mti m-ekundu – **mwekundu** (red tree)
b. moshi m-ingi – **mwingi** (much smoke)

Plural
a. miti mi-ekundu – **myekundu** (red trees)
b. miti mi-ingine – **mingine** (other trees)

KI-VI class

Singular
a. kikombe ki-eupe   – **cheupe** (a white cup)
b. chakula ki-ingi   – **kingi** (much food)

Plural
a. vikombe vi-eupe   – **vyeupe** (white cups)
b. vitu vi-ingi   – **vingi** (many things)

Traditionally, adjectives of foreign origin do not often follow the system of agreement. For example:

a. **mwanafunzi hodari** (a clever student)
b. **mkulima masikini** (a poor farmer)

Despite the absence of agreement in borrowed adjectives, *Zawawi (1974)* shows that there is now a tendency to attach proper prefixes to them. For example:

a. *ma*waziri *ma*tajiri (rich ministers)
b. **wanafunzi *ma*hodari** (clever students)

Word order

Adjectives directly follow the nouns they describe. Thus, unlike in English, adjectives in Swahili are always placed after their nouns. For instance:

a. **kijana *mwema*** (a good youth)
b. **miti *midogo*** (small trees)

Adjectives can follow one another in any order, except those describing possession and quantity. Normally, they come immediately after the nouns they describe. When describing possession and quantity they come at the end of the sentence. For example:

a. **vikombe vyangu *vidogo*** (my small cups)
b. **mizigo myepesi *mingapi*?** (how many light loads?)

Adjectives as head words

Adjectives can function as heads in cases where their deleted nouns can be retrieved, if necessary, from the previous sentences. The heads can operate as subjects, objects or complements of their sentences. Following are some examples:

a. **Watu wazuri wanapendwa duniani.** *Wabaya* **hawapendwi.**
   Good people are liked in this world. *Bad ones* are hated.
b. **Sipendi** *vibaya.*
   I do not like *the bad.*
c. **Huyu ni kijana mwema. Tena ni** *maarufu.*
   This is a good youth. In addition, he is *famous.*

Sometimes, the adjective heads are modified by demonstrative markers, as indicated below:

a. *Wale wakweli* **watazawadiwa vizuri na rais.**
   Those who are sincere will be well rewarded by the president.
b. *Kila kibaya* **kina uzuri wake pia.**
   Every bad thing has its good side as well.

Types of adjectives

Modern grammars classify Swahili adjectives along the following lines:

Descriptive adjectives

Generally, descriptive adjectives, as the name implies, merely describe the quality of things and people. In this group, are found Bantu words which take concords appropriate to the class of the inherent noun. For example:

a. *mw*alimu mkali. (a strict teacher.)
b. *ki*kapu *ki*kubwa. (a big basket.)

Similarly, there are words of foreign origin in this group. As we established earlier, loan words do not usually take concordial agreement. For example:

a. **mkate laini.** (soft bread.)
b. **maji safi.** (clean water.)

Possessive adjectives

Possessive adjectives describe possession on the part of the owners. The possessive roots of these adjectives are: **-angu** (my), **-ako** (your), **-ake** (his or hers), **-enu** (your [pl]), **-ao** (their). These roots take concords appropriate to the class of the inherent noun. For example:

a. **wanafunzi wangu.** (my students.)
b. **mikoba yetu.** (our baskets.)

The possessive root **-ake** is used to refer to antecedents that are plants or inanimate objects. Where the antecedents are human beings or animals, the possessive root **-ao** is adopted. For example:

a.   **miti na majani yake.** (trees and their leaves.)
b.   **kitabu na kurasa zake.** (the book and its pages.)
c.   **wanawake na watoto wao.** (women and their children.)

Numerical adjectives

Numerical adjectives (adjectives of quantity) describe the quantity or number of items or persons in question. The description of the numerical adjectives can be in specific terms. For example:

a.   **wapagazi wawili.** (two porters.)
b.   **viziwi sita.** (six deaf persons.)

On the other hand, the description can also be general. For example:

a.   **watalii wengi.** (many tourists.)
b.   **walimu wachache.** (few teachers.)

Demonstrative adjectives

Adjectives in this group point out objects of all kinds with respect to nearness or remoteness. For nearness, the demonstrative roots are **ha-**, **hi-** and **hu-**. For remoteness, the demonstrative root is **-le**. For example:

a.   **kijana huyu.** (this youth.)
b.   **mshale huu.** (this arrow.)
c.   **simba yule.** (that lion.)
d.   **chumba kile.** (that room.)

Another demonstrative item that is commonly used by Swahili grammars is the **h-o** particle. As described in chapter 19, this demonstrative root is used to refer to an item that was previously mentioned. Some grammars, however, argue that the demonstrative particle also has a locative meaning and that it implies "location near a listener". We shall now examine the usage of this demonstrative particle in the following example:

a.   **mkulima** *huyo.* (that farmer.)
b.   **kitabu** *hicho.* (that book.)

Interrogative adjectives

Interrogative adjectives are used for asking questions. The interrogative particles that are used are **-pi**, **-ngapi** and **gani**. The interrogative particle **-pi**, conveys the meaning of "which". This particle always takes concords appropriate to the class of the noun in question. The interrogative root ngapi also takes concords and the meaning associated with it is "how many". Thus, this interrogative is only used for countable plural nouns. The last interrogative particle is gani. It has an equivalent meaning of "what" or "what sort of". Unlike the two other interrogative roots, the morpheme gani does not take concords. For example:

    a.   mtu *yupi*? (which person?)
    b.   vijana *wangapi*? (how many youths?)
    c.   mti *gani* huu? (what sort of tree is this?)

Adjectives of -A of relationship

Adjectives in this group carry the -A of relationship which is often followed by a noun. For example:

    a.   lugha *ya taifa*. (national language.)
    b.   nguo *za kitoto*. (children's clothes.)

Quasi-adjectives

There are five adjectives in this group. They are -ote (all), -enye (having), -enyewe, (self or selves), -ingine (other) and -o-ote (any). Like possessive adjectives, each adjective in this group takes concords appropriate to the class of the inherent noun. The uses of these five adjectives are illustrated below:

    a.   Nimekula chungwa *lote*.
           I have eaten the whole orange.
    b.   Msichana *mwenye* adabu amepata zawadi.
           The girl with good manners has won a prize.
    c.   Nanasi limeanguka *lenyewe*.
           The pineapple has fallen by itself.
    d.   Vijana *wengine* walichelewa kufika hapa.
           Some youths arrived here late.
    e.   Nipe kitabu *chochote*.
           Give me any book.

VOCABULARY

fuata	imitate	desturi	customs
sherehe	celebrations	anza	start
kwa ubadhirifu	extravagantly	tumia	spend
stahili	deserve	sifa	credit

shinda	win	kiri	confess
madhubuti	firm	udhi	annoy
husudu	admire	hitaji	require
patikana	obtainable	juhudi	diligence
hotuba	speech	karimu	generous
aghalabu	usually	mkaazi	inhabitant
panda	go up	mmea	plant
laini	soft	uwongo	lies
hongo	bribe	punde	recently
maridadi	dandy	-gumu	difficult
uzungu	European life	likizo	leave

Exercise 5

1. Pick out the adjectives in the following sentences:

    a. Sherehe kubwa zitaanza karibuni hapa nchini.
    b. Ouma ametumia mali yote kwa ubadhirifu.
    c. Mtu huyu anastahili sifa zote.
    d. Wanafunzi wengi wamechelewa shuleni leo.
    e. Wanariadha wepi wameshinda katika mashindano ya michezo ya Bara la Afrika katika mwaka 1989?
    f. Mshtakiwa amekiri kosa lake.
    g. Wazee wetu wanafuata desturi za kizamani.
    h. Tusi lolote litamuudhi mama yako tu.
    i. Rais wetu anaizuru Uholanzi hivi sasa.
    j. Vijana wa kisasa wanahusudu uzungu tu.
    k. Watoto wako wamejiangusha wenyewe.
    l. Dhahabu nyingi inapatikana Zambia.
    m. Kazi yoyote inahitaji juhudi tu.
    n. Waziri wa Afya ametoa hotuba nzuri leo.
    o. Wageni wachache walifika hapa mwaka jana.

2. Translate the following sentences:

    a. The cook wants new utensils.
    b. The old woman is a very generous person.
    c. Rich people usually buy expensive clothes.
    d. I have a fierce cat at home.
    e. The other door is very small.
    f. This river is long and narrow.
    g. I carried light loads yesterday.

h. He has a beautiful wife.

i. How many villages have few inhabitants here?

j. Some people are poor, others are rich.

k. The man is firm. I know him very well.

l. The five tall coconut trees have fallen down.

m. The headmaster wants good students this time.

n. The fierce lion has died today.

o. The salaries of all the workers have gone up this year.

3. Translate the following sentences:

a. Mimea mingi imekufa kwa mvua kubwa.

b. Mtumishi alinunua mikate laini leo.

c. Vijana gani wanafanya matata nje?

d. Godoro lako ni kubwa.

e. Vitabu vingi ni ghali sana madukani.

f. Maneno yao yana uwongo mtupu.

g. Uaminifu ni jambo muhimu duniani.

h. Viongozi wengi wanapokea hongo siku hizi.

i. Watu wenye mali ni haba sana hapa kijijini.

j. Mbwa mwenye mkia mweupe mrefu amepita punde.

k. Mwaka ule, mvua ilinyesha kidogo kidogo.

l. Kijana maridadi anaenda dukani sasa hivi.

m. Mzee alinipa kazi ngumu nyumbani.

n. Walimu wangapi wanachukua likizo safari hii?

o. Wasichana wanene wawili wanachukua mizigo mizito.

6 Verbs I: The Infinitive Form, the Imperative and the Subjective

Structurally, the Swahili verb is a complex structure consisting of three parts, namely:

  a. the verb prefixes
  b. the root
  c. the suffixes

The verb root is that part of the Swahili verb stem free of prefixes, infixes and suffixes. It is the part of the verb which cannot be further reduced morphologically. Some Bantu scholars, like *Whiteley (1968)*, prefer to call it "the minimum radical".

The verb root constitutes the lexical meaning of the verb. When the verb root is combined with its affixes, the verb stem is obtained. *Myachina (1982)* refers to the verb stem as the **verbal stem**. With the exception of a few verbs borrowed from Arabic, all verb stems in Swahili end in **-a**. The following are examples of verb stems in Swahili:

  a. **cheza** (play)
  b. **pika** (cook)
  c. **kula** (eat)

The examples of verbs borrowed from Arabic are:

  a. **shukuru** (thank)
  b. **fasiri** (translate)
  c. **samehe** (forgive)

Kinds of verbs

The infinitive form

In Swahili, the infinitive form of the verb is recognized by the presence of the prefix **KU-** before the verb stem for the affirmative forms and **KUTO-** for the negative forms. But the prefix **-to-** does not take any stress. Here are some examples:

  a. **kupika** (to cook)   **kutopika** (not to cook)
  b. **kucheza** (to play)   **kutocheza** (not to play)

The prefix **KU-** occasionally appears as **KW-** before a vowel, but this occurrence is quite rare. For example:

  a. **kwenda** (to go)   **kutokwenda** (not to go)
  b. **kwisha** (to finish)   **kutokwisha** (not to finish)

71

Also, in the case of monosyllabic verbs, a second **KU-** is inserted before the stem, forcing the **-to-** to become the third syllable from the right:

    a.   **kunywa** (to drink)   **kutokunywa** (not to drink)
    b.   **kuja** (to come)   **kutokuja** (not to come)

It should be noted that the negative form of the infinitive is used less often than the affirmative form. The infinitive verb has the following uses:

a.   To function as a verbal noun.
        (i) **Kucheza sana hakufai.**
            Playing excessively is no good.
        (ii) **Kulewa kunakatazwa hapa.**
            Drinking is forbidden here.

The use of the verbal noun is sometimes referred to by grammars as the **gerund**. The verbal noun expresses the act of doing, of becoming or the state of being.

b.   To function as a verbal infinitive.
        (i) **Anapenda kucheza.**
            He likes to play.
        (ii) **Ninapenda kusoma.**
            I like to read.

The use of the verbal infinitive corresponds to the English infinitive form signalled by the use of **to** before the verb stem.

c.   To signal the aspect of manner when preceded by functional items such as **kwa** (by) and **na** (with or by).
        (i) **Alimwua nguruwe kwa kutumia bunduki.**
            He killed the pig by using a gun.
        (ii) **Wanasoma na kuandika madaftarini mwao kwa penseli.**
            They read and write in their books with pencils.

d.   To refer to an activity that is repetitive when co-occurring with the particle **hu-**, as indicated in the examples below:
        (i) **Mjomba huja hapa kupiga domo na wenzake.**
            My uncle comes here to talk with his colleagues.
        (ii) **Hamisi husema kuna simba kichakani.**
            Hamisi says that there is a lion in the bush.

The imperative

The imperative, which has the form of the stem of the verb, that is, without the infinitive prefix **KU-**, is used in the expression of commands.

The following verbs are all examples of imperative forms:

Pika! (Cook!)	**Fungua!** (Open!)
Lima! (Cultivate!)	**Simama!** (Stand up!)
Soma! (Read!)	**Ondoka!** (Get out!)
Lala! (Sleep!)	**Piga!** (Beat!)
Imba! (Sing!)	**Nyanyua!** (Lift!)

Borrowed words also contain the stem of the verb for imperative forms. For example:

Fasiri! (Translate!)	**Samehe!** (Forgive!)
Safiri! (Travel!)	**Tubu!** (Repent!)
Fikiri! (Think!)	**Sahau!** (Forget!)

Monosyllabic verbs, however, take the infinitive **KU-** in order to exert stress on the word. For example:

Kula! (Eat!)	**Kunywa!** (Drink!)

A few exceptions to the rules of the imperative exist, as illustrated below:

Kuja (to come)	becomes	**Njoo** (come)
Kuleta (to bring)	becomes	**Lete** (bring)
Kwenda (to go)	becomes	**Nenda** (go)

The imperative plural

The imperative plural is formed by dropping the infinitive **KU-** and suffixing **-eni** to the verb, as follows:

Pikeni! (Cook!)	**Fungueni!** (Open!)
Limeni! (Cultivate!)	**Simameni!** (Stand up!)
Someni! (Read!)	**Ondokeni!** (Get out!)
Laleni! (Sleep!)	**Pigeni!** (Beat!)
Imbeni! (Sing!)	**Nyanyueni!** (Lift!)

Borrowed words suffix **-ni** to the verb. For example:

Fasirini! (Translate!)	**Sameheni!** (Forgive!)
Safirini! (Travel!)	**Tubuni!** (Repent!)
Fikirini! (Think!)	**Sahauni!** (Forget!)

But monosyllabic verbs again retain the infinitive **ku-**, as indicated in the following example:

Kuleni! (Eat!)	**Kunyweni!** (Drink!)

When utilizing the three verbs which are exceptions to the rules of the imperative, the following trend is observed:

>**Leteni!** (Bring!)
>**Nendeni!** (Go!)
>**Njooni!** (Come!)

In the last verb, the particle -ni is suffixed while in the first two verbs, the suffix is **-eni**.

It is significant to note that an imperative can take an object prefix which is then placed before the verb stem. For example:

>**Mwite!** (Call him!)   **Mchukue!** (Take him!)

As shown above, the suffix of the verb stem changes from -a to -e.

The negative imperative

The original negative imperative of Swahili is no longer in force. Instead, we have the negative subjunctive. It is formed by removing the prefix KU- from the verb infinitive, prefixing u- for the singular second person, infixing the negative particle -si- and finally, changing the suffix of the verb from -a to -e. Thus, the following verbs are formed:

>**Usipike!** (Do not cook!)   **Usifungue!** (Do not open!)
>**Usilime!** (Do not cultivate!) **Usisimame!** (Do not stand up!)
>**Usisome!** (Do not read!)   **Usiondoke!** (Do not go out!)
>**Usilale!** (Do not sleep!)   **Usipige!** (Do not beat!)
>**Usiimbe!** (Do not sing!)   **Usinyanyue!** (Do not lift!)

Borrowed verbs are also treated in the same way except that the final vowel remains unchanged since it is not a suffix. For example:

>**Usifasiri!** (Do not translate!) **Usisamehe!** (Do not forgive!)
>**Usisafiri!** (Do not travel!)   **Usitubu!** (Do not repent!)
>**Usifikiri!** (Do not think!)   **Usisahau!** (Do not forget!)

Monosyllabic verbs are treated like any other Bantu verbs, as shown below:

>**Usile!** (Do not eat!)   **Usiche!** (Do not fear!)
>**Usinywe!** (Do not drink!)   **Usije!** (Do not come!)

The plural negative imperative

The plural form of the negative imperative is formed by inserting the prefix m- in place of u-, as indicated below:

Msipike! (Do not cook!)   Msifungue! (Do not open!)
Msilime! (Do not cultivate!)   Msisimame! (Do not stand up!)
Msisome! (Do not read!)   Msiondoke! (Do not get out!)
Msilale! (Do not sleep!)   Msipige! (Do not beat!)
Msiimbe! (Do not sing!)   Msinyanyue! (Do not lift!)

The subjunctive

The subjunctive is formed by removing the prefix **ku-** from the verb
infinitive, deleting an infix, prefixing an appropriate particle and finally,
changing the suffix of the verb stem from **-a** to **-e**.

Uimbe! (You sing!)   Unyanyue! (You lift!)

The above subjunctive forms are often referred to by grammarians as a
polite imperative.

With verbs borrowed from Arabic, the last vowel of a polite
imperative remains unchanged, as illustrated below:

Ufasiri! (You translate!)   Usamehe! (You forgive!)
Usafiri! (You travel!)   Utubu! (You repent!)
Ufikiri! (You think!)   Usahau! (You forget!)

Similarly, monosyllabic verbs also drop the infinitive prefix KU-. For
example:

Ule! (You eat!)   Unywe! (You drink!)
Uje! (You come!)   Uche! (You fear!)

The plural imperative form is obtained by inserting the plural prefix **m-**
of the second person before a consonant stem and **mw-** before a vowel
stem. For example:

Mpike! (You cook!)   Mfungue! (You open!)
Mlime! (You cultivate!)   Msimame! (You stand!)
Msome! (You read!)   Mwondoke! (You get out!)
Mlale! (You sleep!)   Mpige! (You beat!)
Mwimbe! (You sing!)   Mnyanyue! (You lift!)

Apart from its use in the polite imperative, the subjunctive is also used
to express the second of two commands, especially where the second
affects a third person. For example:

a. **Mwambie apike wali.**
    Tell him/her to cook the rice.
b. **Tulimtaka asome.**
    We wanted him/her to read.

75

Also, the subjunctive is used to signal purpose or intention:

a. **Mwite haraka tumpe zawadi.**
Call him immediately so that we may give him a prize.
b. **Tuliondoka mapema tupate kukutana naye.**
We left early so that we could meet him.

The subjunctive is further used to give the suggestions of "let ...":

a. **Twende nyumbani.**
Let us go home.
b. **Tuanze kazi.**
Let us start work.

It is also used to give a sense of questioned suggestion. For example:

a. **Ningoje hapa?**
Am I to wait here?
b. **Tuanze kula?**
May we start eating?

Finally, the subjunctive is used after some words which express a degree of obligation. For example:

a. **Lazima apike sasa.**
She must cook now.
b. **Yafaa tuondoke hapa kwa haraka.**
It is good that we leave here soon.

The negative subjunctive

The negative subjunctive is formed by inserting the negative particle -si- between the subject prefix and the verb stem. The last vowel of Bantu verbs also changes from -a to -e as shown below:

Nisipike (I shouldn't cook.)
Usipike (You shouldn't cook.)
Asipike (He/she shouldn't cook.)
Tusipike (We shouldn't cook.)
Msipike (You [pl] shouldn't cook.)
Wasipike (They shouldn't cook.)

Borrowed verbs are treated in a similar manner except that the last vowel is retained. For example:

Nisifasiri (I shouldn't translate).
Usifasiri (You shouldn't translate).

Msifasiri	(You [pl] shouldn't translate).
Wasifasiri	(They shouldn't translate).

Monosyllabic verbs also drop the infinitive prefix **ku-**. For example:

Nisile	(I shouldn't eat).
Asile	(He/she shouldn't eat).
Wasile	(They shouldn't eat).

Uses of the negative subjunctive

The negative subjunctive has a number of uses almost resembling those of the affirmative forms. They are described below:

1. As a polite imperative prohibition.
   a. **Usipike chakula.**
      Do not cook the food.
   b. **Asiendeshe gari kwa kasi.**
      He should not drive the car fast.

2. As a signal of purpose or intention.
   a. **Tumekula chakula tusije tukaona njaa njiani.**
      We have eaten food so as not to feel hungry on the way.
   b. **Waliondoka mapema ili wasipate kukutana naye.**
      They left early to avoid meeting him.

3. As a signal of negative obligation.
   a. **Lazima asiondoke sasa.**
      He must not leave now.
   b. **Yafaa tusimwite sasa.**
      We should not call her now.

4. As a signal of negative questioned suggestion.
   a. **Nisiondoke?**
      Am I not to leave?
   b. **Tusilale sasa?**
      Are we not to sleep now?

5. As an expression of the second of two commands and indirect commands when used negatively.
   a. **Mweleze asije hapa.**
      Tell him not to come here.
   b. **Jaribu usilale mapema.**
      Try not to sleep early.

6. After verbs of prohibition.
   a. **Walinizuia nisilale hapa.**
      They forbade me to sleep here.
   b. **Niliwakataza wasitoke nje.**
      I forbade them to go out.

7. As a signal of the suggestion **"Let me not"**, **"Let him not"** etc.
   a. **Nisilale.**
      Let me not sleep.
   b. **Asipike.**
      Let her not cook.

VOCABULARY

mapema	early	**shehena**	load
chagua	elect	**jongea**	come forward
soma	recite/read	**sinzia**	doze
peleleza	investigate	**sita**	hesitate
hujumu	invade	**sherehekea**	celebrate
uwongo	lies	**laumu**	rebuke
bila ya sababu	unnecessarily	**poteza wakati**	waste time
mvua nyingi	downpour	**ghasi**	disturb
kwaruza	scratch	**kosa**	mistake
mlolongo	line	**boga**	pumpkin
shirikiana	co-operate	**kitambulisho**	identity card
fujo	chaos	**nyamaza**	keep quiet
mateka	prisoner	**duru**	round
mgonjwa		**fungua**	release/open
wa ukimwi	AIDS patient	**kirimu**	entertain

Exercise 6

1. Translate the following into Swahili:
   a. Would you elect!
   b. Would you come forward!
   c. Would you recite!
   d. Would you try!
   e. Do not doze!
   f. Do not investigate!
   g. Do not hesitate!
   h. Do not invade!
   i. Let him talk!

j. They came here in order to see us.

k. Should they celebrate the national day?

l. Let the women go away.

m. Are the farmers to grow coffee?

n. Tell them to come back here as soon as possible.

o. I requested them not to tell lies.

p. Tell him not to rebuke me unnecessarily.

q. Do not let the little girl try again.

r. I want her not to come here next week.

s. Let us not waste our time here.

t. You had better not travel by air today because there is a downpour.

2. Translate the following into English:

a. Usighasi!

b. Msikwaruze!

c. Tafadhali msafishe!

d. Uende kupika!

e. Afadhali alale mapema.

f. Lazima akiri makosa.

g. Waambie wajipange kwenye mlolongo.

h. Mtumishi aziweke shehena wapi?

i. Mama anataka niende sokoni ili nikanunue maboga.

j. Yafaa wanasiasa washirikiane vizuri.

k. Mwambie askari akurejeshee kitambulisho.

l. Bora tunyamaze sasa.

m. Waambie vijana wasilete fujo hapa.

n. Yafaa mashindano yasiingie katika duru ya pili wiki hii.

o. Nimemwomba mkulima asilime hapa.

p. Walimu wasifundishe jumamosi.

q. Msiwafungue mateka wote.

r. Afadhali wagonjwa wa ukimwi wasilale upande huu.

s. Anataka tumsaidie kuibeba mizigo hii.

t. Heri asiwakirimu tena wageni wale.

7 Verbs II: Full Verbs, Auxilliary Verbs and Copular Verbs

In the previous chapter, we discussed varieties of verbs, namely: infinitive, imperative and subjunctive. The last two operate in many cases as full verbs.

Full verbs

A full verb is a lexical verb in a verb phrase. It is sometimes referred to as a **main verb**. For example:

a. **Mpishi alikuwa anapika wali.**
   The cook was cooking rice.
b. **Vijana wale wamekwisha fika Kisumu.**
   Those youths have already arrived in Kisumu.
c. **Tafadhali njoo hapa kesho.**
   Please come here tomorrow.

In the sentences above, the full verbs are **pika** (cook), **fika** (arrive) and **njoo** (come).

A full verb tells us a number of things. Firstly, we learn that the actions taking place in the three sentences are *cooking, arriving* and *coming*. Secondly, a full verb tells us the voice; whether the sentence is an active or passive voice. Thus, we learn that sentences a., b., and c. are all active. Finally, we also learn from a full verb about the mood of the sentence; whether the sentence is imperative, subjunctive or indicative. We learn that sentence c. is in imperative form.

Auxiliary verbs

In the grammatical description of the verb phrase, auxiliary verbs are used to refer to the set of verbs subordinate to the main lexical verb. In Swahili, auxiliary verbs accompany main verbs to express a special aspect of an action denoted by the latter. For instance:

a. **Alikuwa anakunywa maziwa.**
   He was drinking milk.
b. **Otieno ataweza kucheza mpira.**
   Otieno will be able to play soccer.

In the above examples, the presence of -li- in the auxiliary **kuwa** (to be) in a. indicates that the activity started in the past. In b. the presence of the particle **-ta-** in the auxiliary verb **weza** (can) shows that the activity will take place in future.

Apart from their function as indicators of time, auxiliary verbs help to produce acceptable sentences. For instance:

a. **Mchezaji anaweza kufunga goli.**
The player can score a goal.

b. **Kijana atataka kuleta maji.**
The youth would want to bring water.

If the auxiliaries **weza** (can) and **taka** (want) are omitted in the two sentences, the constructions produced will be unacceptable as shown below:

a. * Mchezaji kufunga goli.
b. * Kijana kuleta maji.

Finally, auxiliary verbs also signal polarity, that is, whether positive or negative. For example:

a. **Amina alikuwa amelala.**
Amina was sleeping.

b. **Fatuma hakuwa amelala.**
Fatuma was not sleeping.

Sentence a. is positive while b. is negative.

In short, auxiliary verbs help us to make distinctions in areas relating to **mood, aspect, voice,** etc.

In Swahili, auxiliary verbs in existence are **kuwa** (be), **weza** (can), **pata** (get), **kuja** (come), **taka** (want), **kwenda** (go), **wahi** (be in time) and **kwisha** (finish). Below is an analysis of some of them:

Kuwa

The auxiliary **kuwa** (to be) is a monosyllabic verb which can be used to refer to the protracted nature of an action, or action at a definite moment in the past or in the future. It is modulated by tense markers -na-, -li-, -me- and -ta- while the full verb, sometimes called the principal verb, is modulated by markers such as -ki- and -na-. For example:

a. **Mchezaji alikuwa akifunga goli.**
The player was scoring a goal.

b. **Nimekuwa ninapoteza wakati wangu.**
I have been wasting my time.

The auxiliary verb **kuwa** can also be used in negative contexts. In this case, an appropriate negative particle is prefixed to a tense marker, as illustrated below:

a. **Mwalimu hakuwa akisomesha.**
The teacher was not teaching.

  b. **Sitakuwa ninakula embe.**
  I will not be eating a mango.

Weza

The auxiliary verb **weza** (can) assumes the meaning of potentiality and possibility of action at some point in the past, present or future. It is also modulated by the tense markers **-na-**, **-li-**, **-me-** and **-ta-**. But the full verb is always prefixed by the infinitive **ku-**, as shown below:

  a. **Waziri aliweza kuwaona watu wote.**
  The Minister was able to see all the people.
  b. **Mkutano unaweza kumalizika mapema.**
  The meeting can finish early.

  The auxiliary verb **weza** can also be used in negative contexts. Here again, an appropriate negative particle is prefixed to a tense marker, as shown below:

  a. **Mbwa hataweza kula nyama hii.**
  The dog will not be able to eat this meat.
  b. **Mgeni wangu hakuweza kufika hapa jana.**
  My guest could not arrive here yesterday.

Pata

The auxiliary verb **pata** (get) implies ability or opportunity for a subject to accomplish a particular thing or, on the contrary, suffers a stroke of misfortune by the occurrence of the action denoted by the main verb. As an auxiliary, it is followed by a verb stem, with or without the infinitive **KU**, as shown below:

  a. **Mkulima amepata kusafiri.**
  The farmer has travelled before.
  b. **Wale vipofu walipata kugongwa na basi.**
  The blind people were knocked down by the bus.

Like other auxiliaries, the auxiliary **pata** can also be used negatively, sometimes implying the sense of "never". For example:

  a. **Sipati kuja nyumbani kwako kesho.**
  I won't be able to come to your home tomorrow.
  b. **Kijana hatapata kusoma shuleni tena.**
  That youth will never study in a school again.

Kuja

This verb as an auxiliary is used to refer to an action that will take place at an implied time in the near or distant future. It is followed by the verb stem attached to it with the infinitive **KU-**, the subjunctive and the future tense. For example:

- a. **Mti huu utakuja kuanguka.**
  This tree will fall down.
- b. **Uje uwafahamishe wanafunzi wako matatizo yote kesho.**
  Come so that you can explain all the problems to your students tomorrow.
- c. **Anaelewa kuwa atapata mayai sokoni na baadaye sote tutakuja kuyatumia.**
  He knows that he will find eggs in the market, then later, we will use them.

The auxiliary verb **kuja** can also be used in negative contexts. In negative constructions, the auxiliary is usually followed by the particle **-KA-** and often expresses the sense of "lest":

- a. **Alikuja hapa mapema asije kulaumiwa.**
  He came here early lest he be blamed.
- b. **Ondoka sasa hivi usije ukachelewa.**
  Go right away lest you be late.

Taka

The auxiliary verb **taka** suggests the meaning of assurance that a desire or purpose will definitely or most probably be fulfilled. In other words, it is used when a sequel is imminent or practically certain, and thus expresses the meaning of "to be on the verge of" or "to be on the point of". Like the auxiliary **pata**, this verb is followed by the verb stem, with or without the infinitive **KU-**:

- a. **Mgonjwa ataka kunywa maji.**
  The patient wants to drink water.
- b. **Mwizi yule ataka toroka.**
  That thief wants to escape.

The auxiliary verb **taka** is also used in negative constructions:

- a. **Mtoto hataki kuondoka hapa.**
  The child does not want to leave here.
- b. **Mtumishi hataki kufanya kazi tena.**
  The servant does not want to work any more.

Kwenda

The auxiliary verb **kwenda** (to go) has the following uses:

a. When used with -me- or -li- tense markers, **kwenda** assumes the meaning of an action being carried out at the time indicated in the context. It is followed by the infinitive or verb stem:

   (i) **Hamida amekwenda kuleta chakula.**
       Hamida has gone to bring food.
   (ii) **Wageni walikwenda kulala chumbani.**
       The guests went to sleep in the room.

b. When used with or without a subject prefix and with the relative -po- of time, the auxiliary verb **kwenda** gives the meaning of expressions equivalent to "should it happen", "if by chance", and so on. For example:

   (i) **Wendapo hutakuja shuleni kesho, mwalimu wako atahamaki.**
       And if it happens that you do not come to school tomorrow, your teacher will get angry.
   (ii) **Endapo akija leo, nitafurahi sana.**
       Should it happen that he comes today, I will be very happy.

c. When followed by -ka- or -me-, the word **huenda** assumes the meaning of "perhaps" or "maybe". For example:

   (i) **Huenda mvua ikanyesha leo.**
       It may rain today.
   (ii) **Huenda wakulima wale wamevuna asubuhi.**
       Those farmers may have harvested in the morning.

Kwisha

The word **kwisha** (to finish), when functioning as an auxiliary verb, refers to a state of existing or action completed before the point in time indicated in the context. The time indicated could be in the present, past or future. The word "already" frequently assumes the meaning of **kwisha**.

Like some auxiliaries, **kwisha** is followed by the verb stem with or without the infinitive KU-. For example:

a. **Simba amekwisha kuuliwa.**
   The lion is already killed.
b. **Walimu wamekwisha fika mkutanoni.**
   The teachers have already arrived at the meeting.

Copular verbs

Copular verbs have little independent meaning. Their main function is to relate other elements of clause structure, especially subject and complement.

In Swahili, copular verbs are NI, SI, NDI-, SI-, -LI-, -PO, -KO, -MO, -NA, YU, U, WA, etc. The following is a brief description of each of these copulars:

NI

The copular verb NI can also be referred to as **copulative** or **equative** since it describes the quality of a person or thing. *Ashton (1982)* describes it as a marker of predication without a verb. This copular is used to indicate present time references. For example:
a. **Kandege ni mtu hodari.**
Kandege is a clever person.
b. **Amerika ni nchi kubwa.**
America is a big country.

When the copular NI stands at the beginning of a sentence, it gives the sentence prominence or emphasis, as illustrated below:
a. **Ni yeye anayepika sasa.**
It is she who is cooking now.
b. **Ni vitu vyetu vilivyopotea.**
It is our things which got lost.

Structures such as shown above can be referred to as "marked" forms because they give emphasis to particular elements in a sentence.

SI

SI is a copular expressing negation. In other words, it is the negative form of NI. Its uses are shown below:
a. **Omari si mjinga.**
Omari is not a fool.
b. **Nyinyi si wakulima hodari.**
You are not good farmers.

NDI-

NDI-, as a copular verb, is a marker of -O of reference used as an emphatic form of the copular NI. It also carries a positive meaning and is governed by the notion of agreement which subsumes class, person and number. The **NDI-** form is used to define more sharply the referent, which could be a nominal, pronominal or an adverbial antecedent. The following examples illustrate the point:

a. **Huyu ndiye mwizi mwenyewe.**
    This is the real thief.
b. **Kitabu kile ndicho kibovu.**
    That is the bad book.
c. **Wale ndio wahalifu wenyewe.**
    Those are the very culprits.
d. **Vikombe hivi ndivyo vipya.**
    These are the new cups.
e. **Hapa ndipo anapolala.**
    This is where he sleeps.

SI-

The direct opposite counterpart of the copular verb **NDI-** is **SI-** since it is purely used in a negative sense. The **SI-** copular is a marker of **-O** of reference used as an emphatic form of the copular **SI-**. Below are some examples:

a. **Yule siye msafiri.**
    He is not the traveller.
b. **Mti ule sio mnazi.**
    That is not a coconut tree.
c. **Hawa sio wakulima.**
    These are not farmers.
d. **Ile sio mitungi yangu.**
    Those are not my water-jars.
e. **Hapa sipo anapofanya kazi.**
    This is not where he is working.

Personal pronouns also have emphatic forms. For example:

Ndimi ...   It is I ...
Ndiwe ...   It is you ...
Ndiye ...   It is he/she ...
Ndisi ...   It is we ...
Ndinyi ...   It is you (pl) ...
Ndio ...   It is they ...

-LI-

The -LI- marker is also a copular verb used in a relative construction that is affirmative. It is used entirely to denote present time references. This -LI- marker is quite distinct from the particle -LI- of past time. The following examples illustrate the use of this copular verb:

a. **Aliye bahili hataishi kwa raha duniani.**
He who is a miser will not live happily in the world.
b. **Walio wanafunzi hapa ni wawili tu.**
Those who are students here are only two.

The -LI- copular verb co-occurs with the negative copular SI- to express non-identification:

a. **Aliye si tajiri hapati kuishi kwa raha.**
He who is not rich cannot live happily.
b. **Walio si madaktari wazuri hawawezi kuwatibu wagonjwa hawa.**
Those who are not good doctors cannot treat these patients.

In some situations, the copular -LI- also co-occurs with certain adverbial particles to indicate place and manner, as shown below:

a. **Nilipo ni pachafu.**
Where I am is not clean.
b. **Tulivyo ni watu wakweli tu.**
As we are, we are only honest people.

The locative suffix **-PO** can also operate as a copular verb to indicate location with a specified reference. For example:

a. **Nipo hapa.**
I am here.
b. **Tulikuwapo pale jana.**
We were there yesterday.

The **-PO** copular verb also operates in a relative construction. For example:

a. **Aliyepo hapa ni mwanafunzi.**
The one who is here is a student.
b. **Waliokuwapo pale jana ni vijana wawili.**
Those who were there yesterday were two youths.

-KO

Likewise, the locative enclitic -KO is a copular verb. It indicates location without a specific reference. The following is an illustration:

a. **Tuko huku.**
We are here.
b. **Walikuwako kule jana.**
They were there yesterday.

In a relative construction, the -KO copular verb operates in a similar manner. For example:

a. **Tulioko huku ni wachache tu.**
Those of us who are here are few.
b. **Waliokuwako kule jana ni wengi sana.**
Those who were there yesterday were many.

-MO

The -MO locative suffix is a copular verb which indicates location in connection with "withinness", "aroundness" and "alongness". The use of this copular verb is seen in the following sentences:

a. **Mgeni yumo bafuni.**
The visitor is in the bathroom.
b. **Wale vijana wamo vyumbani.**
The youths are in the rooms.

It is worth noting that *Ashton (1982)* refers to the -PO, -KO and -MO locative suffixes as **adverbial enclitics**.

-NA

Adverbial particles, when combined with the -NA of association, also operate as copular verbs to indicate the three basic dimensions of location. For example:

a. **Pana ghasia nyingi hapa.**
There is a lot of fracas here.
b. **Kuna mvua kubwa nje.**
There is a lot of rain outside.
c. **Mna wageni kidogo ukumbini.**
There are few guests in the hall.

The remaining copular verbs are sometimes referred to in grammars as **pronoun prefixes**. They are not, however, used frequently in speech or in writing.

Like other copular verbs, the pronoun prefixes are used to indicate the relationship between two lexical items.

YU

The copular verb YU is used for an antecedent, which is third-person singular possessing an animate semantic feature. For example:

    a. **Kijana yule yu mshari.**
        That youth is troublesome.
    b. **Ominde yu mpole.**
        Ominde is quiet.

U

The copular verb U operates when the antecedent is a singular person possessing a human semantic feature. But it can also be used for third-person reference for non-living things that are singular in form and grouped in M-MI and U-U classes. For example:

    a. **Wewe u mkaidi sana.**
        You are very obstinate.
    b. **Mlango u mdogo.**
        The door is small.
    c. **Ukuta ule u mrefu.**
        That wall is high.

The copular verb U in the three sentences above can be substituted by NI. For example:

    a. **Wewe ni mkaidi sana.**
        You are very obstinate.
    b. **Mlango ni mdogo.**
        The door is small.
    c. **Ukuta ule ni mrefu.**
        That wall is high.

The two copulars U and NI cannot substitute each other in sentences that are "marked" (where a particular element is given prominence). Only the copular NI operates in such contexts. For example:

    a. Mkaidi sana ni wewe.
        * Mkaidi sana u wewe.
    b. Mdogo ni mlango.
        * Mdogo u mlango.

  c. Mrefu ni ukuta ule.
   * Mrefu u ukuta ule.

Similarly, other pronoun prefixes cannot substitute the copular **NI** when the sentences are "marked". For example:

  Yeye ni mjanja.
  * Mjanja yu yeye.

Even in unmarked forms, the copular verb **NI** cannot substitute pronoun prefixes in instances where the predicate is a noun. For example:

  a. Maziwa ya moto.
   * Maziwa ni moto.
  b. Kahawa i baridi.
   * Kahawa ni baridi.

Yet, both the copular **NI** and a pronoun prefix can co-occur to give emphasis to the first element. For example:

  a. **Nyumba hii ni i kubwa.**
   This house is big.
  b. **Yeye ni yu taabani.**
   He is exhausted.

There are other forms of copular verbs referred to in some grammar books as **pronoun prefixes**. As explained earlier, these operate according to class, person and number governing the antecedent.

VOCABULARY

kito	jewel	kumbusha	remind
hatarini	in danger	punde	soon
godoro	mattress	jambazi	villain
iba	steal	hotuba	sermon
kongamano	symposium	safiri	travel
mawingu	clouds	mhojiwa	interviewee
kasha	chest	kiwanda	factory
masaibu	hardships	raha	happiness
chapuchapu	quickly	boya	buoy
bonde	valley	-a thamani	precious
mshtaki	plaintiff	abadan	never
tengeneza	repair	mwembe	mango tree
fundibomba	plumber	malizika	end

majununi	lunatic	**wasili**	arrive
mkalimani	interpreter	**hoi**	tired
-kakamizi	obstinate	**rabsha**	disorder
kamba	prawn	**pwani**	shore
mchuuzi	hawker	**burebure**	without any
sababu	reason		

hakimu mkuu mkaazi   senior resident magistrate

Exercise 7

1. Translate the following sentences:
   a. The man will have arrived by tomorrow.
   b. The porters can carry those heavy loads.
   c. The old lady is at the point of death.
   d. Those are not small valleys.
   e. The windows are open.
   f. My mother has not yet had the chance to travel by air.
   g. The interviewees are in the room.
   h. This is a very precious jewel.
   i. It is I who wanted to go home now.
   j. Those who are not young cannot work in the factory.
   k. The priest came early lest he might miss the sermon.
   l. Those mattresses are about to fall down.
   m. There are many school children outside.
   n. The villain has gone to steal goods in the shop.
   o. Remind us lest we forget.
   p. He who is not a plumber cannot repair water taps.
   q. The symposium can end soon.
   r. It may rain any time now; it is very cloudy outside.
   s. This tea is very hot.

2. Translate the following sentences:
   a. Ile sio miembe kabisa.
   b. Yale ndiyo machungwa mabovu.
   c. Milango yote i wazi.
   d. Mtumishi amekwenda kununua kamba pwani.
   e. Anayeishi huku ni mkalimani mmoja tu.
   f. Sisi tuko hoi leo.
   g. Wewe u mkakamizi ajabu.
   h. Kuna rabsha kubwa sokoni.
   i. Uma huu u mdogo sana.
   j. Walio si wachuuzi hapa ni wawili tu.

k. Mimi ndiye mwenyeji wenyewe.
l. Abiria waliwasili bandarini mapema ili wasije kuikosa safari.
m. Zile boriti zinataka kuporomoka.
n. Mhadhiri anaweza kufika hapa wakati wowote.
o. Wao si majununi.
p. Mjadala unaweza kuanza punde hivi.
q. Lile ndilo boya lenyewe.
r. Uji huu u baridi sana.
s. Mfanyakazi yule anaweza kulima kondeni chapuchapu.
t. Wapishi wamekwisha pika vyakula vyote.

3. Select a suitable copular verb from the brackets and fill in the blank spaces:
   a. Sisi .... hatarini tu. (tumo, tupo)
   b. Watoto wale .... adabu hata kidogo. (hawana, hamna)
   c. Vile .... alivyosema hakimu mkuu mkaazi. (ndicho, ndivyo)
   d. Vyombo vyote .... sandukuni. (vipo, vimo)
   e. Yeye .... anayechunga kondoo. (sio, siye)
   f. Hiki .... kitabu cha sarufi ya Kiswahili. (ni, ki)
   g. Minazi ile .... mirefu mno. (zi, i)
   h. Kuta zote hizo .... nyufa abadan. (zana, hazina)
   i. .... tunaopika wali jikoni. (Ndisi, Ndimi)
   j. Wao .... wasiwasi mwingi. (mna, wana)
   k. Kalamu hizi .... mbovu kwa kukaa sana. (yawa, zawa)
   l. Wewe .... mwenyewe akili kama unapiga watu burebure. (huwa, huwi)
   m. Yale .... masaibu yaliyomfika mzee wiki jana. (ndiyo, ndio)
   n. Kule .... kwenye raha moja kwa moja. (ndipo, ndiko)
   o. Hivi .... ninavyotaka ufanye. (ndio, ndivyo)

8 Adverbs

Traditionally, adverbs have been described as words modifying a verb, an adjective or another adverb. For example:

    a.   **Mtoto mchanga analia** *sana*.
         The baby is crying loudly.
    b.   **Msichana yule ni mzuri** *mno*.
         That girl is very beautiful.
    c.   **Mwanafunzi alikuja jana** *usiku*.
         The student came last night.

In a., the adverb **sana** (loudly) modifies the verb **lia** (cry); in b., the adverb **mno** (very much) modifies the adjective **mzuri** (beautiful) and in c., the adverb **usiku** (night) modifies the adverb **jana** (yesterday).

This syntactic function of an adverb as the modifier of a verb, an adjective and another adverb still stands today, to a large extent.

A sizeable number of adverbs do not have a morphological marker. These are also described by some grammars as "non-derived". For example:

    a.   **Hamisi ameondoka** *sasa hivi*.
         Hamisi has just left.
    b.   **Ninataka vikombe vitatu** *tu*.
         I want three cups only.

A few of these non-derived adverbs are borrowed from Arabic:

    a.   *Labda* **mvua itanyesha kesho**.
         Perhaps it will rain tomorrow.
    b.   *Takriban* **wanafunzi wote walikuja kwenye mkutano**.
         Almost all students attended the meeting.

The second group of adverbs consists of words formed from other parts of speech, mainly from adjectives and nouns. Such words are classified as **derived** and take prefixes **ki-** and **vi-**:

    a.   **Watoto wetu wameharibika** *kiutamaduni*.
         Our children are culturally spoilt.
    b.   **Mtumishi wangu anaifanya kazi** *vizuri*.
         My servant is doing the job well.

Another category of adverbs consists, not of words, but of phrases containing particles followed by nouns. For example:

    a.   Mtalii atasafiri **kwa ndege**.
         The tourist will travel by plane.

    b.   Mzee yule yumo **katika shida**.
         That old man is in difficulties.

Adverbs can also exist in bound morphemes used to denote place, manner and time. For example:

    a.   Mama yangu ameenda dukani.
         My mother has gone to the shop.
    b.   Sielewi anavyofanya kazi ile.
         I do not understand how he does that job.
    c.   Utakapofika nyumbani, niite kutoka nje.
         When you come home, call me from outside.

In the above examples, the particles **-ni, -vyo-** and **-po-** represent the dimensions of place, manner and time.

    Adverbs are not essential to the structure of a sentence but they frequently affect the meaning. Compare the following sentences:

    a.   Mti umeanguka.
         The tree has fallen down.
         Mti umeanguka **punde hivi**.
         The tree has just fallen down.
    b.   Wameimaliza kazi yote.
         They have completed the whole job.
         Wameimaliza **takriban** kazi yote.
         They have almost completed the job.

However, adverbs are sometimes essential in order to produce a meaningful sentence, especially where there is a copular verb:

    a.   Mama yupo **jikoni**.
         Mother is in the kitchen.
    b.   Hawa vijana wamo **taabuni**.
         The youths are in difficulties.

Compare them with:

    (i)   * Mama yupo.
    (ii) * Hawa vijana wamo.

Adverbs are generally mobile in the sense that they can occur in more than one different position in a sentence. For example:

    a.   Tutakwenda Nairobi **kesho**.
         We will go to Nairobi tomorrow.
    b.   Daktari amemtibu mgonjwa hivi **karibuni**.
         The doctor has treated the patient recently.

The two sentences are "unmarked". They contain the adverbs **kesho** (tomorrow) and **karibuni** (recently). These adverbs can be transposed to emphasise a particular element in the sentences, thus becoming "marked" forms. For example:

    a.   Kesho tutakwenda Nairobi.
    b.   Tutakwenda kesho Nairobi.
    c.   Karibuni daktari amemtibu mgonjwa.
    d.   Daktari karibuni amemtibu mgonjwa.
    e.   Daktari amemtibu karibuni mgonjwa.

All these sentences are acceptable in Swahili. However, some adverbs cannot produce acceptable constructions if they are transposed. For example:

    (i)   **Kijana yule anakula wali tu.**
        That youth only eats rice.
    (ii) **Mbona hukuja?**
        Why didn't you come?

The adverbs **tu** (only) and **mbona** (why) would produce unacceptable sentences if they were transposed:

    (i)   * Tu kijana yule anakula wali.
    (ii) * Hukuja mbona?

Adverbs and other word classes

In some cases, there is no difference in form between an adverb and a corresponding noun. Therefore, only the context would help determine which part of speech the word is. For example:

    a.   Ninakupenda **Ulaya** sana.
        I like **Europe** very much. (**Ulaya** operates here as a noun).
    b.   Alikwenda **Ulaya** wiki iliyopita.
        He went to **Europe** last week. (**Ulaya** operates here as an adverb).

Likewise, we can find a similarity in form between an adverb and an adjective in some situations. For example:

    a.   Ni **dhahiri** Juma atakuja kesho.
        It is **clear** that Juma will come tomorrow. (**Dhahiri** operates here as an adjective).
    b.   Aliniambia **dhahiri** kuwa hatanisaidia.
        He told me **plainly** that he would not help me. (**Dhahiri** operates here as an adverb).

Types of adverbs

Adverbs in Swahili are generally classified as follows:

Adverbs of place

Adverbs of place indicate where an action is occurring. They are names of places, seasons and other dimensions connected with the concept of location. For example:

    a.   Mwalimu mkuu anaishi **hapa**.
           The headmaster lives here.
    b.   Msafara umeelekea **mashariki**.
           The caravan has travelled eastward.

Some of the adverbs of place are suffixed with a locative **-ni**, as in the following sentences:

    a.   Mtumishi amekwenda **dukani**.
           The servant has gone to the shop.
    b.   Kuna picha **ukutani**.
           There is a picture on the wall.

Adverbs of place can also exist in bound forms. For example:

    a.   Hatuelewi alikokwenda.
           We do not know where he has gone to.
    b.   Anamoishi yule mkulima ni hapa.
           That farmer lives here.

Adverbs of time

Adverbs of time, as the name implies, indicate the time an action is taking place. Nearly all of these adverbs are free morphemes. They are words which indicate the time of day, days of the week, months, years, as well as other dimensions connected with the time element. For example:

    a.   Mkulima atafika **jioni**.
           The farmer will arrive in the evening.
    b.   Meli itaondoka **Jumanne**.
           The ship will leave on Tuesday.

But adverbs of time can also exist as bound morphemes. For example:

    a.   Alipofika shuleni, hakumkuta mtu yeyote.
           When he arrived in school, he did not meet anyone.
    b.   Ulipokuja nyumbani, nilikuwa nimelala.
           When you came home, I was asleep.

Adverbs of manner

Adverbs of this type describe how an action is taking place. For example:

a. Mwanafunzi ameondoka **kwa haraka**.
   The student has left hurriedly.
b. Mtumishi wangu anafanya kazi **sana**.
   My servant is working hard.

Some adverbs of manner take the prefix ki-:

a. Anafanya mambo **kitoto**.
   He is behaving childishly.
b. Mchezaji yule anacheza mpira **kifundi**.
   That player plays soccer skillfully.

Other adverbs of manner are in the form of ideophones, sometimes functioning as onomatopoeic. For example:

a. Mtoto ameanguka **chubwi**!
   The child has fallen into the water with a splash.
b. Mwanamke yule aliufunga mlango **ndi**!
   That woman closed the door firmly.

Adverbs of frequency

Adverbs of frequency, as the name implies, show the frequency with which the action described by the verb is carried out. These adverbs give general answers to the question "How often?" Adverbs of frequency include single words like **daima** (always) and phrases expressed in specific or general terms like **kila siku** (every day) and **mara kwa mara** (from time to time). For example:

a. Mwanafunzi huyu **daima** anachelewa.
   This student is always late.
b. Mjomba aliizuru Ghana **mara kwa mara** mwaka huu.
   My uncle visited Ghana from time to time this year.

Some grammars group this type of adverbs under the heading "adverbs of number".

Adverbs of degree

Adverbs in this group indicate the extent or degree to which the event described by the verb is carried out. They broadly answer the question "To what extent?" Adverbs of degree, which can also be referred to as **intensifiers**, include phrases like **kidogo kidogo** (a little bit). For example:

a. Mgonjwa anaumwa **sana**.
    The patient is extremely sick.
b. Amekula **takriban** chakula chote.
    He has eaten almost all the food.

VOCABULARY

milele	forever	kwa wingi	abundantly
kwa woga	in fear	kwa salama	peacefully
tapakaa	spread	papo hapo	instantly
karibuni	recently	vipusa	spare parts
beramu	placard	tupa	throw
kwa nguvu	forcefully	theluji	snow
kwa siri	secretly	chirizika	trickle
jasusi	spy	kina	depth
kwa hamu	anxiously	ukimwi	AIDS
labda	probably	kwa ushujaa	gallantly
zamani	formerly	poromoka	fall
nyanyua	raise	kwa uchangamfu	cheerfully
yosayosa	hurriedly	mwendaji	
		kwa miguu	pedestrian

Exercise 8

1. Translate the following sentences:
    a. The hunter shot the lion in fear.
    b. The student asked the questions foolishly.
    c. The pedestrian died instantly after the accident.
    d. Will the woman get married soon?
    e. Recently we travelled the whole day.
    f. Formerly, my parents lived here.
    g. The old man came here thrice to look for the things.
    h. The speaker raised the placard sadly.
    i. The cups fell down forcefully.
    j. I did the job hurriedly.
    k. The cooks cooked the food in the European style.
    l. They came here every day to talk with us.
    m. The spy entered the country secretly.
    n. The year started very badly.
    o. The farmers harvested the crops abundantly.
    p. The train passed here at night.

2. Translate the following sentences:
   a. Wanavijiji walifanya mkutano kwa salama.
   b. Vijana wa siku hizi wanapenda kula kizungu.
   c. Tuliitupa mizigo kwa hasira.
   d. Askari walipigana kwa ushujaa.
   e. Theluji iliporomoka kwa nguvu.
   f. Maji yanachirizika taratibu.
   g. Mimi kadhalika nitaandika tena vitabu vyengine vya sarufi.
   h. Mzee yule amekufa fo-fo-fo.
   i. Bendera ile inapepea kwa kasi.
   j. Vipusa vya magari hupanda bei kila siku.
   k. Waandishi wale walizungumza nasi kwa uchangamfu.
   l. Mkutano wa viongozi utamalizika upesi leo.
   m. Wasafiri walielekea kusini.
   n. Nafikiri itanyesha mvua jioni.
   o. Ugonjwa wa ukimwi umetapakaa haraka duniani.

3. Construct sentences using the following adverbs:
   a. kwa nguvu   b. kando
   c. milele   d. mlangoni
   e. kwa kina   f. ghafula
   g. magharibi   h. upesiupesi
   i. kistaarabu   j. mara tano

9 Prepositions and Conjunctions

Traditional grammars maintain that there are no words of Bantu origin which can be basically called **prepositions**. However, these grammars also explain that a few words based on the -A of relationship may be so termed. These are:

na	–	with, by
kwa	–	by means of, with, by, for, to, at, from, through.

Pronominal concord (**P.C.**) + **-a** of, for example **la**, **wa**, **ya**, **za**, etc.

Simple prepositions

The various examples given above can be classified as **simple prepositions**. In addition to these, some traditional grammars give further examples of prepositions in Swahili. *Ashton (1982)*, for example, shows that a few Bantu nouns, verb forms as well as loan words from Arabic can also be termed as **prepositions**. The following are some of the examples:

mpaka	–	till, as far as
kutoka, toka, tokea	–	from
hata	–	till
kwenye	–	at, in
bila	–	without
kama	–	like
tangu	–	since

Examples of prepositions

Because of their importance and wide usage, some prepositions need more illustrations. Each of them is listed and discussed below:

Kwa

This preposition consists of the locative prefix **KU-** joined to the -A of association, sometimes called **connective -a**. Following is a description of its uses:

a.   To indicate location.
(i)   Nitaenda nyumbani **kwa** Abdi kesho.
I will go to Abdi's house tomorrow.
(ii) Watalii walienda **kwa** mkurugenzi wa idara ya utalii.
The tourists went to see the director of the department of tourism.

b.   To indicate the names of instruments used.
- (i)   Alipigwa **kwa** mawe.
  He was hit with stones.
- (ii) Nilitazama **kwa** darubini.
  I looked through the telescope.

c.   To indicate the manner or mode of an action.
- (i)   Tulisafiri **kwa** basi.
  We travelled by bus.
- (ii) Nilimtambua **kwa** jinsi alivyovaa nguo zile.
  I recognized him by the way he dressed.

d.   To indicate purpose or aim of an action.
- (i)   Alinijia **kwa** ushauri.
  He came to me for advice.
- (ii) Vijana wale hutumia kuni **kwa** kupikia.
  Those youths use firewood for cooking.

e.   To indicate the cause of an action.
- (i)   Wale wakimbizi walikufa **kwa** njaa.
  Those refugees died of hunger.
- (ii) Amewekwa rumande **kwa** kosa la jinai.
  He has been remanded for a criminal offence.

Na

Na consists of the **N- of association** and the **connective -a**. When functioning as a preposition, its uses can be illustrated as follows:

a.   To express an agent or an actor.
- (i)   Wanafunzi walipigwa **na** mwalimu.
  The students were beaten by the teacher.
- (ii) Kazi yangu ilitafsiriwa **na** mkalimani.
  My work was translated by an interpreter.

b.   To express the sense of "together with" or "in company with".
- (i)   Ninataka kusema **naye**.
  I want to speak with him/her.
- ii) Atasafiri **na** watoto wake.
  He will travel with his children.

Tangu

Tangu, meaning "since" or "from", is normally used in reference to time. For example:

a. **Tangu** kunyesha mvua, sijatoka nje.
   Since it began raining, I have not gone out.
b. **Tangu** lini mgeni ameningojea?
   Since when has the visitor been waiting for me?

In some isolated instances, the preposition **tangu** can express the cause of an action. For example:

a. Hamisi haji hapa tena **tangu** nilipomlaumu jana.
   Hamisi has not come here again since I blamed him yesterday.
b. Sili wali tena **tangu** daktari anikataze.
   I will not eat rice again since the doctor forbade me to.

Complex prepositions

Complex prepositions are formed from adverbs, nouns and adjectives with the addition of **kwa, na** or **-a**. The following are examples of various complex prepositions in Swahili:

baada ya	after	**shingoni mwa**	around the neck of
kati ya	between	**ukingoni mwa**	along the bank of
ndani ya	inside of	**mbali na**	far from
mbele ya	in front of	**nyuma ya**	after, behind
karibu	near	**katikati ya**	among
pamoja na	together with	**kwa habari ya**	about
mahali pa	instead of	**zaidi ya**	more than
juu ya	on	**nje ya**	outside
kutoka kwa	from	**kwa sababu ya**	because of
kwa ajili ya	for the sake of	**chini ya**	below, under

It is important to note that compound prepositions formed with **kwa** or **-a** are never used with personal pronouns. Thus, we have:

chini yangu	under me
nyuma yake	behind him
mbele yako	in front of you
pamoja nami	together with me
mbali naye	far from him
kwake	through him

'Katika' as a preposition

Although written as one word, Swahili grammars label the word **katika** as a **compound preposition**. Its basic meaning is "on" or "in" and it refers to both time and place.

102

The time dimension can be compared with any English prepositions indicating duration of time, such as "during", "whilst", "in" and "at":

(i) **Katika** mwaka ule, kulinyesha sana.
During that year, it rained heavily.
(ii) **Katika** kuzungumza, simu mara ikalia.
While speaking, a telephone rang.

The dimension of place concerning the preposition **katika** can be equated with English prepositions "in", "on", "at", "to", "from", "out of", etc. The reference to place of locality performed by **katika** is much the same as the locative suffix -NI. In fact, in many instances, the two may alternate in usage. Here are some examples of the preposition **katika** depicting place:

(i) Wageni waliingia **katika** nyumba hii.
The visitors went into this house.
(ii) Baba alitia sahihi **katika** waraka huu.
My father signed in this document.

Apart from the dimensions of time and place, the preposition **katika** can be used in expressions defining the situation or particular circumstances under which the action of a verb is carried out. For instance:

(i) Kijana yule alikuwa **katika** huzuni kubwa.
That youth was in profound distress.
(ii) Usisadiki hata kidogo **katika** habari zile ulizozisikia.
Do not believe at all the news you have heard.

Conjunctions

Like with prepositions, traditional grammars point out that there are no words of Bantu origin which are basically conjunctions except those which consist of the **N-** of association and the connective **-a**. Nevertheless, there are various methods of joining words and sentences. For example:

a. By borrowing from Arabic, e.g, **lakini** (but), **ama** (or), etc.
b. By phrases, many of them being based on **kwa**.
c. By the use of certain tense forms. e.g. **-ka-**, **-ki-**, **-japo-**, etc.

Traditionally, conjunctions are divided into two main clauses: **coordinating** and **subordinating**. Coordinating conjunctions, sometimes referred to as **coordinators**, are connective items which join linguistic units of equivalent syntactic structures. Coordinators may be further divided according to the function they perform. In Swahili, there are two main divisions of coordinating conjunctions:

Additive

na´	and, also
pia	also, too
tena	again
isitoshe	furthermore
vilevile	moreover
juu ya hayo	furthermore
fauka na hayo	in addition
pamoja na hayo	moreover
au	or
ama	either ... or
wala	neither ... nor

Adversative

lakini	but
ila	but, except, unless
bali	but rather, on the contrary

Other connective items like **kwa vile** and **kwani** — all meaning "because" — are grouped in this book under the rubric of **subordinating conjunctions**. Thus, unlike *Ashton (1982)*, this book treats these two connective items as subordinating conjunctions because they do not join units of paratactic structures, that is, structures of equal status.

Subordinating conjunctions join linguistic units of non-equivalent status. In the case of sentences, they introduce clauses which are subordinate to the main clause. Likewise, subordinating conjunctions can also be grouped. In Swahili, we can have the following groups:

Purpose

ili	so that
ili kwamba, kusudi, etc.	in order that, etc.

Concession

ingawa	although
ijapokuwa	even though
ingawaje, etc.	albeit, etc.

Comparison

kuliko	more than
kuzidi,	better than, etc.
kushinda, etc.	

Condition

mpaka kama	until
ikiwa	if
kama kwamba	whether, etc.

Reason

kwa vile	for
kwa kuwa,	because
kwa sababu,	
kwani	
kwa maana, etc.	the reason being, etc.

Temporal

tangu,	
hadi, etc.	since, etc.

Some modern Swahili grammarians, such as *Kapinga (1983)*, do not make a distinction between prepositions and conjunctions. Thus, they group these two categories of grammatical items under one heading, namely **vihusishi** (connecting items). More research, however, is needed to support the claims of these grammarians.

VOCABULARY

muogeleaji	swimmer	zuga	deceive
ugua	suffer	kandanda	soccer
bakora	stick	endelea	progress
kwa kasi	fast	bahili	miser
jitimai	sorrow	sumbua	vex
dhihaki	mock	ficha	hide
raha	happiness	andama	sight
mahuluku	human being	ongea	talk
saidia	assist	gulio	market
jukumu	responsibility	vita	war
tusi	insult	jeshi	army

105

matumaini	spirits, hope	**mpishi**	cook
jaza	fill	**sabahi**	greet
maziko	funeral	**kopesha**	lend
zana	implements	**daftari**	book
kabili	face	**toroka**	escape
chumba cha		**hofu**	fear
wageni	visitors' room		

Exercise 9

1. Pick out the **prepositions** in the following sentences:
   a. Yule mwanafunzi alipigwa kwa bakora.
   b. Chuo kikuu cha Moi kinaendelea vizuri.
   c. Mama alieleza kwamba yule mtu hatoki nje ila usiku
   d. Mali bila daftari hupotea bila habari
   e. Mimi nilikuwa katika jitimai kubwa.
   f. Wanataka kwenda mbio sana kushinda wenzake.
   g. Taarifa yako inanisumbua kama nini.
   h. Fika hapa kesho kusudi uonane na mama yangu.
   i. Tangu kuja kwake nyumbani, nimekuwa sina raha.
   j. Kwenye miti hakuna wajenzi.
   k. Hawakopeshi wazima sembuse wagonjwa.
   l. Ikiwa mwezi utaandama kesho, basi Waislamu watafunga siku ya pili yake.
   m. Mwanariadha Carl Lewis anakimbia mbio sana kuliko wanariadha wengi duniani.
   n. Kijana yule alinisaidia bila ya kutaka malipo yoyote.
   o. Paka wako ameiba nyama ya mpishi wetu.
   p. Wanavijiji hawa wanaishi karibu na mto.

2. Translate the following sentences:
   a. The old man lives behind the market.
   b. Mariamu will travel to Dar es Salaam by road.
   c. They beat the young boy because he insulted them.
   d. I saw him outside the visitors' room.
   e. The army was in great spirits before winning the war.
   f. The girl passed us quietly as if she was a stranger.
   g. Since he arrived here last Sunday, a lot of people like to greet him on the way.
   h. Either you or he will go to the shop tomorrow.
   i. From here to the lake is quite far.

    j. All attended the funeral except their uncle.
    k. Stay here and do not go out.
    l. Little by little fills up the measure.
    m. I can do the job but I do not have the implements.
    n. Three prisoners escaped from jail yesterday at dawn.
    o. They waited for us from afternoon to evening.

3. Translate the following sentences:
    a. "Mwanariadha wa mwaka" safari hii ni James Ngugi.
    b. Hatukwenda shambani kwa vile mvua ilinyesha sana.
    c. Mtu hawezi kuishi bila ya kula chochote.
    d. Msasi alimkabili nguruwe bila ya hofu.
    e. Utakuja kesho kwenye mashindano au vipi?
    f. Wanafunzi wale walikimbia tangu nyumbani mpaka shuleni.
    g. Afadhali kufa kuliko kuugua kwa muda mrefu.
    h. Napenda kucheza kandanda lakini mimi sasa ni mgonjwa.
    i. Hamsaidii mama yake sembuse wewe.
    j. Muogeleaji alipiga mbizi katikati ya ziwa.
    k. Ama yeye anakuzuga au anakudhihaki tu.
    l. Huyu kijana huimba; tena huimba vizuri sana.
    m. Mwizi alizificha nguo chini ya kitanda chake.
    n. Toka ardhini mpaka mwezini ni umbali gani?
    o. Ndege huenda kwa kasi kuliko gari.

4. Fill the blank spaces in the following sentences by using an appropriate **preposition** or **conjunction**:
    a. Mzee wako ana mali nyingi ajabu _____ ni bahili mno.
    b. Shoga yako ameolewa _____ rafiki yangu.
    c. Lazima akimbie kwa haraka _____ ataikosa treni.
    d. Hawajui wasemalo _____ wafanyalo.
    e. Maliza hadithi yote _____nielewe vizuri.
    f. Sasa imepita miaka mingi _____ marehemu mama alipofariki.
    g. Wageni watakunywa kahawa _____ chai?
    h. Yeye ni mahuluku _____ sisi.
    i. Omino ana jukumu kubwa _____ kuwasaidia wazee wake.
    j. Tumesikia _____ wewe unapenda kula ndizi.
    k. Wasafiri wote walisafiri _____ gari.
    l. Nilifika karibu yake _____ nipate kuongea naye.
    m. Wale wanawake sita walikufa _____ njaa.
    n. Hamidu atafika tu leo _____ anaweza kuchelewa.
    o. Hapa ni karibu sana _____ sokoni.

10 Pronouns and Pronominalization

Pronouns have often been defined as closed sets of items which can be used to replace or substitute nouns or noun phrases. Look at the example below:

Kariuki ameenda sinema.
Kariuki has gone to the cinema.

It is grammatically correct to expand the above sentence by saying **Yeye atakuja hapa baadaye** (He will come here afterwards). This construction is more acceptable than repeating the noun **Kariuki** in place of the word **yeye** (he). Thus, **yeye** is a pronoun since it is replacing the noun **Kariuki** in the expanded sentence.

Types of pronouns

Like adjectives and adverbs, Swahili pronouns are of various types. They are described below.

Personal pronouns

There are two forms in this group. First, we have personal independent pronouns. Other grammars refer to them as **self standing pronouns**. There are six in all. Each refers to animate beings. For example:

mimi	I, me
wewe	you
yeye	he, him, she, her
sisi	we, us
ninyi	you (pl)
wao	they

Personal independent pronouns can stand on their own. They are, therefore, free morphemes. All the six pronouns can serve as "actors" or "agents" (traditional grammars refer to them as **subjects**) of their sentences. For example:

a. **Mimi nitaendesha gari.**
   I will drive the car.
b. **Yeye anacheza mpira sasa.**
   He is playing soccer now.
c. **Wao waliimba vizuri jana.**
   They sang well yesterday.

In the three examples, the pronouns **mimi** (I), **yeye** (he or she) and **wao** (they) are clearly actors of their sentences.

Conversely, the six persons can also become "goals" or "patients" (traditional grammars refer to them as **objects**) of their sentences as shown below:

a. **Mwalimu atanipa mimi zawadi.**
The teacher will give me a prize.

b. **Mama atatuandalia sisi chakula.**
Mother will prepare food for us.

c. **Juma atakwita wewe.**
Juma will call you.

Here, the pronouns **mimi** (me), **sisi** (us) and **wewe** (you) function as "patients" or "goals" of their sentences.

Apart from personal independent pronouns, we also have **subject prefixes**. This is another category of personal pronouns. Subject prefixes are bound morphemes. As we have seen in the preceding chapters, subject prefixes are attached to the various verbs as shown below:

a. **Nitasafiri kwa ndege kesho.**
I will travel by air tomorrow.

b. **Wanapika wali kila siku.**
They cook rice everyday.

c. **Atakuja mapema leo.**
She will come early today.

Our subject prefixes **ni** (I), **wa** (they) and **a** (she) are attached to the verbs **safiri** (travel), **pika** (cook) and **ja** (come) respectively. The subject prefixes function as subjects of their sentences. But they can also operate as objects of their sentences as demonstrated in the following examples:

a. **Tulimlaumu sana.**
We blamed him a lot.

b. **Nilikivunja kiti.**
I broke the chair.

c. **Ulitufahamisha vizuri.**
You explained to us well.

The morphemes **m** (him), **ki** (it) and **tu** (us) function here as objects. As shown in the previous chapters, they are referred to as **object prefixes**. Some grammars refer to them as **object markers**.

Possessive pronouns

The roots of possessive pronouns are similar to those of possessive adjectives. These are **-angu** (mine), **-ako** (yours), **-ake** (his) or (hers), **-etu** (ours), **-enu** (yours) (pl) and **-ao** (theirs). There is, however, a difference between these two categories of grammatical items. Possessive adjectives are accompanied by nouns while possessive pronouns stand alone. The following examples show the use of possessive pronouns:

a. **Yeye ni wangu.**
   She/He is mine.
b. **Mahala hapa ni pake.**
   This place is hers.
c. **Kwao ni mbali sana.**
   Their place is too far.

Possessive pronouns in Swahili take concordial agreements which must be with the possessed and not the possessor. The agreements operate according to the class of the noun in existence. Therefore, we have these various forms of conjugation:

M-WA class

Singular

Mtumishi wangu	My servant.
Mtumishi wako	Your servant.
Mtumishi wake	His/her servant.
Mtumishi wetu	Our servant.

Plural

Watumishi wangu	My servants.
Watumishi wako	Your servants.
Watumishi wake	His/her servants.
Watumishi wetu	Our servants.

M-MI class

Singular

Mkoba wangu	My basket.
Mkoba wako	Your basket.
Mkoba wake	His/her basket.
Mkoba wetu	Our basket.

Plural

Mikoba yangu	My baskets.
Mikoba yako	Your baskets.

110

Mikoba yake	His/her baskets.
Mikoba yetu	Our baskets.

JI-MA class

Singular

Nanasi langu	My pineapple.
Nanasi lako	Your pineapple.
Nanasi lake	His/her pineapple.
Nanasi letu	Our pineapple.

Plural

Mananasi yangu	My pineapples.
Mananasi yako	Your pineapples.
Mananasi yake	His/her pineapples.
Mananasi yetu	Our pineapples.

KI-VI class

Singular

Kiti changu	My chair.
Kiti chako	Your chair.
Kiti chake	His/her chair.
Kiti chetu	Our chair.

Plural

Viti vyangu	My chairs.
Viti vyako	Your chairs.
Viti vyake	His/her chairs.
Viti vyetu	Our chairs.

Demonstrative pronouns

Demonstrative pronouns point out objects of all kinds. Being pronouns, they stand alone and, therefore, are not followed by adjectives. Furthermore, the roots of these pronouns are similar to those of demonstrative adjectives. For nearness, the roots are **ha-**, **hu-** and **hi-**. For remoteness, the root is **-le**. For example:

    a.   **H*a*wa ni wakulima kutoka Nakuru.**
        These are farmers from Nakuru.

    b.   **H*u*yu ndiye mkaidi sana.**
        This is the one who is very obstinate.

    c.   **H*i*ki ni kizuri sana.**
        This one is very good.

111

The last kind of demonstrative pronoun is the **h-o** particle which, as we have seen in the earlier chapters, refers to an item that was either previously mentioned or has a locative meaning (see Chapter 5). For example:

    a.   **Hicho ni kibaya sana.**
        That is very bad.
    b.   **Hayo ni maneno mazuri.**
        Those are good words.

Interrogative pronouns

Interrogative pronouns are only used for asking questions. Unlike interrogative adjectives, interrogative pronouns are not accompanied by nouns. Certain interrogative pronouns take concords. These are **-pi** (which) and **-ngapi** (how many). For example:

    a.   **Yupi anafanya kelele?**
        Who is making noise?
    b.   **Wangapi wamesafiri leo?**
        How many have travelled today?

Other interrogative pronouns, however, do not take concords. These are **nani** (who) and **nini** (what). For example:

    a.   **Nani ataifanya kazi hii?**
        Who will do this work?
    b.   **Nini kinakukera mwanangu?**
        What is pestering you, my child?

Relative pronouns

Some grammars refer to relative pronouns as **pronouns of -O of reference**. As we will see later, relative pronouns may refer either to the subject or object of the sentence. The type of relative pronoun used is dependent upon the class of the antecedent.

A number of grammars have shown that in Swahili, relative pronouns can operate along the following three dimensions:

a.   By inserting the appropriate relative pronoun within the verb. For example:
     (i)   **Mtu anayefundisha vizuri ni John.**
         The person who teaches well is John.
    (ii) **Kitabu kilichoanguka chini ni changu.**
         The book which has fallen down is mine.

b. By attaching the appropriate particle to the word **amba-**.
    (i) **Mtu ambaye anakaa katika hii nyumba ni mjomba yangu.**
         The person who lives in this house is my uncle.
    (ii) **Sahani ambayo imevunjika ni yangu.**
         The plate which is broken is mine.

c. By suffixing the appropriate relative particle to the last element of the verb:
    (i) **Msichana azungumzaye sana ni Jane.**
         The girl who talks a lot is Jane.
    (ii) **Sentensi zifuatazo ni ndefu.**
         The following sentences are long.

Quasi pronouns

Certain pronouns cannot belong to any of the categories discussed above. *Steere (1976)* uses the term **quasi pronouns** to refer to such grammatical items. Other grammars refer to them as **generalizing pronouns**. Like quasi adjectives, quasi pronouns also take concords appropriate to the class of the noun in question.

Quasi pronouns are few in number and thus can be listed. They are **-ote** (all), **-ingine** (other), **-enyewe** (self) and **-o-ote**, (any). They are used in the following way:

    a. **Chote kimevunjika.**
        The whole thing is broken.
    b. **Wengine wamechelewa.**
        Others are late.
    c. **Mwenyewe ameanguka chini.**
        He has fallen down by himself.
    d. **Yeyote aje hapa kwa haraka.**
        Anyone should come here quickly.

Emphasis of pronouns

Pronouns in Swahili are emphasized by the reduplication of the concord marker of each noun class. Such emphasized grammatical items are sometimes referred to as **emphatic pronouns**. They are always used together with the demonstrative pronouns of the first degree so as to reinforce their meaning. For example:

    Kitabu hiki.
    This book.

To reinforce the meaning of the above construction, we would say:

Kitabu kiki hiki.
This very book.

When used with the demonstrative pronouns which refer to an already mentioned object, the emphatic pronouns are formed from the class concords and the relative particle:

Jambo lilo hilo.
This same affair.

Pronominalization

This is a term used by generative grammarians to refer to a rule which replaces a lexical noun phrase with a pronoun. Generative grammarians have pointed out that pronominalization can take place along two axes: **backward** and **forward**. To explain these concepts, let us consider the following sentences:

a. **Alipoingia chumbani tu, John akaanza kula chakula.**
    As soon as he entered the room, John started to eat food.

b. **Huko walikokwenda, wazee wale wangeweza kumkosa kijana mwenyewe.**
    Where they had gone, those old men could have missed the young man.

The two sentences above can be rewritten in this manner:

c. **John alipoingia chumbani tu, John akaanza kula chakula.**
    As soon as John entered the room, John started to eat food.

d. **Huko wazee wale walikokwenda, wazee wale wangeweza kumkosa kijana mwenyewe.**
    Where those old men had gone, those old men could have missed the youth.

In sentences c. and d., the noun phrases used in subordinate or dependent clauses are identical to those used in the main clauses. Since **John** and **wazee wale** (those old men) are definite, it is possible to argue that sentence a. is derived from sentence c. while b. is derived from d. Thus, sentences (a) and (b) are instances of **backward pronominalization**. In each of these sentences, the first pronoun occurs in a subordinate clause that does not include the antecedent, whereas the antecedent is not in a clause that includes the first pronoun.

In forward pronominalization, a pronoun in a subordinate clause refers to the preceding main clause. Thus in both forms of pronominalization, the pronoun and the antecedent, which is generally a noun phrase, must be co-referential to each other. Here are a few examples:

a. **Salima kauza gari mpya aliyoinunua hivi karibuni.**
    Salima sold the new car that she bought recently.

b. **John kaona sega la nyuki alipotazama juu.**
    John saw the honeycomb when he looked upwards.

These two examples show that a pronoun can indeed refer to a preceding antecedent even though it is not in a clause to the one that contains the antecedent.

Constraints in pronominalization

Although pronominalization is sometimes necessary in order to avoid repetition of particular words, there are constraints surrounding it. One such constraint is the fact that there may be the need to repeat a noun phrase to avoid ambiguity in meaning, especially if there is a relatively great distance between the pronominal form and its referent noun phrase. Worse still, the occurrence of more than one noun phrase in a discourse is likely to make the processing of anaphoric items more difficult for the listener or reader.

Furthermore, it should be remembered that the repetition of a particular word or noun phrase constitutes an accepted rhetorical device for the purpose of emphasis. It is for this reason that orators make use of this technique to impress a message upon their audience. This same device is used in our daily speech. While we may contend that pronominalization may be permissible syntactically, the intended rhetorical effect would certainly be lost. And finally, the repetition of a word or noun phrase is sometimes necessary so as to produce grammatically acceptable constructions.

VOCABULARY

fukara	poor person	bwege	stupid
jabari	brave	dhahiri	clear
-zembe	lazy	dhifa	reception, banquet
upelelezi	investigation	panda	grow
maonyesho	exhibitions	mdahalo	debate
asherati	prostitute	gololi	marble

115

dosari	flaw	**kera**	disturb
mlingoti	mast	**boriti**	pole
mkwasi	rich person	**paa**	deer
sihi	advise	**mchoraji**	artist
mrembo	dandy	**chukiza**	disgust
upuuzi	rubbish		
kitalu	courtyard		
askari wa mgambo	militia people		
zirai	faint		

Exercise 10

1. Pick out the pronouns in the following sentences:
   a. Wao ni watu majabari.
   b. Mimi nimo katika furaha kubwa.
   c. Vingapi vimepotea tangu majuzi?
   d. Ni dhahiri kwamba vyenu ni vizuri sana.
   e. Yao na yetu ni mamoja.
   f. Vijana walio warefu wameondoka punde hivi.
   g. Tutachelewa kufika kwenye dhifa yako.
   h. Maneno yasemwayo ni mazuri sana.
   i. Kwao kuna vitu vya kufurahisha.
   j. Hilo halisemeki.
   k. Nani anaandika kwa mkono wa kushoto?
   l. Wewe ni kijana mzembe sana.
   m. Askari wanafanya upelelezi mkubwa.
   n. Yupi anapanda viazi katika shamba lake?
   o. Papi pamejaa askari wa mgambo?

2. Find suitable pronouns to fill in the blank spaces of the following sentences:
   a. .... ni kiti chako.
   b. .... si mtu bwege hata kidogo.
   c. .... mna njia kidogo.
   d. Mimi nitakwenda .... kwenye maonyesho.
   e. .... pana uchafu mwingi sana.
   f. .... ndivyo tunavyoelewa hapa.
   g. .... si machungwa bali ni chenza.
   h. .... mmekuwa wasemaji wakubwa katika mdahalo huu.
   i. .... ni mlima wa Mt. Elgon na sio Mt. Meru.

j. .... amekuwa sasa mwanamke asherati.

k. .... wamekwisha yasema?

l. .... watumiavyo ni vizuri sana.

m. .... mna kila kitu cha thamani.

n. .... ni gololi zangu.

o. .... vina dosari kubwa.

3. Translate the following sentences:
   a. This is a rabbit and not a cat.
   b. What they say is not true.
   c. Do not disturb me every now and again.
   d. These are masts and not poles.
   e. We know him well; he is a very rich person.
   f. His long arrow hit the lion. Mine hit the deer.
   g. Those books are expensive. These are cheap.
   h. He is very tall but I am short.
   i. Who has hidden the gold?
   j. Your shirts are all new.
   k. They are very stingy.
   l. Which has a long tail?
   m. How many has he bought? (mangoes)
   n. This is Ominde and that is Ochieng.
   o. I have a lot of problems; he has none.

4. Translate the following sentences:
   a. Yule ni msichana mrembo.
   b. Vingapi vimeanguka chini?
   c. Sisi tumemsihi sana karibuni.
   d. Ule ni mnazi na huu ni mtende.
   e. Asemayo kila siku ni upuuzi mtupu.
   f. Wale ni wakulima na hawa ni wapagazi.
   g. Wewe una saa nzuri sana.
   h. Mimi si mhandisi; mimi ni mchoraji.
   i. Hicho ni kitabu chetu.
   j. Nani amechukua chakula changu jikoni?
   k. Nyinyi ni watu wachochole sana.
   l. Zile ni nyumba mpya.
   m. Kwa maoni yangu, sisi tutazirai kwa machovu.
   n. Nini kinakuchukiza mwanangu?
   o. Kule ni kwa mjomba na hapa ni kwangu.

11 Interjections

Interjections are terms used in traditional grammar to refer to a class of words that is unproductive and that does not enter into syntactic relations with other classes. The function of these words is purely emotive.

In Swahili, there are two kinds of interjections, namely:

1. Words that are essentially used as interjections
2. Words that may have other functions besides that of being interjections.

Terms that are essentially interjections

A few examples of terms that are essentially interjections are illustrated below:

Ala!

This is an exclamation of annoyance or impatience. It can be compared with other kinds of interjections which perform a similar function such as **ka! aka!**

Ati!

This interjection is sometimes written as **eti**. It is an expletive expression of surprise. It is also used as an exclamation for calling attention.

> **Alituambia ati anaweza kufanya kazi ile.**
> He told us that he could do that work.

It is worth noting that the interjection **ati** is commonly used in Kenya to correspond to English expressions such as "I beg your pardon" and "pardon."

Buu!

This interjection is sometimes written as **fu!** The two forms are used to stress the noise of something, like that of a falling bag of rice.

Wa!

This is a term of assent used by inferiors towards superiors. The interjection is sometimes written as **Ewallah!**

The term **ewa** is also used to show approval. It carries the meaning of "alright", "O.K.", etc.

Kumbe!

This interjection expresses slight astonishment or surprise at the occurrence of the reverse of what was anticipated.

    a.   **Kumbe umekuja. Mimi nilifikiri hutakuja kabisa.**
          Lo! You have come. I thought you would not come at all.

    b.   **Tulifikiri wewe ndiye mshindi mwenyewe. Kumbe si wewe.**
          We thought that you were the victor. Lo! It is not you!

Laiti!

This interjection is an expression of regret at an unfulfilled wish, when it is used with contrary-to-fact conditional forms. When used in the simple future tense, it introduces a wish because of the difficulty involving the fulfilment.

    a.   **Laiti tungalikuwa kitu kimoja duniani.**
          I wish we were all united in this world.

    b.   **Laiti dawa ile itawafaa.**
          I only hope that the medicine may be of use to them.

Lo!

This interjection is an exclamation of intense feeling, pleasant or unpleasant. With the prolongation of the vowel, an intense feeling is expressed.

    a.   **Lo! Wewe umeiba pesa zetu.**
          Oh! You have stolen our money!

    b.   **Lo! Timu ya Cameroon imeifunga Argentina.**
          Oh! Cameroon's team has beaten Argentina.

Sometimes the exclamations **salale!** or **masalale!** are added:

    a.   **Lo salale! Mama yako hakupi chakula kingi.**
          Oh! Your mother is not giving you enough food.

    b.   **Lo masalale! Watu wengi wamekufa katika ajali ile.**
          Oh! A number of people have died in that accident.

Terms sometimes used as interjections

a.   **Ajabu!**
       Surprising! Isn't that strange!

b.   **Asante! Asanteni!**
       Thanks

c.   **Basi! Bas!**
     This interjection expresses disgust, resignation, agreement, etc.
     i.)   **Basi sasa!**
           Enough now!
     ii.) **Njoo basi!**
           Well, come then!
d.   **Haraka!**
     Quickly!
e.   **Hodi!**
     Anyone in there?

The interjection in (e) is a polite inquiry before entering a house or a room. It has the same meaning as "knock at the door", an expression found in European cultures.

f.   **Pole!**
     Be well! I am sorry!

This word is used in contexts where someone has experienced suffering, for instance, the death of a relative. The polite answer to this is generally: **Nimekwisha poa** (I am feeling better now).

g.   **Sumile!**
     Make way! Get out of the way!
h.   **Wapi!**
     Alas! This interjection expresses regret, sorrow, etc.

The list of terms used as interjections is quite long, but the ones exemplified in this chapter are more commonly used by Swahili speakers.

VOCABULARY

kufuru	blasphemy	motoni	hell
ruka	fly	msafiri	passenger
kataza	forbid	binafsi yangu	personally
mkaguzi	inspector	endelea	continue
fanya	do	-tamu	pleasant, nice
riziki	necessities of life	mazungumzo	conversation

Exercise 11

1. Construct short sentences using the following interjections:
   a. khaa!   b. salale!
   c. subhanallah!   d. pole!
   e. kweli!   f. mashallah!
   g. ebu!   h. ha!
   i. la!   j. abwa!

2. Select an appropriate interjection from the list below for each of the blank spaces:

   taibu   alaa
   ajabu   toba we
   alhamdulilah   ati
   haya   la hasha
   pole   hongera

   a. ....! Hivyo unakufuru utaingia motoni tu.
   b. ....! Ng'ombe huruka hewani.
   c. ....! Tumesikia leo ajali ya ndege yenye kumhusu mumeo aliyekuwa msafiri.
   d. ....! Umefaulu vizuri kwenye mtihani.
   e. ....! Riziki yangu nimeipata. Mungu si Athumani.
   f. ....! Sisi hatuwezi kufanya hayo.
   g. ....! Unaona mambo yalivyotokea. Mimi binafsi yangu nilikukataza usifanye vile.
   h. ....! Waendapi sasa hivi?
   i. ....! Mazungumzo yako ni matamu. Endelea tu.

12 Tenses I: Present Tense, the -A- Tense Marker and Simple Past Tense

Present verb tense

-NA-

Steere (1976) was the first grammarian to describe the marker -na- as a present tense, and all other grammarians after him have accepted this definition. *Ashton (1982)* qualifies this by stating that the marker refers to the present if nothing in the context indicates the past or future. However, she continues to refer it to the present. *Brain (1977)* states that this tense corresponds to the "I am doing", "You are going" tense in English.

The tense marker -na- is inserted between the subject prefix and the verb stem. Thus, using the verb **kupika**, (to cook), we get:

Ni-na-pika	Ninapika	I am cooking
U-na-pika	Unapika	You are cooking
A-na-pika	Anapika	He/she is cooking
Tu-na-pika	Tunapika	We are cooking
M-na-pika	Mnapika	You (pl) are cooking
Wa-na-pika	Wanapika	They are cooking

Monosyllabic verbs used with this tense retain the infinitive KU-. For example:

Ni-na-kunywa	Ninakunywa	I am drinking
U-na-kunywa	Unakunywa	You are drinking
A-na-kunywa	Anakunywa	He/she is drinking
Tu-na-kunywa	Tunakunywa	We are drinking
Wa-na-kunywa	Wanakunywa	They are drinking

But verbs of Arabic origin, like other Bantu verbs of more than one syllable, drop the infinitive KU-. For example:

Ni-na-safiri	Ninasafiri	I am travelling
U-na-safiri	Unasafiri	You are travelling
A-na-safiri	Anasafiri	He/she is travelling
Tu-na-safiri	Tunasafiri	We are travelling
M-na-safiri	Mnasafiri	You (pl) are travelling
Wa-na-safiri	Wanasafiri	They are travelling

Wilson (1970) argues that the present tense is only used when the action is definitely taking place at the present time. He adds that this tense cannot be used when there is an implication that the action will occur in the future. This, however, is a misleading statement since this tense, when it co-occurs with adverbial markers, can refer to three different points in time: future, present and past. For example:

a. **Anatoa hotuba wiki ijayo.**
    He is giving a lecture next week.

b. **Mama anasikiliza taarifa ya habari sasa hivi.**
    Mother is listening to the news now.

c. **Wanasikiliza habari kila siku.**
    They listen to the news everyday.

d. **Alikuwa anasikiliza habari jana.**
    He was listening to the news yesterday.

In example a., the action refers to the future. In b., the action occurs at the exact moment of speech. In c., the action occurs generally, with no reference to time. And finally, in d., the action refers to the past by using the adverbial indicator **jana** (yesterday). It is safer to argue that the present tense marker -na- is basically used for the exact moment of speech. Yet, when the marker co-occurs with adverbial indicators, it can signal different meanings: present, past and future. Thus, it can be contended that the analysis of -na- by traditional grammars as merely indicating an action happening at the time of speaking is misleading.

VOCABULARY

baharia	sailor	waka	burn / light
bendera	flag	zungumza	talk
pandisha	hoist	vuma	blow
mgonjwa	patient	jificha	hide
teremka	disembark	mhadhiri	lecturer
bafuni	in the bathroom	sinzia	doze
omba	beg	shona	sew
jaribu	try	stawi	flourish
sana	hard	embe	mango
lima	cultivate		

Exercise 12a

1. Translate the following sentences:
    a. The young lady is crying.
    b. The policeman is hoisting the flag.
    c. The sailor is disembarking from the ship.
    d. You (pl) are dozing.
    e. They are begging.
    f. He is reading the book.
    g. We are selling mangoes.
    h. The headteacher is coming here.
    i. The doctor is treating the patient.
    j. We are trying hard.
    k. The baby is drinking milk.
    l. The cook is cooking now.
    m. The lecturer is lecturing.
    n. She is cultivating.
    o. They are laughing loudly.
2. Translate the following sentences:
    a. Anaimba polepole.
    b. Mama anaoga bafuni.
    c. Moto unawaka.
    d. Ndege anaruka.
    e. Mwalimu anazungumza.
    f. Watoto wanacheza nje.
    g. Mtumishi anaosha vyombo.
    h. Vijana wanachukua mizigo.
    i. Simba anakula majani.
    j. Mti unaanguka.
    k. Wageni wanafika sasa hivi.
    l. Wanawake wanashona nguo.
    m. Upepo unavuma vibaya.
    n. Miti inasitawi.
    o. Wezi wanajificha.

The -A- tense marker

A number of grammars have defined the tense marker -a- as indefinite. *Ashton (1982)* states that the -a- tense is used "to describe facts and ask questions regardless of the time factor, and this grammatical marker is, therefore, in opposition to -na- tense." *Wilson (1970)* points out that the sign -a- is used to signify an action made periodically without necessarily implying that it is in the process of going on at the time of speaking. *Brain (1977)* does not say much about the tense sign -a- except to refer to it as the present indefinite. *Mbaabu (1985)* describes it along similar lines. He argues that the sign -a- does not refer to any particular time. To illustrate these various arguments with the verb **kulala** (to sleep), we get the following:

nalala	I sleep
walala	you sleep
alala	he/she sleeps
twalala	we sleep
mwalala	you (pl) sleep
walala	they sleep

Monosyllabic verbs drop the infinitive KU- when used with this tense. For instance:

nanywa	I drink
wanywa	you drink
anywa	he/she drinks
twanywa	we drink
mwanywa	you (pl) drink
wanywa	they drink

Loan words also drop the infinitive KU-. For example:

naamini	I believe
waamini	you believe
aamini	he/she believes
twaamini	we believe
mwaamini	you (pl) believe
waamini	they believe

We have already illustrated that a number of grammars have described the -a- tense sign as referring to indefinite time vis-a-vis the -na- marker which refers to the exact moment of speaking. Ashton gives the following example to support her argument:

Mpishi asema ataka sukari.
The cook says he wants some sugar.

Here, Ashton argues that the verbs **asema** and **ataka** state facts regardless of the time dimension. But in the case of:

Mpishi asema anataka sukari,

Ashton contends that the use of **na** in **anataka** signifies that the cook is "in immediate need of sugar" for his or her work. This argument of the

-a- tense sign as referring to indefinite time versus the -na- marker as an indicator of the exact moment of speech as shown in the above example may be true in some cases but should not be taken as a standard rule for all Swahili sentences. Consider, for example, the following sentence:

> Alisema kwamba yeye mtu mwenye pesa, aweza kufanya shughuli nyingi na mambo yake yanaweza yakanyoka.

> He said that, being a person who has money, he can do a lot of business and that he can be successful.

The use of affixes -a- and -na- in the bold type verbs are mutually interchangeable and thus, are not in opposition. This shows that grammars that have contended the use of na as referring to the exact moment of speech and -a- as an indicator of indefinite time may be misleading. What is correct is the fact that the -a- tense is merely a dialectical variant of the -na- marker and both indicate, by and large, the same meaning.

VOCABULARY

peperuka	fly away	gari	vehicle
zaa	bear	shetani	devil
pinduka	overturn	kimbunga	hurricane
kuku	hen	kanisa	church
msiba	disaster	lia	ring
mfungwa	prisoner	teseka	suffer
kwa nguvu	loudly	ushairi	poetry
tamthiliya	play	kipupwe	cold season
toroka	run away	paa	go up
kishada	kite	sebule	sitting room
ujenzi wa taifa	nation building		

Exercise 12b

1. Translate the following sentences:
   a. They eat.
   b. She works hard.
   c. The old man arrives here in the evening.
   d. Those trees bear fruits.
   e. The knife cuts badly.
   f. You drink porridge.
   g. The wind blows.

h. The vehicles overturn.
i. The devil comes every day.
j. The workers wake up early in the morning.
k. Healthy people live long.
l. Those beggars beg on Fridays.
m. Hurricanes bring disasters.
n. The women sing in the church.
o. The prisoners stay here.
p. The bells ring loudly.
q. Men and women suffer a lot.
r. Writers write plays, novels and poems.
s. The messenger comes at 9 o'clock.
t. Human beings need water and food.

2. Translate the following sentences:
a. Njia hii yafika Kisumu.
b. Viongozi wa chama waanza mikutano asubuhi.
c. Daktari afika hapa kila Alhamisi.
d. Mkuu wa jeshi akagua kikosi chake kila asubuhi.
e. Wanafunzi wasoma lugha mbalimbali mashuleni.
f. Maelfu washiriki katika ujenzi wa taifa nchini.
g. Vijana wale watoroka shuleni kila mara.
h. Kazi hii yasumbua sana.
i. Majani ya miti yaanguka wakati wa kipupwe.
j. Kishada hiki chapaa juu sana.
k. Arudi hapa jioni.
l. Twazungumza sebuleni.
m. Njiwa yule ala vitu vidogo vidogo.
n. Karatasi hii yapeperuka.
o. Mwalimu mkuu aapiza sana.
p. Tanzania yatoa kahawa nzuri.
q. Kuku huyu azaa watoto wengi.
r. Mtumishi wangu afanya kazi chapuchapu.
s. Aimba vizuri.
t. Twadurusu masomo kila Ijumaa.

Simple Past Tense (-LI- OR -ALI-)

The simple past tense, as the name implies, refers to a past activity without reference to a specific time. The tense marker for this past activity is -li- and, in some situations, -ali-. If we take the verb **cheza**, the following conjugation results:

Ni-li-cheza	Nilicheza	I played
U-li-cheza	Ulicheza	You played
A-li-cheza	Alicheza	He/she played
Tu-li-cheza	Tulicheza	We played
M-li-cheza	Mlicheza	You (pl) played
Wa-li-cheza	Walicheza	They played

Monosyllabic verbs, however, retain the infinitive KU-:

Ni-li-kunywa	Nilikunywa	I drank
U-li-kunywa	Ulikunywa	You drank
A-li-kunywa	Alikunywa	He/she drank
Tu-li-kunywa	Tulikunywa	We drank
M-li-kunywa	Mlikunywa	You (pl) drank
Wa-li-kunywa	Walikunywa	They drank

Verbs of Arabic origin, like other polysyllabic Bantu verbs, drop the infinitive KU-:

Ni-li-shukuru	Nilishukuru	I thanked
U-li-shukuru	Ulishukuru	You thanked
A-li-shukuru	Alishukuru	He/she thanked
Tu-li-shukuru	Tulishukuru	We thanked
M-li-shukuru	Mlishukuru	You (pl) thanked
Wa-li-shukuru	Walishukuru	They thanked

With first and second persons, the past tense marker -ali- can sometimes be used. This is contrary to the argument put forward by *Ashton (1982)*, that it can only be used with the first person, as shown below:

N-ali-penda	Nalipenda	I liked
Tw-ali-penda	Twalipenda	We liked
W-ali-penda	Walipenda	You liked
Mw-ali-penda	Mwalipenda	They (pl) liked

VOCABULARY

vua	undress	nyesha	rain
kohoa	cough	nguruwe	pig
pumzika	rest	ingia ndani	enter
saka	hunt	mto	cushion
mwembe	mango tree	viazi vikuu	yams
pasuka	split	taratibu	slowly
vunja	break	teleza	slip

128

goma	strike	mbinguni	in the sky
zama	sink	fagia	sweep
waza	ponder	mwaga	spill
staajabu	wonder, be surprised		

Exercise 12c

1. Translate the following sentences:
   a. I coughed very much yesterday.
   b. It rained in the morning.
   c. They tried very hard.
   d. We slept here.
   e. I ran fast yesterday.
   f. John rested here.
   g. The hunter hunted pigs.
   h. The blind man entered slowly.
   i. He spoke English.
   j. The mango tree fell down.
   k. The cushion split.
   l. The servant waited.
   m. The old man arrived the day before yesterday.
   n. The patient died in hospital.
   o. We ate some yams.

2. Translate the following sentences:
   a. Tulitembea usiku.
   b. Wezi walivunja duka.
   c. Nyumba iliporomoka.
   d. Mwezi uliandama jana.
   e. Kijana aliteleza vibaya.
   f. Usiku uliingia.
   g. Niliangalia mbinguni.
   h. Wafanyakazi waligoma bandarini.
   i. Mama alioga mapema.
   j. Tuliwaza sana.
   k. Jahazi ilizama jana.
   l. Mtumishi alifungua mlango taratibu.
   m. Walimwaga maziwa.
   n. Nilistaajabu mno.
   o. Tulikubali asubuhi.

3. Construct sentences in Swahili using the past simple form
    containing the following verbs:

    a. imba   b. shinda
    c. andika   d. tumia
    e. osha   f. iba
    g. vua   h. fagia
    i. nywa   j. leta

13 Tenses II: Present Perfect Tense and Future Tense

Present perfect tense (-ME-)

Swahili grammars have frequently argued that the tense marker -li- is used to indicate a past action which took place a long time ago, while -me- refers to what is termed as the "immediate past". Certain studies by *Zawawi (1971)*, however, show that this is not always the case. For example, she cites the following discourse extracted from a newspaper:

Shughuli hizo za uchaguzi zimeanzia Kinondoni tarehe 28 Februari, na mnamo tarehe 1 na 2 Mechi uchaguzi uliendeshwa Magomeni.

The preparations for the elections had started at Kinondoni on February 28, and on March 1 and 2 the election was conducted at Magomeni.

We can see from the above example that the event which occurred on February 28 takes a tense marker -me- while that of March 1 and 2 has a -li- marker. Thus, according to Zawawi, native speakers tend to use -me- where grammatical rules would require the use of -li-.

Kapinga (1983) shows that the tense marker -me- is used to indicate an activity that occurred in the recent past and which continues to show relevance to the present time. The author gives this example to support his argument:

Mti umeanguka.
The tree has fallen down.

Kapinga (1983) contends that the above sentence shows that the tree has fallen down and the fact that it has done so is still being observed at the moment. *Maw (1985)* also thinks along the same lines; that is, the -me- tense implies a completed action with reference to the present.

Ashton (1982) points out that the tense marker -me- is used to express the completion of an action and the resultant state. For example:

a. **Amefika.**
   He has arrived.
b. **Amechoka.**
   He is tired.

Ashton's arguments about the completion of an action and the resultant state make a lot of sense as far as the above sentences are concerned. Yet, in the following example, Ashton's arguments lack the necessary validity:

Amesimama.
He is standing.

The sentence **'Amesimama'** states that the person is still standing up. In other words, he has stood up and is still in the process of doing so. This clearly shows that Kapinga's arguments of defining -me- as a tense marker of a past activity which has relevance to the present time is also valid. *Mbaabu (1985)* also shares the views on relevance to the present time.

Other grammars, however, do not make a detailed analysis of the tense marker -me-. *Brain (1977)*, for example, merely points out that the -me- tense gives the meaning of the perfect tense in English. Similarly, *Wilson (1970)* explains that the -me- tense is used when the words "has" or "have" occur in English and is also frequently found in stative verbs. These arguments can be illustrated in the following manner:

Ni-me-pika	Nimepika	I have cooked
U-me-pika	Umepika	You have cooked
A-me-pika	Amepika	He/she has cooked
Tu-me-pika	Tumepika	We have cooked
M-me-pika	Mmepika	You have cooked

Like in the previous tenses, monosyllabic verbs retain the infinitive **KU-**. For example:

Ni-me-kunywa	Nimekunywa	I have drunk
U-me-kunywa	Umekunywa	You have drunk
A-me-kunywa	Amekunywa	He/she has drunk
Tu-me-kunywa	Tumekunywa	We have drunk
M-me-kunywa	Mmekunywa	You (pl) have drunk
Wa-me-kunywa	Wamekunywa	They have drunk

Verbs of Arabic origin again drop the infinitive **KU-**, as indicated below:

Ni-me-sahau	Nimesahau	I have forgotten
U-me-sahau	Umesahau	You have forgotten
A-me-sahau	Amesahau	He/she has forgotten

With stative verbs, the use of the tense marker -me- can be illustrated as follows:

Kikombe kimevunjika	The cup is broken
Shati limechanika	The shirt is torn
Mlango umefunguka	The door is open
Chakula kimechomeka	The food is burnt

132

Wilson (1970) states that we also use the present tense marker **-na-** in stative verbs. For instance:

Mlango unafunguka	The door is openable
Chakula kinachomeka	The food is roastable
Shati linachanika	The shirt can be torn
Kikombe kinavunjika	The cup is breakable

Although Wilson's argument is valid, there is a slight shift of meaning between sentences used with the tense marker **-me-** and those used with **-na-**.

VOCABULARY

punde hivi	just now		batamzinga	turkey
kiwanda	industry		oza	rot
mpango	plan		mkalimani	interpreter
kataa	refuse		potea	lose
vimba	swell		kwisha	already
mpagazi	porter		mgeni	guest
ondoka	leave		jadili	discuss
lalamika	complain		sungura	rabbit
haribika	spoil		Mzungu	European
upesi	rapidly		ota	grow

Exercise 13a

1. Translate the following sentences:
    a. The ladies have arrived.
    b. The six men are drunk.
    c. The long spear is broken.
    d. The umbrellas have fallen down.
    e. The plan has begun.
    f. The servant is very tired.
    g. The youth has married today.
    h. The interpreter has refused.
    i. The workers have brought water.
    j. The arm has swollen.
    k. The room is untidy.
    l. The guests have complained.
    m. I have eaten mangoes.
    n. The cup is lost.

o. The porters have carried loads.
p. The milk is spilt.
q. The doctor has just come.
r. The farmers have already gone.
s. The Europeans have left.
t. The book is torn.

2. Translate the following sentences:
   a. Wazee wamejadili.
   b. Masikini amechoka sana.
   c. Viatu vimepotea.
   d. John amekwisha haribika.
   e. Wanawake wamesimama.
   f. Sungura amekimbia.
   g. Jua limechomoka.
   h. Mgeni amekwisha ingia chumbani.
   i. Mshtakiwa amekiri kosa.
   j. Mimea imeota upesi.
   k. Samaki wameoza.
   l. Walinzi wametoroka.
   m. Chombo kimewasili.
   n. Maziwa yameharibika.
   o. Vijana wamerejea hapa.
   p. Mwalimu amejaribu sana.
   q. Mpishi amekwenda sokoni.
   r. Nimeondosha viti punde hivi.
   s. Nchi yetu imeendelea sana.
   t. Bata mzinga amelala kibandani.

The future tense

The tense marker -TA- refers to a verbal activity that will take place in future. To illustrate, here are some examples:

Ni-ta-cheza	Nitacheza	I will play
U-ta-cheza	Utacheza	You will play
A-ta-cheza	Atacheza	He/she will play
Tu-ta-cheza	Tutacheza	We will play
M-ta-cheza	Mtacheza	You (pl) will play
Wa-ta-cheza	Watacheza	They will play

Monosyllabic verbs retain the infinitive **KU-**. For example:

Ni-ta-kunywa	Nitakunywa	I will drink
U-ta-kunywa	Utakunywa	You will drink
A-ta-kunywa	Atakunywa	He/she will drink
Tu-ta-kunywa	Tutakunywa	We will drink
M-ta-kunywa	Mtakunywa	You (pl) will drink
Wa-ta-kunywa	Watakunywa	They will drink

Borrowed words, mainly from Arabic, drop the infinitive **KU-**. For example:

Ni-ta-amuru	Nitaamuru	I will order
U-ta-amuru	Utaamuru	You will order
A-ta-amuru	Ataamuru	He/she will order
Tu-ta-amuru	Tutaamuru	We will order
M-ta-amuru	Mtaamuru	You (pl) will order
Wa-ta-amuru	Wataamuru	They will order

The marker **-ta-** can co-occur with another tense marker like **-na-** in a different verb to signal futurity. For example:

Nitakuwa ninapika	I shall be cooking
Atakuwa anapika	He/she shall be cooking
Watakuwa wanapika	They shall be cooking

VOCABULARY

hakika	certainly	**bahati nasibu**	lottery
maliza	complete	**kwa bidii**	diligently
ndovu	elephant	**gundi**	glue
majira	season	**chana**	tear
chuma	pick	**lambo, bwawa**	dam
tuwa	land	**teka**	fetch
panda	climb	**mtoto mdogo**	infant
zaa	bear	**zagaa**	prevail
mpito	transition, interim	**gwaride**	parade

Exercise 13b

1. Translate the following sentences:
    a. He will certainly forget.
    b. The fork will fall.
    c. Those elephants will die.

d. The shopkeeper will arrive here on Monday.
e. I will go to the shop to buy meat.
f. She will complete the work soon.
g. The salaries will go up next month.
h. He will grow millet next season.
i. The glue will dry soon.
j. Those farmers will pick flowers.
k. They will be writing letters in the evening.
l. She will get married soon.
m. The servant will bring a pillow.
n. The children will eat good food.
o. The light loads will arrive just now.
p. The tailor will tear the cloth.
q. The man will do the job.
r. The plane will land later.
s. Mary will visit the dam.
t. The insect will pass here.

2. Translate the following sentences:
a. Kila mtu atakufa tu.
b. Nitaupanda ule mlima.
c. Mnazi huu utazaa mwakani.
d. Rais atachagua serikali ya mpito kesho.
e. Mwanamke atateka maji kisimani.
f. Yule mtoto mdogo atalala punde.
g. Upepo utavuma vibaya sasa hivi.
h. Ukimwi utazagaa kijijini.
i. Mwanafunzi atapata adhabu kali.
j. Nitashiriki katika bahati nasibu katika safari hii.
k. Ufunguo huu utafungua mlango.
l. Gwaride litaanza punde hivi.
m. Mama atatayarisha chai.
n. Gari la moshi litaondoka punde.
o. Hiki kikombe kitavunjika.
p. Ile nyumba itaanguka.
q. Samaki ataungua jikoni.
r. Wageni wangapi watawasili leo?
s. Kijana huyu atakuwa analima shamba.
t. Watajifunza Kiswahili kwa bidii.

14 Tenses III: The Habitual -HU- and Negative Tenses

The habitual HU-, and Negative Tenses

The first educator to define the habitual **hu-** sign was Steere. He described it as a tense which marks customary actions without distinction of time. In later stages, other grammars agreed with this definition although slight changes were made in the wording. *Ashton (1982)* points out that the **hu-** tense occurs in situations which signal "habitual or recurrent action". *Brain (1977)* simply states that the tense sign indicates "habitual action". *Perrot (1985)* describes it as a tense which shows customary, frequent or habitual action. *Wilson (1970)* points out that "the sense of this tense is habitual or usual action". Polomé calls it a tense which marks habitual or recurrent action. Similarly, *Mbotela (1979)* states that the tense is used "to describe actions or activities that are habitual or usual and thus, it is always referred to as the "habitual " tense sign. Thus, with the verb **kucheza** (to play) we get the following:

> **Hucheza mpira kila siku.**
> I usually play footbal every day.
> You usually play football every day.
> He/she usually plays football every day.
> We usually play football every day.
> You (pl) usually play football every day.
> They usually play football every day.

As we can see from the above Swahili example, the **hu-** tense has taken no subject prefix. We can, therefore, argue that a subject ellipsis has taken place. Sometimes, however, it is necessary to define a subject and in this case, an appropriate noun or a self-standing pronoun is used. For example:

Mimi hucheza	I usually play.
Wewe hucheza	You usually play.
Yeye hucheza	He/she usually plays.
Sisi hucheza	We usually play.
Nyinyi hucheza	You (pl) usually play.
Wao hucheza	They usually play.

For monosyllabic verbs, the infinitive **KU-** is also dropped:

Mimi hula	I usually eat
Wewe hula	You usually eat
Yeye hula	He/she usually eats

137

Words borrowed from other languages, notably Arabic, also drop the infinitive **KU-**:

Mimi hujaribu	I usually try
Wewe hujaribu	You usually try
Yeye hujaribu	He/she usually tries

Apart from **M-WA** classes, the **hu-** tense sign can be used for all other classes in both singular and plural forms. For example:

Mto huu hufurika	This river usually overflows.
Mito hii hufurika	These rivers usually overflow.
Kiti hiki huanguka	This chair usually falls.
Viti hivi huanguka	These chairs usually fall.
Ua hili huchanuka	This flower usually blooms.
Maua haya huchanuka	These flowers usually bloom.
Wimbo huu husisimua	This song usually stimulates.
Nyimbo hizi husisimua	These songs usually stimulate.

Some grammars also indicate that the **hu-** tense sign is used to describe the activities that are almost permanent or that are of universal truth. *Ashton (1982)*, for example, points out that this tense marker is commonly found "in proverbs and everyday maxims" as shown in the following examples:

a. **Jua huchomoza Mashariki.**
   The sun rises in the east.
b. **Ubishi mwingi huleta matata.**
   Too much joking causes quarrels.
c. **Haba na haba hujaza kibaba.**
   Little by little fills up the measure.

Zawawi (1971) has also given an analysis of the **hu-** tense sign. She reckons that the tense sign has other meanings apart from the traditional interpretation of the **hu-** marker as habitual. These multiple meanings are explained in the following sentences:

a. **Mzee hufika hapa kila Ijumaa.**
   The old man arrives here every Friday.
b. **Ng'ombe hula nyasi.**
   Cows eat grass.
c. **Kila ninapokwenda, huwa amesikiliza habari.**
   Whenever I go, he has listened to the news.
d. **Huenda ikanyesha mvua kesho.**
   It may rain tomorrow.

In the first sentence, the **hu-** marker indicates repetition. But here, the reference is specified. The action of coming takes place every Friday. In the second sentence, the reference is unspecified. It takes place any time. In the third sentence, the **hu-** marker with the copular verb **-wa** (be) indicates "it becomes". In the last sentence, the **hu-** occurs with the verb of motion **enda** (go) indicating a meaning of "probability". This last interpretation has been overlooked by other grammars and is, thus, worth mentioning.

Another significant analysis of Zawawi's work is the interchangeable nature of the **hu-** marker and the present tense marker **-na-**. Traditional grammars, as we have already mentioned, described the **hu-** tense sign as basically habitual and **-na-** as a present tense marker. Zawawi, however, cites instances (both in writing and in speech) of native speakers who frequently use the two tense markers interchangeably to signal the same meaning, namely customary activities. Following is an example cited by Zawawi from her studies:

> **Huko aghalabu *hu*kuta watu wanawake na wanaume wa*na*wangojea ...**
> Here, men often find women waiting for them ...

These studies by Zawawi are important since they reflect a slight deviation from traditional analysis of the **hu-** tense sign and the **-na-** marker.

The negative HU- tense

The negative of the **hu-** tense marker is the normal present negative form. For example:

> **Ndugu yangu husoma riwaya.**
> My brother usually reads novels.

The negative form of this sentence is:

> **Ndugu yangu hasomi riwaya.**
> My brother doesn't read novels.

VOCABULARY

nzi	fly	**mara kwa mara**	frequently
zuru	visit	**fuga**	domesticate
kima	monkey	**subira**	patience
ukumbi	hall	**mhariri**	editor

chapisha	publish	kwa makelele	loudly
mfadhili	donor	mfanyakazi	workman
simama	stop	mwanakijiji	villager
vuja	ooze	rais-mteule	president-elect
ghala	store	rushwa	bribe
kiazi kikuu	yam	bweka	bark
daktari wa meno	dentist		

Exercise 14a

1. Translate the following sentences:
   a. We usually eat potatoes.
   b. Maina usually comes here in the evening.
   c. Workmen usually get compensation.
   d. I usually wake up early every day.
   e. They generally get many eggs every week.
   f. Flies bring diseases.
   g. Heavy rains usually come in March.
   h. She usually travels by train.
   i. Zanzibar people are generally hospitable.
   j. We don't usually speak French in school.
   k. That lady sings in the hall every Saturday.
   l. Patience attracts happiness.
   m. My sister normally sleeps early.
   n. Our country exports coffee.
   o. The villagers normally rest in the huts.
   p. The editor normally publishes poems.
   q. The dentist usually arrives here in the afternoon.
   r. Those men usually speak loudly.
   s. Monkeys like to eat bananas.
   t. That president-elect usually talks a lot.

2. Translate the following sentences:
   a. Viongozi wale hufanya mikutano mara kwa mara.
   b. Baba yangu huamka mapema kila siku.
   c. Mpishi hupika viazi vikuu kila Jumatano.
   d. Wafadhili mbalimbali husaidia sana nchi yetu.
   e. Mimi hunywa maziwa kila asubuhi.
   f. Kijana yule husafiri kwa ndege.
   g. Watalii huzuru sana Kenya.
   h. Waziri alipokea rushwa.

i.   Ghala hii huhifadhi vitu vingi.
j.   Mzee yule hufikiri sana.
k.   Saa hii husimama mara kwa mara.
l.   Barua zako aghalabu huchelewa kufika.
m. Mbwa huyu hubweka sana usiku.
n.   Mimi na mama huenda sokoni asubuhi.
o.   Rubani huendesha ndege juu sana.
p.   Debe lile halivuji.
q.   Mshoni huyu hushona nguo vizuri.
r.   Watu wale hufuga wanyama mbalimbali.
s.   Magari huhitaji petroli.
t.   Wapagazi hawa hubeba mizigo mizito.

Negative tenses

In general, negative tenses in Swahili carry a negative subject prefix in accordance with the agreement principle. In the **M-WA** class, the situation is somewhat different. Here is a full illustration of the negative subject prefixes:

M-WA class

si-	I ... not	hatu-	we ... not
hu-	you ... not	ham-	you ... not
ha-	he/she ... not	hawa-	they ... not

M-MI class

| hau- | it ... not | hai- | they ... not |

JI-MA class

| hali- | it ... not | haya- | they ... not |

KI-VI class

| haki- | it ... not | havi- | they ... not |

N-N class

| hai- | it ... not | hazi- | they ... not |

U-U class

| hau- | it ... not | hazi- | they ... not |

The negative present

Ashton (1982) refers to the negative present as the **General Negative**. It is termed so because the primary function of this form is to express the fact of negation with no particular reference to time. Thus, this form is not merely the negative form of the present tense. It can also mean the negative form of the habitual sentence, referred to by some grammars as **Present Indefinite**. For example:

> **Kijana yule hapendi maziwa.**
> That youth does not like milk.

A sentence like the one above merely states the fact of the matter, that is, **that youth does not like milk.** Thus, the sentence is not the negative form of the present tense.

The negative present has a zero morpheme. In other words, it has no tense sign. But the last vowels of the Bantu affirmative verbs is changed from **-a** to **-i** in order to construct the negative present form. Thus, in the case of the verb **kupika** (to cook), we can have this kind of conjugation. For example:

M-WA class

si-pik-i	sipiki	I do not cook
hu-pik-i	hupiki	You do not cook
ha-pik-i	hapiki	He/she does not cook
hatu-pik-i	hatupiki	We do not cook
ham-pik-i	hampiki	You (pl) do not cook
hawa-pik-i	hawapiki	They do not cook

M-MI class

hau-ot-i	hauoti	It does not grow
hai-ot-i	haioti	They do not grow

JI-MA class

hali-anguk-i	halianguki	It does not fall
haya-anguk-i	hayaanguki	They do not fall

KI-VI class

haki-anguk-i	hakianguki	It does not fall
havi-anguk-i	havianguki	They do not fall

N-N class

hai-anguk-i	haianguki	It does not fall
hazi-anguk-i	hazianguki	They do not fall

U-U class

hau-anguk-i	hauanguki	It does not fall
hazi-anguk-i	hazianguki	They do not fall

Monosyllabic verbs drop the infinitive **KU-** but their last vowels also change from **-a** to **-i**. For example:

si-l-i	sili	I do not eat
hu-l-i	huli	You do not eat
ha-l-i	hali	He/she does not eat
hatu-l-i	hatuli	We do not eat
ham-l-i	hamli	You (pl) do not eat
hawa-l-i	hawali	They do not eat

Borrowed verbs, mainly from Arabic, retain the last vowel of the affirmative verb, as in the examples below:

si-tafsiri	sitafsiri	I do not translate
hu-tafsiri	hutafsiri	You do not translate
ha-tafsiri	hatafsiri	He/she does not translate
hatu-tafsiri	hatutafsiri	We do not translate
ham-tafsiri	hamtafsiri	You (pl) do not translate
hawa-tafsiri	hawatafsiri	They do not translate

The present negative of the verb "to have"

The present negative tense of this verb is obtained by attaching a negative marker to the **na**. For example:

M-WA class

sina	I have not
huna	You have not
hana	He/she has not
hatuna	We have not
hamna	You (pl) have not
hawana	They have not

M-MI class

hauna	It has not
haina	They have not

JI-MA class

halina	It has not
hayana	They have not

KI-VI class

hakina	It has not
havina	They have not

N-N class

haina	It has not
hazina	They have not

U-U class

hauna	It has not
hazina	They have not

VOCABULARY

pokea	accept	kibarua	labourer
shamba	plantation	ladha	taste
mchimba migodi	miner	dari	ceiling
vizuri	properly	halmashauri	council
tajiri	employer	mwanariadha	athlete
mali	property	durusu	revise
ghala (ya nafaka)	barn	chokoza	tease
mwiba	thorn	mzigo	luggage
kifungo	button	chagua	appoint
salimu	greet	hundi	cheque
majinato	pomposity	busara	wisdom
jalada	cover	manyoya	feathers
nyama ya nguruwe	pork	hamaki	get angry

Exercise 14b

1. Translate the following sentences:
   a. The farmers do not grow yams in this plantation.
   b. Those labourers do not work on Saturdays.
   c. This house does not have a ceiling.
   d. This date tree does not have long leaves.
   e. The food does not have any taste.
   f. That door does not close properly.
   g. The knife does not cut meat.
   h. Those ladies do not drink milk.
   i. The students do not revise their lessons regularly.

j. The miners do not have much property.
k. The children do not tease the madman everyday.
l. The employer does not pay well.
m. The dog does not have a long tail.
n. The old man does not have a wife.
o. The tourists do not have any luggage.
p. The government does not like corruption in the country.
q. The council does not appoint members.
r. The animals do not live in the barn.
s. We do not have athletes in the school.
t. The tree does not have many thorns.

2. Translate the following sentences:
a. Mwanafunzi yule haelewi kitu.
b. Mfanyabiashara huyu hapokei hundi.
c. Kijana yule hasalimu watu.
d. Kitabu hiki hakina jalada.
e. Waislamu hawali nyama ya nguruwe.
f. Mwalimu yule hahamaki upesi.
g. Suruali hii haina vifungo.
h. Mashindano ya riadha hayaanzi leo.
i. Sisi hatusafiri kwa jahazi.
j. Chama chetu hakina wanachama wengi.
k. Mzazi yule hana busara.
l. Watoto wale hawana majinato.
m. Lugha nyingine hazikui.
n. Ndege yule hana manyoya.
o. Mimi siamki mapema sana asubuhi.
p. Watoto wa siku hizi hawana adabu.
q. Mamba hakai msituni.
r. Mwenye duka hana bidhaa nyingi.
s. Baskeli haina mnyororo.
t. Kwa nini hatupi ukweli wenyewe?

The negative future

Like in the affirmative, the verbal marker is -ta- for the negative form. In Lamu and Zanzibar, Swahili speakers tend to use the allomorph -to-. The negative future is made by the use of the verbal markers -ta- or -to- preceded by the negative prefixes. But the last vowel of the affirmative verb remains unchanged. Thus, the verb **kuanguka** (to fall) conjugates in the following manner:

M-WA class

si-ta-anguka	sitaanguka	I will not fall
hu-ta-anguka	hutaanguka	You will not fall
ha-ta-anguka	hataanguka	He/she will not fall
hatu-ta-anguka	hatutaanguka	We will not fall
ham-ta-anguka	hamtaanguka	You (pl) will not fall
hawa-ta-anguka	hawataanguka	They will not fall

M-MI class

hau-ta-anguka	hautaanguka	It will not fall
hai-ta-anguka	haitaanguka	They will not fall

JI-MA class

hali-ta-anguka	halitaanguka	It will not fall
haya-ta-anguka	hayataanguka	They will not fall

KI-VI class

haki-ta-anguka	hakitaanguka	It will not fall
havi-ta-anguka	havitaanguka	They will not fall

N-N class

hai-ta-anguka	haitaanguka	It will not fall
hazi-ta-anguka	hazitaanguka	They will not fall

U-U class

hau-ta-anguka	hautaanguka	It will not fall
hazi-ta-anguka	hazitaanguka	They will not fall

Monosyllabic verbs tend to retain the infinitive **ku-**. For example:

si-ta-kunywa	sitakunywa	I will not drink
ha-ta-kunywa	hatakunywa	He/she will not drink
hawa-ta-kunywa	hawatakunywa	They will not drink

Borrowed words, mainly from Arabic, drop the infinitive **ku-**. For example:

si-ta-sahau	sitasahau	I will not forget
ha-ta-sahau	hatasahau	He/she will not forget
hawa-ta-sahau	hawatasahau	They will not forget

146

VOCABULARY

badili	change	**masharti**	terms
uza	sell	**karibu**	soon
dungu	cockpit	**kashfa**	scandal
dumu	last	**jirafu**	fridge
ratiba	programme	**chochea**	incite
kipele	pimple	**kizibao**	waistcoat
chemka	boil	**rudi**	shrink
birika	kettle	**sumu**	poison
enea	spread	**athiri**	affect, influence
masihara	joke	**ubao**	plank
tengeneza	repair	**chanua**	blossoms
hika moto	start	**mbolea**	fertilizer
mwizi wa nyumba	burglar		

Exercise 14c

1. Translate the following sentences:
   a. We will not travel by train tomorrow.
   b. The fisherman will not sell the fish today.
   c. He will not read the poem.
   d. This dog will not bite you.
   e. The passenger will not sit in the cockpit.
   f. The scandal will not affect the government.
   g. The spareparts will not last long.
   h. The enemies will not come here.
   i. I will not buy the fridge.
   j. The athletes will not change the programme.
   k. The soldiers will not march here.
   l. We will not incite anyone.
   m. The doctor will not remove the pimples soon.
   n. The animal will not pass here.
   o. They will not need to discuss the matter here.
   p. The translators will not translate the new books.
   q. The long masts will not fall down.
   r. Those students will not understand anything.
   s. The waistcoats will not arrive here soon.
   t. He will not accept the terms.

2. Translate the following sentences:
   a. Walimu hawatakubali kugoma kesho.

b. Mipango yetu haitabadilika.
c. Shangazi yako hatawasili hapa juma lijalo.
d. Shida hii haitamalizika.
e. Suruali mpya hii haitarudi.
f. Maji hayatachemka upesi katika hilo birika.
g. Sumu ile haitapakaa mara moja.
h. Wezi wa nyumba hawataogopa kuiba mchana.
i. Mhandisi hataitengeneza mashini leo.
j. Chakula hiki hakitatosha.
k. Kwa nini mbao hizi hazitapasuka?
l. Yale maua hayatachanua upesi.
m. Mimi sitamdharau mtu yeyote.
n. Baba hatamlazimisha Saidi kwenda shuleni.
o. Gari haitashika moto upesi.
p. Wakulima hawatatumia tena mbolea.
q. Wewe hutastahamili na masihara yake.
r. Mwezi hautaandama kesho.
s. Mimi sitamkopesha mtu yeyote.

The negative past

Some grammars point out that there is one particle which can operate as a negative marker for the two affirmative past tense forms -li- and -me-. This negative particle is **-ku-**. Its method of conjugation operates in the following manner:

M-WA class

si-ku-cheza	sikucheza	I did not play
hu-ku-cheza	hukucheza	You did not play
ha-ku-cheza	hakucheza	He/she did not play
hatu-ku-cheza	hatukucheza	We did not play
ham-ku-cheza	hamkucheza	You (pl) did not play
hawa-ku-cheza	hawakucheza	They did not play

M-MI class

hau-ku-fungua	haukufungua	It did not open
hai-ku-fungua	haikufungua	They did not open

JI-MA class

hali-ku-fungua	halikufungua	It did not open
haya-ku-fungua	hayakufungua	They did not open

KI-VI class

haki-ku-fungua	hakikufungua	It did not open
havi-ku-fungua	havikufungua	They did not open

N-N class

hai-ku-fungua	haikufungua	It did not open
hazi-ku-fungua	hazikufungua	They did not open

Monosyllabic verbs drop the infinitive **ku-** which is replaced by the past tense marker of **KU-**. For example:

hau-ku-fa	haukufa	It did not die
hai-ku-fa	haikufa	They did not die

Borrowed verbs, like some Bantu words, drop the infinitive **ku-**. For example:

si-ku-tafsiri	sikutafsiri	I did not translate
hu-ku-tafsiri	hukutafsiri	You did not translate
hawa-ku-tafsiri	hawakutafsiri	They did not translate

VOCABULARY

boga	pumpkin	**toboa**	pierce
ondosha	abolish	**shawishi**	persuade
kiri kosa	plead guilty	**funga**	close
bilauri	tumbler	**tumia**	exploit
kinyozi	barber	**malighafi**	raw materials
toa	extract	**asali**	honey
nyoa	shave	**mkurufunzi**	tutor
ufalme	kingdom	**askari wa polisi**	policeman
zuia	ban	**upepo**	wind
vizuri	effectively	**utumwa**	slavery
ziara	visit	**kwa nguvu**	forcefully
kiranja	prefect	**teka**	conquer
saga	grind	**mjeledi**	whip

Exercise 14d

1. Translate the following sentences:
   a. The accused did not plead guilty.
   b. We were not able to persuade him.
   c. The traveller did not come here by boat.
   d. The tumbler did not break.
   e. The messenger did not shut the door.
   f. We did not exploit our raw materials well.
   g. The handle did not fall down here.
   h. The doctor did not extract my tooth yesterday.
   i. The barber did not shave his beard.
   j. The crocodile did not eat the child.
   k. The honey did not spill here.
   l. The wind did not blow heavily.
   m. She did not open those windows.
   n. The fisherman did not bring the fish home yesterday.
   o. His kingdom did not please the subjects.
   p. The tutor did not teach the students properly yesterday.
   q. The government did not ban foreign films.
   r. The policeman could not arrest the thief.
   s. The soap factory did not function effectively last year.
   t. Ominde did not write that book alone.

2. Translate the following sentences:
   a. Sikuweza kwenda kwa daktari jana.
   b. Hatukufungua mlango kwa nguvu.
   c. Wazungu hawakuondosha utumwa hata kidogo.
   d. Mtoto mchanga hakunywa maziwa ya moto.
   e. Kiranja wa shule hakuipiga kengele kwa wakati.
   f. Ziara yake kijijini haikuwafurahisha watu.
   g. Madaktari wale hawakuwatibu vizuri wagonjwa wetu.
   h. Hatukutaka kununua mananasi mengi jana.
   i. Seremala hakuutoboa ubao wote.
   j. Ukimwi haukuenea sana mjini.
   k. Wale wanajeshi hawakuweza kuuteka mji wote.
   l. Msasi hakuwinda paa mwezi uliopita.
   m. Msichana hakupenda kuusaga mtama.
   n. Mazungumzo yetu ukumbini hayakumalizika upesi.
   o. Mimi sikutaka kula yale maboga.
   p. Mzee wangu hakugombana na mtu yoyote.

q. Mgonjwa hakutaraji kama atapona.
r. Mijeledi yote haikuanguka chini.
s. ˙Sukari haikupanda bei kufuatana na tangazo la serikali.
t. Sisi hatukuichafua mipango yenu.

The -JA- tense

Earlier, we demonstrated the contention of some grammars that the past tense marker -KU- is the negative particle of the two affirmative tenses -li- and -me-. Other grammars, however, do not think along these lines. *Brain (1977)*, for example, indicates that the negative particle -me- is -ja. Thus, like others, he calls it the **-JA- tense** or **not yet tense**.

Zawawi (1971) does not make a distinction between the negative past and the -JA- tense. In her Masters dissertation, she also points out that the affirmative marker -li- has two negative particles: -ku- and -ja-. Similarly, she argues that the affirmative marker -me- has two negative particles: -ku- and -ja-. These differences between grammars are trivial since both tense markers -ku- and -ja- are basically indicators of previous activities. The differences between them are minor, as shown in the following examples:

a. **Hakumwona.**
   She/he did not see him/her.
b. **Hajamwona.**
   She/he has not seen him/her.

The two sentences refer to activities in the past. But in a., there is no relevance to the present. In other words, the fact of not seeing him/her in the past does not indicate any possibility that so and so would do so in the future. In b., the fact of not seeing him/her in the past does not rule out the possibility of it happening in the future.

The tense particle -ja-, like other tense markers, operates across different noun classes. It conjugates in the following manner:

si-ja-lala	sijalala	I have not (yet) slept.
hu-ja-lala	hujalala	you have not (yet) slept.
ha-ja-lala	hajalala	he/she has not (yet) slept.
hatu-ja-lala	hatujalala	we have not (yet) slept.
ham-ja-lala	hamjalala	you (pl) have not (yet) slept.
hawa-ja-lala	hawajalala	they have not (yet) slept.

Monosyllabic verbs drop the infinitive **ku-**, as indicated below:

si-ja-la	sijala	I have not (yet) eaten.
hu-ja-la	hujala	you have not (yet) eaten.
ha-ja-la	hajala	he/she has not (yet) eaten.

Borrowed words also drop the infinitive **ku-**. For example:

si-ja-fahamu	sijafahamu	I have not (yet) understood.
hu-ja-fahamu	hujafahamu	you have not (yet) understood.
ha-ja-fahamu	hajafahamu	he/she has not (yet) understood.

The word **bado** (not yet) is commonly used in the -JA- tense to emphasize the sense of "not yet":

Umemwona?	(Have you seen him/her?)
Sijamwona bado.	(I have not yet seen him.)

VOCABULARY

vunja	dissolve	**buibui**	spider
ambia	inform	**mhunzi**	blacksmith
ondoka	take off	**pendeza**	impress
jela	prison	**kama maziwa**	milk
kiwanja	pitch	**futa**	wipe
pata nafuu	recover	**kesi**	case
zindua	awaken	**taga**	lay eggs
tangazo	announcement	**vutia**	attract
uhamisho	transfer	**sega**	honeycomb
safirisha	export		
mzamili	postgraduate student		

Exercise 14e

1. Translate the following sentences:
    a. The queen has not yet dissolved parliament.
    b. The doctor has not attended to the patient.
    c. We have not come here to write books.
    d. The presidential plane has not yet landed.
    e. The woman has not yet arrived.
    f. The spider has not laid eggs on the wall.

g. The car has not yet passed here.
h. I have not informed him of anything.
i. The blacksmith has not yet done a good job.
j. The small plane has not taken off.
k. The plant has not died.
l. Those shoes have not impressed me.
m. The farmer has not yet milked the cow.
n. The players have not yet attended the pitch since morning.
o. Party meetings have not taken place for a long time now.
p. I have not yet received new guests.
q. It has not yet rained this week.
r. The prisoner has not yet escaped from the prison.
s. The beautiful lady has not yet given birth.
t. The postgraduate student has not wiped the blackboard.

2. Translate the following sentences:
   a. Wajumbe wa mkutano bado hawajawasili.
   b. Hakimu yule hajahukumu vizuri kesi yetu.
   c. Wavuvi hawajarudi bado kutoka kuvua.
   d. Mgonjwa bado hajapata nafuu.
   e. Mimi sijaelewa vizuri hotuba yake.
   f. Mlango haujafungika vizuri.
   g. Kelele zenu hazijamzindua msimamizi hata kidogo.
   h. Kuku wako bado hajataga mayai.
   i. Mfumo mpya wa kiuchumi wa nchi yetu bado haujaathiri nchi nyingine zinazoendelea.
   j. Tangazo lao la mkutano halijafika mbali.
   k. Ule moshi haujaenea sana.
   l. Mkurugenzi wa shirika la bima hajapata bado uhamisho wowote.
   m. Wale nyuki hawajaondoka kutoka sega lao.
   n. Ujumbe haujamfika mtumishi wako asubuhi.
   o. Mimi sijamtukana hata kidogo.
   p. Hicho kikombe hakijavunjika.
   q. Mpagazi bado hajaichukua mizigo yetu.
   r. Juma hajasafirisha bidhaa zozote.
   s. Ukulima wa kisasa haujawavutia wakulima kijijini.
   t. Mjane hajarithi mali nyingi kwa mumewe.

The -KI- and -SIPO- tenses

Conditional use

When the subject prefix precedes the **-KI-** tense and the verb stem follows it, grammarians point out that the concept of conditional use is implied. We can classify this conditional use as real because there is still the possibility of an action taking place at some point in the future. Some grammars argue that the **-KI-** tense gives the sense of "if" and "when", and all these are considered to have referential meanings. For example:

a. **Ukifika kesho, nitakupa pesa zako.**
   If you arrive tomorrow, I will give you your money.

b. **Ikinyesha mvua jioni, sitatoka nje.**
   If it rains in the afternoon, I will not go out.

The conditional use of the **-KI-** tense can be made more emphatic by the addition of **kama**, meaning "if" or "whether". For example:

a. **Kama akipika wali, atatuambia.**
   If he/she cooks rice, he/she will tell us.

b. **Kama ukimuuliza maswali mwalimu, atahamaki.**
   If you ask the teacher some questions, he will get angry.

For other noun classes, subject prefixes preceding the **-KI-** tense will change according to the noun class of a word. Following are some examples:

M-MI class

u-ki-anguka	ukianguka	if it falls.
i-ki-anguka	ikianguka	if they fall.

KI-VI class

ki-ki-anguka	kikianguka	if it falls.
vi-ki-anguka	vikianguka	if they fall.

JI-MA class

li-ki-anguka	likianguka	if it falls.
ya-ki-anguka	yakianguka	if they fall.

N-N class

i-ki-anguka	ikianguka	if it falls.
zi-ki-anguka	zikianguka	if they fall.

U-U class

u-ki-anguka	ukianguka	if it falls.
zi-ki-anguka	zikianguka	if they fall.

Like other kinds of verbs, monosyllabic verbs drop their infinitive, thus avoiding the **KU-** stress-carrier. For example:

ni-ki-la	nikila	if I eat.
u-ki-la	ukila	if you eat.
a-ki-la	akila	if he/she eats.
tu-ki-la	tukila	if we eat.

Conditional sentences in Swahili are also introduced by other markers, mainly **ikiwa** and **iwapo**, all meaning "if" and thus implying some degree of uncertainty or doubt. For example:

    a.   **Iwapo Juma atakuja leo, nitakuarifu.**
        If Juma arrives today, I will inform you.

    b.   **Ikiwa atafanya kelele darasani, mwalimu wake atampiga.**
        If he/she makes noise in class, his/her teacher will beat her.

Present participle function

When the -ki- tense occurs in a compound verbal construction, grammars describe it as functioning as a **participle**. *Ashton (1982)* points out that the tense marker conveys the idea of imperfect, continuous or incomplete action. For example:

    a.   **Tuliwaona vijana wakiimba.**
        We saw the youths singing.

    b.   **Nilimwona baba akilala.**
        I saw father sleeping.

Zawawi (1971) argues that the -KI- marker seems to be neutral with respect to time or action point. She adds that when -KI- occurs in a compound verb, its meaning of "in the event of" resembles that of -na-, "unended action". But when -KI- occurs in a simple verb, its referential meaning is equivalent to that of "if" or "when", which -na- does not possess.

    Brain (1977), like other grammars, points out that it is possible in Swahili to use both forms of -KI-. For example:

    a.   **Ukimwona akiruka, mzuie.**
        If you see him/her jumping, hold him/her.

   b. **Ukimwona akicheza, mpige.**
       If you see him/her playing, beat him/her.

Although the above sentences are grammatically correct, they are less common among native speakers of Swahili. More common is the use of the present tense **-na-** in the second or subsequent verbs. For example:

   a. **Ukimwona anaruka, mzuie.**
       If you see him/her jumping, hold him/her.
   b. **Ukimwona anacheza, mpige.**
       If you see him/her playing, beat him/her.

Past and future imperfect

The -KI- marker, in its function as a particle, can be used with the auxiliary **KUWA** (to be) to produce a compound verbal construction denoting the sense of continuity. For example:

   a. **Nilikuwa nikipika kutwa nzima.**
       I was cooking the whole day.
   b. **Nitakuwa nikipika kutwa nzima.**
       I will be cooking the whole day.
   c. **Nimekuwa nikipika kutwa nzima.**
       I have been cooking the whole day.

Negative conditional tense

There are two different ways of negating the -KI- conditional tense, which in English would be interpreted as "if not" or "unless".

1. By using the word **kama** and the present negative:

   a. **Kama hupiki chakula, mama yako atakasirika.**
       If you don't cook the food, your mother will get angry.
   b. **Kama haendi sokoni, mimi nitamfukuza kazini.**
       If he does not go to the market, I will dismiss him from work.

2. By using the negative participle **-sipo-** preceded by a positive or an affirmative subject prefix:

   a. **Usipopika chakula, mama yako atakasirika.**
       If you don't cook the food, your mother will get angry.
   b. **Asipoenda sokoni, mimi nitamfukuza kazini.**
       If he doesn't go to the market, I will dismiss him from work.

But with monosyllabic verbs, the infinitive **KU-** is retained so as to give stress to the verb stem:

  a. **Usipokuja kesho, mwalimu wako atakuadhibu.**
      If you do not come tomorrow, your teacher will punish you.
  b. **Asipokunywa maziwa, mtoto ataanza kulia.**
      If she does not drink the milk, the baby will start crying.

VOCABULARY

karafuu	cloves	kwa hadhari	carefully
tunza	reward	rithi	inherit
jiunga	join	kokota	pull
fasiri	translate	jitahidi	work hard
ajali	accident	angamia	perish
adhibu	punish	vibaya	severely
sifu	praise	shiriki	participate
funga	fast	anika	dry
neemeka	prosper	rejea	return
kifungu		mahari	dowry
cha habari	passage		

Exercise 14f

1. Translate the following sentences:
    a. If you go to Zanzibar, you will see cloves.
    b. If it doesn't rain heavily today, I will go out.
    c. If Ominde comes tomorrow, I will give him the eggs.
    d. If the lady sings well, I will reward her.
    e. If his father dies, he will inherit a lot of money.
    f. We saw our students pulling a cart.
    g. She will be writing a letter tomorrow morning.
    h. If he joins the university, he will work hard.
    i. If you do not go to school on Monday, the headmaster will be angry.
    j. If I do not translate the article, who will do it?
    k. We saw the old man fetching water from the well.
    l. If they see the coconut tree falling, they will run away.
    m. If you buy those flowers, you will like them.
    n. If he drives the car very fast, he will have an accident.

o. If the accused does not speak the truth, the judge will punish him severely.
p. If you obey old people, they will like you.
q. If Fatuma goes there, they will receive her.
r. Unless she comes early, she will not finish the job.
s. They saw us returning from town.
t. If you look carefully, you will see the cats running away.

2. Translate the following sentences:
   a. Ukilima vizuri, utavuna vizuri.
   b. Usipomsaidia mdogo wako, baba atasikitika.
   c. Nikisafiri kesho, nitakuarifu tu.
   d. Tuliona jirani zenu wakienda mazikoni.
   e. Atakuwa akiningoja nyumbani.
   f. Kama akijifunza Kiswahili sasa, mwalimu atafurahi.
   g. Akishiriki katika kujenga taifa, chama kitamsifu.
   h. Asiponiandikia barua ndugu yako, nitamlaumu sana.
   i. Mama yako amekuwa akikupenda sana.
   j. Nikimsikia kijana yule akilia, nitampiga.
   k. Likitoka jua leo, nitaanika nguo zangu.
   l. Mwezi ukiandama kesho, Waislamu nchini watafunga.
   m. Ukitoka nje, funga mlango.
   n. Msichana yule akiolewa, mwanamume atatoa mahari.
   o. Maendeleo yakipatikana nchini, wananchi wataneemeka.
   p. Ukiingia ndani, piga hodi kwanza.
   q. Wanajeshi wakirejea kambini, wataanza kwenda gwaride.
   r. Vita vya Dunia vikitokea, watu wengi wataangamia.
   s. Akisoma kitabu, anasoma kwa makelele.
   t. Ukimwona daktari wako, mpe salamu zangu.

3. Complete the following constructions:
   a. Mzee akiamka ....
   b. Ukiwaza sana ....
   c. Usipofanya kazi yako kwa bidii ....
   d. Nikiwa waziri wa elimu ....
   e. Akitukodisha nyumba yake ....
   f. Mgema akisifiwa ....
   g. Ukimwona akiiba kuku wangu ....
   h. Usipoendesha gari kwa hadhari ....
   i. Nikizuru nchi za Ulaya ....
   j. Akikutukana tena ....

k. Rais akiwasili kwenye maonyesho ....
l. Ukimwona nyoka njiani ....
m. Aibu ikikupata ....
n. Mkijifunza Kiswahili kwa juhudi ....
o. Usipolala mapema ....
p. Tukiwaona wakulima wanachunga wanyama ....
q. Ukiwaona wakichezacheza njiani ....
r. Mjomba akikupa mzigo wangu ....
s. Paka akiondoka ....
t. Ukame ukitokea nchini ....

The -KA- Tense

The -KA- tense has generally been associated with the notion of consecutiveness. *Steere (1976), Ashton (1982)* and other grammars all point out that the -KA- tense is used to express an action or state which follows another action. For example:

> **Nilikwenda dukani, nikanunua maembe mengi, nikampa sita ndugu yangu.**
> I went to a shop and bought many mangoes, I gave six to my brother.

Here, the -KA- tense is used to give narrative meaning to single observations that are recounted. Used this way, the -KA- is usually first introduced by an ordinary past tense marker, affirmative or negative. Normally, it is the -LI- tense which is used for the introduction. However, it is acceptable to argue, as other grammars have done, that the -KA- tense is not used at the beginning of a sentence unless it is closely allied to the verb in the previous sentence. *Zawawi (1971)* notes that the opening sentence of a novel by Katalambula, *Simu ya Kifo*, contains the -KA- tense in the first verbs of the sentence, as indicated below:

> **Inspekta Wingo akasikia kengele ya simu, ikalia pale mezani. Akaonekana kutojali ...**
> Inspector Wingo heard the telephone on the table ringing. He seemed not to care ...

Traditional grammars have also tried to associate the -KA- morpheme with the past tense. *Loogman (1965)*, for example, contends that the -KA- form is used exclusively with the past tense. This is a weak argument because, as exemplified in the following example, the -KA- form does not indicate the past tense:

Huenda ikanyesha jioni.
It may rain in the evening.

The -KA- above follows hu-, which implies probability.

An additional use of -KA- is found in certain situations, such as newspaper headlines, to give an immediacy effect and thus arrest the curiosity of the reader. *Brain (1977)* calls this a **Headline Tense**. For example:

a. **Waziri kafa.**
The minister is dead.
b. **Mwizi kakamatwa.**
The thief is arrested.

But *Wilson ('1970)* has confined the use of the initial -KA- only to newspaper headlines. This is misleading since structures such as those above are often heard among Swahili speakers. *Mshindo (1987)* argues that such structures are heard frequently among Swahili speakers of both Standard and Pemba varieties. It is worth noting that in the above two examples, the subject marker in the verb has been deleted. This deletion takes place in Swahili if the subject marker refers to a third person singular. The -KA- under such consideration embodies two grammatical functions: a tense marker and a subject prefix.

In brief, whether -KA- is a tense marker or a subject prefix or a combination of both is hard to say. But it is clear that the -KA- morpheme can be preceded by different tenses to provide different interpretations as the following examples prove:

a. **Waliondoka wa*ka*ona moto mbele.**
They left and saw a fire ahead.
b. **Huamka tu*ka*piga mswaki.**
We wake up and brush our teeth.
c. **Amka u*ka*mwite.**
Wake up and call him.
d. **Nitakwenda ni*ka*le chakula.**
I will go to eat food.
e. **Tumeanguka tu*ka*jiumiza.**
We have fallen down and hurt ourselves.

f.   **Mchana, nalala kidogo ni*k*aamka baadaye.**
At noon, I sleep a little and then wake up.

g.   *Kateleza vibaya.*
He has slipped terribly.

In the first example, the -**KA**- morpheme is used to convey narrative meaning whereas in the second, there is a habitual activity. In the third and fourth examples, the subjunctive form of the two verbs indicate that the notion of purpose is implied. In the fifth and sixth sentences, there is, again, a narrative meaning. In the last example, the indicative form suggests that some emotional use is implied; most probably in newspaper headlines.

All these are different interpretations explaining the use of the particle -**KA**-. Thus, contrary to some traditional views, the -**KA**- morpheme can also occur after various other tenses, apart from -**li**-.

Narrative use of -KA-

Following is a summary of the narrative use of the -**KA**- morpheme for all the noun classes in Swahili:

M-WA class (A - WA)

nikacheza	(and) I played.
ukacheza	(and) you played.
akacheza	(and) he/she played.
tukacheza	(and) we played.
mkacheza	(and) you (pl) played.
wakacheza	(and) they played.

M-MI class (U - I)

ukaota	(and) it grew.
	(and) they grew.

JI-MA class (LI - YA)

likaanguka	(and) it fell.
yakaanguka	(and) they fell.

KI-VI class (KI - VI)

kikavunjika	(and) it broke.
vikavunjika	(and) they broke.

N-N class (I - ZI)

ikalia	(and) it rang.
zikalia	(and) they rang.

U-U class (U - ZI)

ukaanguka	(and) it fell.
zikaanguka	(and) they fell.

PA- KU- MU- (PA-KU-MU)

pakajaa	(and) it was filled with.
kukajaa	(and) it was filled with.
mkajaa	(and) it was filled with.

For monosyllabic verbs, the **KU-** infinitive is dropped, thus enabling the -**KA**- tense to take stress, as in the following cases:

nikanywa	(and) I drank.
ukanywa	(and) you drank.
akanywa	(and) he/she drank.
tukanywa	(and) we drank.
mkanywa	(and) you(pl) drank.
wakanywa	(and) they drank.

Negation

The negative form of -**KA**- is identical with its negative subjunctive. For example:

a. **Tulimtazama hapa na pale tusimwone.**
   We looked for him here and there but did not find him.

b. **Watafanya kazi hapa na pale wasifanye?**
   How can they work only here without working there?

Now compare the positive forms for the above sentences, presented below:

a. **Tulimtazama hapa na pale tukamwona.**
   We looked for him here and there and found him.

b. **Watafanya kazi hapa na pale wakafanye pia?**
   How can they work here and also work there?

VOCABULARY

ukoo	family	**pamba**	cotton
sera	policy	**chungua**	examine
jogoo	cock	**njiwa**	pigeons
abadan	never	**mwishoni**	in the end
shirika	corporation	**uadui**	enmity
ndoa	marriage	**kaanga**	fry
mwanzoni	in the beginning	**mhasibu**	accountant
kagua	check		

Exercise 14g

1. Translate the following sentences:
   a. We first grew cotton and then planted maize.
   b. Go to school now and get my books.
   c. We bought pigeons, roasted them and then ate all of them.
   d. Her marriage may take place next week.
   e. The visitor woke up, brushed her teeth and then walked to the bathroom.
   f. The accountant first checked the books and then threw me some questions.
   g. The government examined the company's policy and then took the necessary action.
   h. The nice mule bent her neck downwards and in the end, she drank water.
   i. Go now to the market to buy some fish.
   j. The old woman came here, took her things and went away. She never asked me at all about the marriage.

2. Translate the following sentences:
   a. Alifika uwanja wa ndege mapema. Alipofika huko, akaona wasafiri kidogo tu wamewasili. Akasalimiana nao, kisha akateremka chini kununua vitu katika duka moja.
   b. Siku moja, mjomba wangu alikwenda sokoni kutafuta mayai ya kuku. Kwa bahati mbaya, akakuta mayai ya bata. Akauliza bei yake. Mwenye duka akamwambia kwamba yai moja ni shilingi tano.
   c. Nenda jikoni ukaoshe vyombo vyote mara moja. Vyombo vyote jikoni ni vichafu.

163

d. Usiku ule, nilitoka nje kwa hofu. Mbele kidogo, nikawakuta watu watatu wanazungumza. Wakanisalimu na mimi nikawaitikia.

e. Twende shuleni tukawachukue watoto wetu sasa hivi. Au nenda pamoja na kaka mkawalete hao watoto.

f. Yule jirani alituambia tukatafute nyama kwenye duka la ushirika. Sisi tukakataa kwenda.

g. Jogoo akasikia maneno yake asiseme neno; akakaa kimya.

h. Walikuja wakakaa mpaka magharibi wasipate hata tende na kahawa.

i. Twende kwa mzee wetu tukamwulize habari zenyewe.

j. Mpishi alikwenda kijijini akatafuta viazi na muhogo, asipate chochote.

3. Construct five sentences in Swahili containing the particle **-ka-**.

15 Tenses IV: NGE, NGALI and NGELI Tenses

NGE Tense

Traditional grammars have clarified that the **NGE** tense is used in a suppositional sense and that it is known as the present conditional. In other words, the tense is used when we begin to talk of events that are imaginary and, therefore, very unlikely to take place. For example:

a. **Ungefika hapa mapema, ungeweza kumwona baba yako.**
    If you were to come here early, you would be able to see your father.
b. **Ningekuwa tajiri, ningewasaidia masikini.**
    If I were rich, I would help the poor.

M-MI class

u-nge-anguka	ungeanguka	if it were to fall down.
i-nge-anguka	ingeanguka	if they were to fall down.

KI-VI class

ki-nge-vunjika	kingevunjika	if it were to break.
vi-nge-vunjika	vingevunjika	if they were to break.

Monosyllabic verbs retain their infinitive **KU-**.

ni-nge-kula	ningekula	if I were to eat.
a-nge-kunywa	angekunywa	if he/she were to drink.

Borrowed words drop the infinitive **KU-**.

ni-nge-jaribu	ningejaribu	if I were to try.
a-nge-fikiri	angefikiri	if he/she were to think.

In some instances, the word **kama** (if) is used to introduce or emphasize the conditional clause. For example:

a. **(Kama) ungekuwa daktari ungewatibu wagonjwa wengi.**
    If you were a doctor, you would treat many patients.
b. **(Kama) angelala mapema, wangeamka mapema.**
    If they would sleep early, they would wake up early.

In the above sentences, the word **kama** (if) has been bracketed to show that its presence is optional. As we have said, its use is merely intended to introduce or emphasize the conditional clause.

Some grammars point out that the **NGE** tense may also replace the **-KI-** tense to give the sense of supposition. For example:

165

a. **Ukifanya bidii, utafaulu tu.**
If you work hard, you will succeed.

Ungefanya bidii, ungefaulu.

b. **Nikimpiga sana, atalia.**
If I beat her severely, she will cry.

Ungempiga sana, angelia.

Although the use of the -KI- tense in the above examples produce grammatically correct sentences, the notion of supposition is not at all implied. The -KI- tense, as we have noted in the previous chapter, indicates a real situation and not a suppositional or unreal one. Therefore, the argument that the -KI- tense can replace -NGE- as advanced by some grammars is misleading since each tense conveys a different meaning.

In some instances, the -NGE- tense can be used in an unconditional sense to correspond to the English words "would" and "should", as shown in the following examples:

a. **Angependa kuja.**
He would like to come.
b. **Ungejaribu mara ya pili.**
You should try again.

NGALI tense

Unlike the **NGE** tense, traditional grammars have labelled **NGALI** as a past conditional or hypothetical condition. In other words, it is used when one is thinking about a past event and imagines it to be different from what it really was. Hence, the possibility of fulfilment of that condition is out of the question, as the proposition in the main clause shows. For example:

a. **Angalijua Kifaransa, angaliweza kutafsiri makala haya.**
If he knew French, he would have translated this article.
b. **Ungalikwenda sokoni jana, ungalipata samaki.**
If you would have gone to the market yesterday, you would have got the fish.

Like in the **NGE** tense, the word **kama** (if) can also be used in **NGALI** tense to introduce or emphasize the conditional clause. For example:

a. **(Kama) ningalikimbia, ningalianguka.**
If I would have run, I would have collapsed.

b. **(Kama) angaliibeba mizigo hii, ningalimpa pesa.**
   If he would have carried these loads, I would have given him money.

Maw (1985) also makes a distinction in the usage of **NGE** and **NGALI** forms. She contends that the latter may be thought of as "further back in conceptual time" than the former. Such a distinction does not at all correspond to the actual usage of the forms by native speakers of Swahili.

NGELI tense

Traditional grammars have not discussed this tense, yet native speakers of Swahili use it quite often in their speech. It is also intended to denote unreal situations. The following examples illustrate the point:

a. **Ungelipika wali jana, ningeliula wote.**
   If you had cooked rice yesterday, I would have eaten all of it.

b. **Ningelikuwa ndege, ningeliruka.**
   If I were a bird, I would have flown.

Combination of the tenses

Depending upon the sense of the context, it is possible in Swahili to combine two tenses, so that a condition in one tense is followed by a condition in another tense. For example:

a. **Tungekwenda nyumbani, tungalimkuta mama.**
   Had we gone home, we would have met mother.

b. **Ungalininunulia kalamu jana, ningelifurahi mno.**
   If you had bought me a pen yesterday, I would have been very happy.

Syntactic function of the tenses

Maw (1969) states that the three tenses function as exponents of interdependence.

a. **Ungekifuata, ungekiona.**
   If you really looked for it, you would find it.

b. **Ningalifanya kama tungalisema hivi.**
   I would have done if we had said this.

Recent findings on conditional tenses

Recent studies on the use of **NGE, NGALI** and **NGELI** tenses have shown that all three forms are considered free variants of the same morpheme. *Zawawi (1971)* points out that the three variants have the same function, namely to indicate a hypothetical condition with no reference to a particular time. Likewise, *Salone (1983)* differs significantly from the analysis of traditional grammarians on the question of **NGE, NGELI** and **NGALI** tenses. In his doctoral dissertation, he contends that the **NGE** marker is not associated with any particular tense. He also contends that the **NGELI** and **NGALI** markers tend to favour a past interpretation, and that implies having a low possibility of occurrence.

Unlike traditional grammarians, therefore, *Salone (1983)* has not restricted the **NGE** tense to present reference only. The possibility of occurrence in the use of **NGELI** and **NGALI** tenses still exists although she thinks it is minimal. This means that the traditional analysis of **NGE** as present conditional and **NGALI** as past conditional does not correspond to the actual usage of these forms by native speakers of Swahili.

Negative conditional

There are two different ways of expressing the negative forms of the three conditional tenses.

a. By inserting the negative particle **-SI-** immediately after the subject prefix as shown here:

ni-singe-lala	nisingelala	if I had not slept.
u-singe-lala	usingelala	if you had not slept.
a-singe-lala	asingelala	if he/she had not slept.
tu-singe-lala	tusingelala	if we had not slept.
m-singe-lala	msingelala	if you(pl) had not slept.
wa-singe-lala	wasingelala	if they had not slept.

M-MI class

u-singe-anguka	usingeanguka	if it had not fallen down.
i-singe-anguka	isingeanguka	if they had not fallen down.

KI-VI class

ki-singe-vunjika	kisingevunjika	if it had not broken.
vi-singe-vunjika	visingevunjika	if they had not broken.

168

With monosyllabic verbs, the infinitive **KU-** is retained. For example:

ni-singe-kula	nisingekula	if I had not eaten.
u-singe-kunywa	usingekunywa	if you had not drunk.

With borrowed words, the infinitive **KU-** is dropped like in Bantu verbs. For example:

ni-singe-jaribu	nisingejaribu	if I had not tried.
u-singe-fikiri	usingefikiri	if you had not thought.
a-singe-samehe	asingesamehe	if he/she had not forgiven.

b. By using **HA-** before the subject prefix (except in the case of the first person singular where **NI-** is always preceded by **SI-**). But with this construction, the word **kama** (if) is usually used to introduce and emphasize the conditional clause as shown below:

Kama (ni-si-nge-andika) nisingeandika ...
If I had not written ...

Kama (ha-u-nge-andika) hungeandika ...
If you had not written ...

Kama (ha-a-nge-andika) hangeandika ...
If he/she had not written ...

VOCABULARY

tapika	vomit	mwandishi	writer
uchumi	economy	andama	chase
maendeleo	progress	azima	lend
tarishi	messenger	piga kura	vote
kosa	crime	leta	bring
mara moja	at once	bidii	effort
hakimu	judge	vunja	cancel
achia huru	acquit	mashindano	competition
siri	secret	raia	citizen
-kali	wild, fierce	ponya	treat

Exercise 15

1. Translate the following sentences:
   a. If John had vomited here, his father would have punished him.
   b. If you knew, you would have told me.
   c. If this tree had fallen down, it would have hurt me badly.
   d. If the messenger did not know, he would have asked you.
   e. If the accused had confessed his crime, the judge would have probably acquitted him.
   f. If you had gone there at once, you would have seen the old man.
   g. If the cook had looked for the knife, she would have found it.
   h. If I had known, would I not have told you the secret?
   i. If the lady had come last week, she would have helped us.
   j. I would not have caught the animal if it was wild.
   k. She would not have lent you the book if she did not know you.
   l. If it had rained yesterday, I would not have gone out.
   m. If the bird had flown over here, he would have caught it.
   n. If I were a magician, I would have treated your child.
   o. If this hut was large, I would have slept in it.

2. Translate the following sentences:
   a. Ungalimleta mdogo wako hapa, ningalifurahi sana.
   b. Angeonyesha bidii katika kazi, tajiri wake angempandisha cheo.
   c. Ningelikuwa kiziwi, nisingelisikia vizuri maneno yote.
   d. Tungeondoka sasa hivi, tungemkuta nyumbani.
   e. Kama taa zisingezimika, tungeendelea na kazi yetu.
   f. Kama usingeliamka mapema, ungalikosa gari la moshi.
   g. Ningepoteza ufunguo wa nyumba, baba angehamaki.
   h. Asingelipika ndizi leo, nisingelikula chakula chochote.
   i. Kama simba angekuona, angekuandama.
   j. Kama uhuru usingelipatikana nchini, maendeleo katika uchumi yasingalionekana.
   k. Ungesikia habari, ungeniarifu mara moja.
   l. Kama ningekosa kusafiri leo, ningeivunja safari yangu.
   m. Kama asingalikuwa mtu masikini, angewasaidia watu wengi.

n. Tungeshiriki katika mashindano, tungeshinda bila ya wasiwasi.

o. Kama nisingelikuwa raia nchini, nisingelishiriki katika kupiga kura.

3. Complete the following constructions:
   a. Tungekuwa wakulima ....
   b. Angelisafiri kwa ndege ....
   c. Ungeandika vitabu vya Kiswahili ....
   d. Ningeendesha gari kwa kasi sana jana ....
   e. Usingeliinunua mikoba hii ....
   f. Angelikutana na simba msituni ....
   g. Kama kijana yule angelikuwa mwanariadha ....
   h. Nisingekwenda hospitali jana ....
   i. Ingeanguka nyumba hii leo ....
   j. Kingelitokea kimbunga nchini ....
   k. Usingalimpelekea barua mjomba wako ....
   l. Angejifunza Kiarabu ....
   m. Tungekwenda kule ....
   n. Ungekuwa mwaandishi mashuhuri ....
   o. Angelikuwa kiongozi wa nchi ....

16 Demonstratives of Reference

Traditionally, grammarians have differentiated demonstrative pronouns of Swahili along the following lines:

The **h-** root is used for proximity and the **-le** for non-proximity. *Ashton (1982)* states that these grammatical items are used in contexts where proximity or non-proximity of place or time is implied. However, *Ashton* further explains that when the root is **h-o**, the question of proximity or non-proximity is immaterial because it always refers to something previously mentioned. *Polomé (1967)* also thinks that the **h-** and the **-le** roots signal "proximity or non-proximity in time and space". And with **h-o**, Polomé states, the root points to something already mentioned. Other grammars, such as *Kapinga (1983)*, *Perrot (1951)*, *Wilson (1970)* and *Zawawi (1971)*, only mention place and make no reference to time. Others, such as *Loogman (1965)*, merely refer to **h-** as "this" and **-le** as "that" and make no explicit statement regarding proximity or non-proximity.

Demonstrative of proximity

If we follow the analysis of some grammars, such as that of Ashton, we will see that the **h-** is used for proximity. This demonstrative marker takes an appropriate subject prefix and then between the two, the same vowel occurring in the subject prefix is repeated. For instance, in the KI-VI class, the construction "this chair" will be translated as follows:

kiti h + ki = kiti hiki

The subject prefix for **kiti** (chair) is KI- and this contains the vowel **i**. Hence, the vowel **i** is repeated and then inserted between the demonstrative marker and the subject prefix as shown above. The same principle is applicable when the construction **kiti hiki** is pluralized. Nouns belonging to other classes are also treated in this manner. But with M-WA class, there is an exception. This exception, however, is found only in the singular form. According to the rules of grammar, we expect the subject prefix **a** to be used. But instead, the demonstrative root **-yu** is used. This grammatical marker is derived from an old Bantu form. For the plural form, the grammatical rule is still valid and hence, the subject prefix **wa-** is used. Thus the following construction results:

| this man | = | mtu h + u + yu | = | **mtu huyu** |
| these men | = | watu h + a + wa | = | **watu hawa** |

In each case, the vowel is repeated, as was discussed in other noun classes.

Demonstrative of non-proximity

For reference to non-proximity, the demonstrative particle **-le** is used. This demonstrative begins with an appropriate subject prefix. Again, this rule does not apply to M-WA class nouns when used in the singular form. Instead, the demonstrative root **yu-** is utilized. Therefore we have the following construction:

those men = watu wa + le = **watu wale**

Demonstrative of mentioned items

Most of the grammars agree that the third demonstrative, namely **H-O**, is used to refer to an item that was previously mentioned. Other grammars, however, disagree with Ashton's contention that location is immaterial and instead argue that the demonstrative particle can also have a locative meaning. *Zawawi (1971)*, for example, thinks that the h-o demonstrative can also take the meaning of "location near a listener". Let us examine this construction:

that man = **mtu huyo**

The expression **mtu huyo** can carry two meanings: the man who was previously mentioned and the man near the listener. Table 6 gives a summary of the forms of demonstrative markers.

Maw (1985) describes the h-o demonstrative item as a kind of reference, thus distinguishing it from the first two which denote nearness and distance. To label **h-o** alone as a marker of reference and exclude the other two is misleading. All the three items deserve to be grouped under the label **reference**.

Demonstrative forms of reference in Swahili operate according to class and the number of the item in question. As can be seen in Table 6, we have fifteen forms of demonstrative markers.

Word order

In a sentence structure, demonstrative words precede or follow their nouns. *Ashton (1982)* says that when the demonstrative forms precede the nouns, their function approximates that of the English article "the" in similar situations. When they follow the noun, their function is similar to that of the English words "this", "these", "that" and "those". These arguments need extensive research. What is clear, however, is that some Swahili speakers do not make such distinctions when they use demonstrative forms either to precede or to follow their nouns.

Class	Proximity (near speaker)	Already mentioned or near listener	Non-proximity (away from speaker and listener)
M-WA (1)	huyu	huyo	yule
M-WA (2)	hawa	hao	wale
M-MI (3)	huu	huo	ule
M-MI (4)	hii	hiyo	ile
JI-MA (5)	hili	hilo	lile
JI-MA (6)	haya	hayo	yale
KI-VI (7)	hiki	hicho	kile
KI-VI (8)	hivi	hivyo	vile
N-N (9)	hii	hiyo	ile
N-N (10)	hizi	hizo	zile
U-U (11-14)	huu	huo	ule
U-U (11-14)	hizi	hizo	zile
PA (16)	hapa	hapo	pale
KU (17)	huku	huko	kule
MU (18)	humu	humo	mle

Table 6: Forms of demonstrative markers in Swahili

Grammars, such as *Myachina (1981)*, point out that demonstrative forms can be used regardless of whether their coefficients are textually present or not. The following example demonstrates this:

Nataka kitabu hiki. (I want this book.)

Myachina notes that it is possible to delete the noun **kitabu** (book) and simply use the demonstrative form. This contention seems viable, in which case we should classify the demonstrative marker as a pronoun. But when it is used with a noun, the demonstrative marker should be referred to as an adjective rather than a pronoun.

Emphatic forms

Demonstrative forms function as emphatic when the process of reduplication takes place. Here, the concord of the noun prefix is repeated

174

to give emphasis, as shown below:

Nataka kitabu kiki hiki. (I want this very book.)

Emphasis can also take place by repeating the whole demonstrative word:

Nataka kitabu hiki hiki. (I want this very book.)

Recent findings on demonstrative forms

There have been recent studies on the use of demonstrative forms by some educators. The most striking contribution is that of Robert Leonard who seems to depart from the traditional analysis. *Leonard (1982)* argues that the traditional analysis which refers to **h-** as proximate and **-le** as non-proximate cannot be adequately accounted for in all cases. In other words, Leonard contends that in his study of Swahili discourse, the demonstrative particle **-le** can refer in certain situations to an item whose context indicates it to be in a proximate position. Conversely, the demonstrative root **h-** can refer to an item situated in a non-proximate position.

As regards the **h-o** root, *Leonard (1982)* points out that the demonstrative can, in certain contexts, refer to an item that is being mentioned for the first time. All these arguments obviously contradict the traditional analysis of the mentioned demonstrative particles. Further research is still necessary to substantiate Leonard's arguments.

VOCABULARY

kijana	youth	**mwewe**	hawk
maandamano	demonstrations	**kwa wakati**	in time
fanya	hold	**amini**	believe
nasaha	advice	**kifaranga**	fowl
taraji	expect	**chopi**	a lot
imara	firm	**msafara**	caravan
tafsiri	translate	**tua**	land
umoja	unity	**mpaka**	till
hifadhi	maintain	**kwa hadhari**	cautiously
puuza	ignore, dislike	**kiongozi**	leader
mlevi	drunkard	**mgomo**	strike
amua	decide	**ardhi**	land

Exercise 16

1. Translate the following sentences:
   a. Those youths will arrive here in time.
   b. We have brought these cups today.
   c. I have never seen that hawk before.
   d. If you believe those words, everyone will laugh at you.
   e. Those workers held demonstrations in the afternoon.
   f. I like your advice; I think that advice will help me a lot.
   g. The ladies will cook these fowls today.
   h. I did not expect that woman to come yesterday.
   i. Those drunkards drank a lot that week.
   j. I like that politician. He is quite firm.
   k. We saw those caravans but we ignored them.
   l. That plane landed safely.
   m. Our leaders want to maintain this unity.
   n. I bought the shoes yesterday. Those shoes are very nice.
   o. We followed those thieves cautiously until we arrested them.

2. Translate the following sentences:
   a. Kitabu hiki si kizuri sana.
   b. Baba yangu amenunua vikombe hivi karibuni.
   c. Yule mwewe anafanya nini pale?
   d. Migomo hii itauharibu sana uchumi wetu.
   e. Nimeisikia taarifa ile tangu jana.
   f. Ukimpiga mzee yule, watu watakulaumu sana.
   g. Msafara huu utaanza siku ya Ijumaa.
   h. Kiongozi yule hafai kutuongoza.
   i. Mtumishi wako amenunua nazi zile sokoni.
   j. Wanasiasa wale wanapenda kutudanganya kila siku.
   k. Ardhi hii haina rotuba hata kidogo.
   l. Mapapai yale yameiva sana.
   m. Hakimu amemtaka mkalimani yule atafsiri tena maneno yale.
   n. Nimeamua kulinunua zulia lile.
   o. Mwenyeduka anauza chupa zile kwa bei kubwa.

17 Relatives I: Tensed Relatives

Relative English words such as "who", "whom", "which", "whose" and "that" are expressed in Swahili by the use of appropriate relative particles either as infixes or suffixes of the verb. These relative particles refer back to the subject or object of the sentence - in other words, to its antecedents - to form what is known as a **relative clause**. A relative clause is that part of a sentence which is embedded in a noun phrase. The relative particles for all classes of nouns are shown in Table 7 below.

Noun class	relative particles
1	-ye-
2	-o-
3	-o-
4	-yo-
5	-lo-
6	-yo-
7	-cho-
8	-vyo-
9	-yo-
10	-zo-
11	-o-
14	-o-
15	-ko-
16	-po-
17	-ko-
18	-mo-

Table 7: Relative particles

In Swahili, three types of relativization exist: tensed relatives, "amba" relatives and tenseless relatives.

Tensed relatives

Tensed relatives are sometimes known as "reduced relative clauses". Here, the pronoun **amba** does not occur. Instead, a relative particle agreeing with the class of the noun referred to is attached to the verb. Using different tense markers, tensed relatives can be illustrated in the following manner:

-NA- tensed relative particle

M-WA class

ni-na-ye-fundisha	ninayefundisha	I who am teaching.
u-na-ye-fundisha	unayefundisha	you who are teaching.
a-na-ye-fundisha	anayefundisha	he/she who is teaching.
tu-na-ye-fundisha	tunayefundisha	we who are teaching.
m-na-ye-fundisha	mnayefundisha	you(pl) who are teaching.
wa-na-o-fundisha	wanaofundisha	they who are teaching.

M-MI class

u-na-o-anguka	unaoanguka	it which falls.
i-na-o-anguka	inaoanguka	they which fall.

JI-MA class

li-na-lo-anguka	linaloanguka	it which falls.
ya-na-yo-anguka	yanayoanguka	they which fall.

KI-VI class

ki-na-cho-anguka	kinachoanguka	it which falls.
vi-na-vyo-anguka	vinavyoanguka	they which fall.

N-N class

i-na-yo-anguka	inayoanguka	it which falls.
zi-na-zo-anguka	zinazoanguka	they which fall.

U-U class

u-na-o-anguka	unaoanguka	it which falls.
zi-na-zo-anguka	zinazoanguka	they which fall.

-LI- tensed relative particle

M-WA class

ni-li-ye-fundisha	niliyefundisha	I who taught.
u-li-ye-fundisha	uliyefundisha	you who taught.
a-li-ye-fundisha	aliyefundisha	he/she who taught.
tu-li-o-fundisha	tuliofundisha	we who taught.
m-li-o-fundisha	mliofundisha	you(pl) who taught.
wa-li-o-fundisha	waliofundisha	they who taught.

M-MI class

u-li-o-anguka	ulioanguka	it which fell.
i-li-yo-anguka	iliyoanguka	they which fell.

JI-MA class

| li-li-lo-anguka | lililoanguka | it which fell. |
| ya-li-yo-anguka | yaliyoanguka | they which fell. |

KI-VI class

| ki-li-cho-anguka | kilichoanguka | it which fell |
| vi-li-vyo-anguka | vilivyoanguka | they which fell |

N-N class

| i-li-yo-anguka | iliyoanguka | it which fell |
| zi-li-zo-anguka | zilizoanguka | they which fell |

U-U class

| u-li-o-anguka | ulioanguka | it which fell |
| zi-li-zo-anguka | zilizoanguka | they which fell |

With monosyllabic verbs, the infinitive **KU-** is retained irrespective of whether the tense marker is **-NA-** or **-LI-**:

| a-na-ye-kuja | anayekuja | he/she who comes |
| a-li-ye-kuja | aliyekuja | he/she who came |

Borrowed verbs, notably from Arabic, drop the infinitive **KU-**:-

| ni-na-ye-fahamu | ninayefahamu | I who understand |
| ni-li-ye-fahamu | niliyefahamu | I who understand |

Future tensed relative particle

When a relative clause is used to signal futurity, the future tense marker **-TA-** takes an extra syllable **-KA-** to become **-TAKA-**. The following examples illustrate this:

ni-taka-ye-fundisha	nitakayefundisha	I who shall teach
u-taka-ye-fundisha	utakayefundisha	you who will teach
a-taka-ye-fundisha	atakayefundisha	he/she who will teach
tu-taka-o-fundisha	tutakaofundisha	we who will teach
m-taka-o-fundisha	mtakaofundisha	you(pl) who will teach
wa-taka-o-fundisha	watakaofundisha	they who will teach

M-MI class

| u-taka-o-anguka | utakaoanguka | it which will fall |
| i-taka-o-anguka | itakaoanguka | they which will fall |

JI-MA class

| li-taka-lo-anguka | litakaloanguka | it which will fall |
| ya-taka-yo-anguka | yatakayoanguka | they which will fall |

N-N class

| i-taka-yo-anguka | itakayoanguka | it which will fall |
| zi-taka-zo-anguka | zitakazoanguka | they which will fall |

U-U class

| u-taka-o-anguka | utakaoanguka | it which will fall |
| zi-taka-zo-anguka | zitakazoanguka | they which will fall |

In tensed relatives, a relative particle operates with one of the four tense markers: **na-**, **-li**, **-taka-** and the negative **-si**. It cannot operate when the tense affixes are **-me-** and **-ta-** alone, as shown below:

> * **ua limeloanguka** the flower which has fallen
> * **watu wataokula** people who will eat

Russel (1992) points out that as early as the nineteenth century, the tense affix **-me-** could be used in tensed relatives. For example, in the poem of *Ayubu* compiled by Allen, J.W.T., we notice the use of **-me-** in the relative clause of the following stanza:

> *Na ng'ombe na ngamize*
> *Na farasi na pundaze*
> *hesabuye niweleze*
> *ni kama nimezotaja*

> *And his cattle and camels*
> *and horses and asses*
> *let me tell you their number*
> *it was the same I have mentioned*

Amba relatives

This is the second type of relativization in Swahili. Here, the relative clause is introduced by a relative pronoun **amba**, to which a relative particle functioning as the suffix is obligatorily attached in agreement with the class and number of the antecedent. For example:

M-WA class
mtu ambaye anakula   the person who is eating
watu ambao wanakula   the people who are eating

M-MI class
mti ambao unaanguka   the tree which is falling
miti ambayo inaanguka   the trees which are falling

JI-MA class
ua ambalo linaanguka   the flower which is falling
maua ambayo yanaanguka   the flowers which are falling

KI-VI class
kikapu ambacho kinaanguka   the basket which is falling
vikapu ambavyo vinaanguka   the baskets which are falling

N-N class
nyumba ambayo inaanguka   the house which is falling
vyumba ambazo zinaanguka   the houses which are falling

U-U class
uma ambao unaanguka   the fork which is falling
nyuma ambazo zinaanguka   the forks which are falling

In both relative strategies, the antecedent, sometimes known as the **head**, must precede its modifying clause and the relative particle. Furthermore, although we argued earlier that the tense affix -me- cannot operate in tensed relatives, this restriction does not prevail in **amba** relatives. For example, it is acceptable to say the following:

mtu ambaye amefika leo   the person who has arrived today
watu ambao wamefika leo   the people who have arrived today

Tenseless relatives

In tenseless relatives, the relative particle is suffixed to the last element of the verb and is mutually exclusive with a tense marker. The relativized verb thus functions as a qualifier to the head. In other words, it possesses an adjectival function hence, depicting the action of the verb as habitual.

Some grammars refer to tenseless relatives as **general relatives**. They are always translated in the present tense although no overt tense marker exists in them. Thus, in the verb **kupenda** (to love), we have the following forms:

ni-penda-ye	nipendaye	I who loves
u-penda-ye	upendaye	you who loves
a-penda-ye	apendaye	he/she who loves
tu-penda-ye	tupendaye	we who love
m-penda-ye	mpendaye	you (pl) who love
wa-penda-ye	wapendaye	they who love

M-MI class

u-anguka-o	uangukao	it which falls
i-anguka-yo	iangukayo	they which fall

JI-MA class

li-anguka-lo	liangukalo	it which falls
ya-anguka-yo	yaangukayo	they which fall

KI-VI class

ki-anguka-cho	kiangukacho	it which falls
vi-anguka-vyo	viangukavyo	they which fall

N-N class

i-anguka-yo	iangukayo	it which falls
zi-anguka-zo	ziangukazo	they which fall

U-U class

u-anguka-yo	uangukayo	it which falls
zi-anguka-zo	ziangukazo	they which fall

Monosyllabic verbs, like other verbs, drop the infinitive **ku-**. For example:

ni-la-ye	nilaye	I who eats
a-la-ye	alaye	he/she who eats
wa-la-o	walao	they who eat

Similarly, borrowed verbs, mainly from Arabic, also drop the infinitive **ku-**. For example:

ni-fasiri-ye	nifasiriye	I who translates
u-fasiri-ye	ufasiriye	you who translates

Functional definition of relative clauses

Functionally, relative clauses are defined in two ways: **defining** and **non-defining**. The defining relative clause attempts to define or identify a particular item which serves as the antecedent. The clause is sometimes referred to as **restrictive**. For example:

> **Kijana aliyefika hapa jana ni ndugu yangu.**
> The youth who arrived here yesterday is my brother.

The construction **aliyefika hapa jana** (who arrived here yesterday) is known as a **defining clause**. It can also be interpreted as a post-modifying clause because it describes the noun **kijana** (youth).

The non-defining relative clause, however, merely gives further information about the item to which it refers. It does not specifically define or identify the item. The non-defining clause is sometimes referred to in grammar books as **non-restrictive** or **continuative**. In Swahili, this clause is generally introduced by the **amba** construction:

> **Aliendesha gari kwa kasi sana pamoja na ndugu zangu, ambao sasa wameenda sokoni.**
> He drove very fast with my brothers, who have now gone to the market.

Here, the relative clause **ambao sasa wameenda sokoni** (who have now gone to the market) does not identify which brothers accompanied him during the drive. The clause merely gives more information about them.

Non-defining clauses also differ from defining relatives in phonology. While they are spoken with a separate intonation contour, defining clauses are attached prosodically to their antecedent. Thus, we would expect that in written form, non-defining clauses generally carry a comma, and possibly a dash, before and after them.

Multiple uses of relative clauses

Relative clauses are widely used in Swahili. In situations where English would utilize the present or past participle, Swahili would employ relativization. For example:

> A stolen purse.

The expression "A stolen purse" would be paraphrased as "a purse which is stolen". In Swahili, participles are expressed by means of relativizing them. Thus, "A stolen purse" would be translated as **mkoba ulioibiwa**. The expression **ulioibiwa** is a relative clause.

Also, in situations where English would use a covert relative pronoun, Swahili would employ an overt one. For instance:

> The man I saw.

The relative pronoun "whom" has been deleted in the above sentence. Yet the expression "I saw" is considered to be a relative clause. In English, while we have an option of retaining or deleting the relative pronoun, Swahili does not. In other words, it must use a relative marker.

The relative with object

When an object is relativized, it has to come first, followed by the **amba** and by the subject. There is an obligatory object agreement on the verb as shown in the following examples:

    a.   **Miti ambayo niliipanda jana, imeng'olewa.**
         The trees that I planted yesterday have been uprooted.

    b.   **Watu ambao tumewaona leo ni Wayunani.**
         The people whom we have seen today are Greeks.

The object agreement affix also appears obligatorily when the object is relativized in tensed relatives:

    a.   **Mayai nitakayoyaona mabovu yatatupwa.**
         The eggs that I will find to be rotten will be thrown away.

    b.   **Barua ulizozichukua ni zangu.**
         The letters that you have taken are mine.

All these sentences are instances of what is known as **object relativization** because it is the object which is relativized. When it is the subject which is relativized, then it is termed as **subject relativization**. For example:

    a.   **Watu ambao walimtukana jirani yangu ni wahuni.**
         The people who insulted my neighbour are hooligans.

    b.   **Gari ambalo lilimgonga mwendeshaji baiskeli hivi karibuni ni la serikali.**
         The vehicle which knocked down a cyclist recently belongs to the government.

Syntactic function of the relative clauses

All three types of relative clauses are considered as **rankshifted clauses** since they can function as a single word acting as a qualifier to the antecedent or, in systemic linguistics, to the **headword**. Sometimes, these relative constructions are also referred to as **embedded clauses** since they are clauses which operate within the main clause.

Constraints in relative clauses

We have shown that the tense marker -me- cannot operate in tensed relatives. Such grammatical restrictions can also govern amba relatives, although in a different way. We have seen in the previous examples that the word **amba** immediately precedes the head of the relative. For example:

> **Wanafunzi ambao walikisoma kitabu kile ni wengi.**
> The students who read that book are many.

An ill-formed sentence would be produced by transposing **amba** in such a way that it does not immediately occur after the head of the relative. For instance:

> a. *Wanafunzi kitabu kile ambao walikisoma ni wengi.
> b. *Wanafunzi kitabu kile walikisoma ambao ni wengi.

Such sentences, as we have just shown, are not acceptable because, since Swahili is a post-specifying language, the relative word **ambao** must come immediately after the head of the relative construction.

A similar constraint prevails in tensed relatives where we find that two noun phrases cannot occur adjacent to one another:

> a. **Vitu alivyovichukua Paul ni vizito.**
> The things which Paul has carried are heavy.
> b. **Mitungi aliyoinunua Mary ni mizuri.**
> The water-jars which Mary has bought are beautiful.

If, however, we use two noun phrases adjacent to one another, we would produce unacceptable sentences. For example:

> a. ***Vitu Paul alivyovichukua ni vizito.**
> The things Paul has carried are heavy.
> b. ***Mitungi Mary aliyoinunua ni mizuri.**
> The water-jars which Mary has bought are beautiful.

Constraints associated with subject relativization also exist in passive relative constructions. Here, we find that the agentive preposition **na** must be obligatorily attached to the relative particle:

> (i) **Mtu ambaye watoto waliponywa naye ni mganga.**
> The man who the children were cured by is the medicine man.
> (ii) **Kijana ambaye watalii waliongozwa naye ni rafiki yangu.**
> The youth who the tourists were led by is my friend.

185

Compare them with the sentences below whose agentive preposition **na** stands alone and, therefore, produces unacceptable Swahili forms:

a.   *Mtu ambaye watoto waliponywa na ni mganga.
     The man who the children were cured by is the medicine man.

b.   *Kijana ambaye watalii waliongozwa na ni rafiki yangu.
     The youth who the tourists were led by is my friend.

A restriction governing **amba** relatives is connected with adverbs of time and manner. Consider the following examples:

(i)   **Mtu ambaye alifika jana ni mwalimu.**
      The person who arrived yesterday is our teacher.

(ii) **Mtu ambaye alisoma vizuri kitabu kile ni wewe.**
      The person who read that book well is you.

The sentences above have the adverbial markers **jana** (yesterday) and **vizuri** (well) modifying their verbs. If these adverbial markers are transposed such that they modify the relative pronoun **amba** instead of the verbs, the sentences produced become less acceptable:

(i)   * Mtu ambaye jana alifika ni mwalimu
(ii) * Mtu ambaye vizuri alisoma ni wewe.

Constraints surrounding relative clauses are also associated with the relative marker **kwamba** (that). This word occurs in non-relative embedded sentences. It never occurs internally in a sentence. Thus, the following sentence is acceptable:

Tulihisi kwamba mvua itanyesha tu.
We felt that it would definitely rain.

In the **amba** relative, the word **kwamba** (that) cannot occur internally.

* **Mimi ambaye kwamba niliumwa zamani, sasa nimepona.**
I who was sick in the past have now recovered.

Pseudo-cleft and cleft constructions

In pseudo-cleft and cleft constructions, a single clause is divided into two separate parts, each with its own verb. One part contains a main clause and the other a dependent one. Thus, the single clause has a main clause-dependent clause relationship. For example:

Wewe ni mtu tajiri.
You are a rich person.

The above sentence, which has a single clause, can be written in the following manner:

>**Ulivyo wewe ni mtu tajiri.**
>What you are is a rich person.

Such a construction is known as **a pseudo-cleft sentence**. In the case of a cleft sentence, we can have another variation of the given single clause:

>**Aliye mtu tajiri ni wewe.**
>It is you who is rich.

The kinds of construction discussed above have relative features. They are sometimes used in determining the existence of noun phrases.

The negative relative clauses

A relative clause is negated by inserting the particle -si- immediately after the subject prefix. But the presence of this particle does not indicate time preference. It merely describes the negative character of a person or thing. The following sentence indicates this:

>**Msichana asiyependa kusoma.**

The construction **msichana asiyependa kusoma** can refer to three tenses: present, past and future. It can mean either "a girl who does not like to read"; "a girl who did not like to read"; or "a girl who will not like to read". To avoid ambiguity, some grammars prescribe the use of **amba** for expressing a negative relative sentence. For instance:

>a. **Msichana ambaye hapendi kusoma.**
>   A girl who does not like to read.
>b. **Msichana ambaye hakupenda kusoma.**
>   A girl who did not like to read.
>c. **Msichana ambaye hatapenda kusoma.**
>   A girl who will not like to read.

VOCABULARY

shida	problems	**ropoka**	prattle
muhimu	important	**kipanga**	falcon
vuma	blow	**mashariki**	east
nyati	buffalo	**kwa furaha**	happily
-aminifu	honest	**riwaya**	novel
-bovu	rotten	**ng'ara**	glitter

jibu	answer	**endesha**	operate
mkutano	meeting	**tembelea**	tour
mashuhuri	famous	**dondoka**	drip
motokaa	motorcar	**bakunja**	stupid person
farasi	horse	**jamii**	community

Exercise 17

1. Translate the following sentences:
   a. The lady who passed here yesterday is Mary.
   b. The six eggs that are broken are mine.
   c. The wind which is blowing now comes from the east.
   d. The buffalo that killed the child last year has died.
   e. A person who doesn't work hard will not live happily.
   f. The cook who will cook the food at home is honest.
   g. The plane that is flying now belongs to Kenya Airways.
   h. The woman you saw yesterday is my sister.
   i. The pineapples that are falling are rotten.
   j. The spoons that are glittering are not mine.
   k. I who has written this book comes from Zanzibar.
   l. He has seen the broken chair.
   m. We who do not know the answer are five.
   n. Those who brought the present are few.
   o. The shops which we operate here are well known in the village.
   p. The meeting that is taking place now is very important.
   q. The clock which arrived today is new.
   r. The president who is touring the region is very famous.
   s. The dogs which will arrive tomorrow are quite fierce.
   t. The novel that I like best is *Nyota ya Rehema*.

2. Translate the following sentences:
   a. Maelfu watakaofika kesho ni wageni.
   b. Mtoto anayelia sana ni mwanangu.
   c. Samaki niliyemnunua jana ni mbovu.
   d. Ndege warukao juu sana si kunguru.
   e. Paka yule asiyekula chakula ni mgonjwa sana.
   f. Motokaa ambayo uliendesha jana ni nzuri sana.

g. Maji yanayodondoka sasa hivi ni machafu sana.

h. Mizigo isiyofika wiki ijayo ni mingi.

i. Wale ambao wanazungumza sana hapa ni wachache.

j. Mzee aliyekuja leo ni mtu bashasha.

k. Yeye asemaye maneno yale ni bakunja.

l. Yule asiyesitahi wakubwa zake hafai katika jamii yetu.

m. Ndege achukuaye vifaranga ni kipanga.

n. Mfanyakazi ambaye ataleta vitu vyako ni mtu karimu.

o. Sauti inayonguruma ni ya simba.

p. Wewe ulalaye hapa kila siku wajua shida zangu zote.

q. Mti ambao umeanguka punde hivi ni mnazi.

r. Mnyama aliyepita hapa ni farasi.

s. Mtoto anayeropoka kila mara ni Ali.

t. Mtihani uliofanya jana ni mgumu.

3. Complete the following sentences by filling in the gaps with the correct relative particle.

a. Maziwa yali _____ fika leo si mazuri

b. Mtungi uli _____ vunjika jikoni ni wangu.

c. Gari ili _____ pinduka jana ni ndogo sana.

d. Wimbo usi _____ sahaulika daima ni "Mapenzi ni Hiari".

e. Wapagazi wali _____ beba mizigo yetu ni wanne.

f. Misikiti ili _____ jengwa Arabuni ni mingi.

g. Viyoo vili _____ vunjika leo ni vikubwa.

h. Mahali pale pana _____ pa'ikana chai nyingi ni Kenya.

i. Barua zili _____ wasili leo ni zangu.

j. Wananchi wasi _____ fanya kazi kwa bidii nchini ni wengi.

k. Yule asema _____ maneno ya upuuzi ni Okello.

l. Njia ifika _____ hadi Dar es Salaam ina mashimo mengi.

m. Maswali yana _____ fika hapa kila mara ni magumu.

n. Kuta zili _____ anguka punde hivi ni kubwa.

o. Kilima kina _____ fuata sasa ni kikubwa.

p. Mlevi ana _____ lewa sana mtaani ameondoka.

q. Nguzo zili _____ kuja ni madhubuti.

r. Walimu wataka _____ pata uhamisho karibuni ni wawili.

s. Mnyama ana _____ tisha sana ni simba.

t. Nyimbo zina _____ sikikana siku hizi ni nyingi.

4. Rewrite the following sentences using the marker **amba**.

   Example:
   Kijana aliyefika leo ni Hamisi.
   Kijana ambaye amefika leo ni Hamisi.

   a. Ugonjwa unaotapakaa sana ni wa kipindupindu.
   b. Uchaguzi utakaofanywa nchini ni wa urais.
   c. Vitabu vilivyopotea karibuni sasa vimeonekana.
   d. Mpishi asiyepika vizuri hatakiwi nyumbani.
   e. Wateja wanaokuja dukani kwangu ni wengi sana.
   f. Sauti inayosikika vibaya ni yake.
   g. Mnyama asiyetisha sana ni paka.
   h. Wakulima wataikata mipapai yote isiyozaa.
   i. Mikahawa yote itakayoleta uchafu kijijini itafungwa.
   j. Funguo zote zisizofungua milango ni nyingi.
   k. Redio iliyokuja majuzi ni mbovu.
   l. Mwanajeshi aliyepata ajali ya gari wiki iliyopita sasa amefariki.
   m. Tume itakayochaguliwa na waziri karibuni inaweza kuleta manufaa makubwa nchini.
   n. Vikombe vinavyoanguka hivi sasa ni vyangu.
   o. Sahani iliyoanguka punde hivi, imevunjika vipande vipande.
   p. Mikoa itakayoshiriki katika ujenzi wa taifa ni mingi.
   q. Wazee wote wanaopata shida waende katika ofisi ya ustawi wa jamii.
   r. Blanketi lililochanika litatupwa tu.
   s. Wanariadha watakaoshinda katika michuano ya "Olympics" watapata zawadi nzuri.
   t. Meli inayopakia mizigo bandarini inaitwa "Mapinduzi".

5. Discuss the three forms of relative clauses in Swahili. Give two examples for each form.

18 Relatives II: Relatives of Time, Manner and Place

Relatives of time

The particle -po- is used to indicate the relative of time. Its equivalent meaning in English is the word "when" if used in statement form. *Ashton (1982)* describes the uses of this relative marker in two ways: as a "point" and as a "going on" in time.

The relative marker -po- is believed to derive from the locative class of **PA**. When used to express the relative of time, it is attached to the verb and thus functions as a bound morpheme. The particle -po- is, however, never attached to the **amba** marker.

The following examples illustrate the points made above:

Nilipoamka	When I woke up
Atakapoamka	When he/she wakes up
Tunapoamka	When we wake up
Walipoamka	When they woke up

In some instances, the -po- particle appears at the end of the verb instead of being affixed within it:

Uonapo, hutaamini.
When you see, you won't believe it.

To denote a persistent action, the word **kila**, literally meaning "every", is employed, preceding the verb containing the particle -po-.

Kila anapokuja, watu humzomea.
Whenever he comes, people boo at him.

Relatives of manner

The particle -vyo- as a relative is used basically to signal manner. *Ashton (1982)* mentions five uses of this relative marker, all of them being closely associated to one another: **manner, likeness, reason, cause** and **degree**, whether stated or unstated. *Wilson (1970)* points out that the relative marker -vyo- conveys the equivalent meaning of "how", "as", "like", etc. For example:

a. **Sielewi anavyopika.**
    I do not know how she cooks.

    b.   **Fanya ninavyokuambia.**
       Do as I tell you.
    c.   **Sema asemavyo.**
       Say as he does.

Certain words, as demonstrated below, are sometimes used, together with the relative particle -vyo- to convey different meanings.

    a.   **Chukua *kadiri* uwezavyo.**
       Carry as much as you can.
    b.   **Sifahamu *jinsi* anavyotenda.**
       I do not understand how he performs.
    c.   **Fuata *kama* ninavyotaka.**
       Follow as I want.

Like the -po- participle, the -vyo- marker can also be suffixed to its verb:

    Nionavyo, utafaulu.
    As I see it, you will succeed.

Syntactic position of the relative clause

The two kinds of relative clauses, that is, of time and manner, can precede or follow their main clause. For example:

    a.   **Alipokuja nyumbani, nilikuwa nimelala.**
       When he came home, I was asleep.
    b.   **Anavyofanya, sielewi.**
       How he does, I do not understand.

If we reorganize the position of the relative clause, we get:

    a.   **Nilikuwa nimelala alipokuja nyumbani.**
       I was asleep when he came home.
    b.   **Sielewi anavyofanya.**
       I do not understand how he does (it).

Usually, when the two kinds of relative clauses precede their main clause, they function as "topic" or "given". In other words, they function as the entity about which something is said. The "comment" or the "new" information is in the main clause. The "comment" or "new" information is the further statement made about this entity. (See also the section on "topic").

VOCABULARY

mada	topic	**chumvi**	salt
tia	put	**amkia**	greet
jeneza	coffin	**chunguza**	investigate
boriti	pole	**fahamisha**	explain
tukio	incident	**maringo**	boasting
ita	call	**kemea**	reprimand
abiria	passengers	**maiti**	corpse

Exercise 18a

1. Translate the following sentences:
   a. We will discuss the topic when he arrives.
   b. I will do what I can to help him.
   c. When the messengers come, we shall tell you.
   d. When I spoke to him, he agreed.
   e. They arrived last week as I said.
   f. When the old man comes here, he will want the money.
   g. Do not believe what he tells you.
   h. When the guards saw me, they greeted me.
   i. It turned out just as you said.
   j. When the bell rings, we shall enter the class.
   k. Do as you can.
   l. I shall investigate the incident when I get time.
   m. When the farmer gets the milk, he will bring it.
   n. Tell him as you saw the incident.
   o. When the sun rises, people go to work.

2. Translate the following sentences:
   a. Fanya uwezavyo.
   b. Kila wanapocheza, hufanya kelele.
   c. Niliporudi nyumbani, nilimwona mama akilia.
   d. Kwa nini hukuniita uliponiona?
   e. Vijana wale walitusaidia kadiri wawezavyo.
   f. Kama ujuavyo, kila kitu kina mwisho.
   g. Watakapokuja wapagazi kesho, watachukua mizigo hii.
   h. Nilimfahamisha yote mara tu alipowasili.
   i. Nenda utakavyo lakini mimi siyapendi hayo maringo.
   j. Gari lilipofika, abiria wakateremka.
   k. Nisemavyo sivyo nifanyavyo.

l. Jinsi anavyonikemea, hutaamini.

m. Boriti zilipoanguka, nyumba nayo ikaanguka.

n. Wanapopika mchuzi, hutia chumvi nyingi.

o. Jeneza lilipopita, watu wakasimama kutoa heshima zao kwa maiti.

Relative of place

Traditional grammars have defined the adverbial particles **PA-** as referring to some definite place, **KU-** as being more indefinite and **MU-** as being of "inside-ness" or "within-ness". Thus, by using a relative construction in the verb **kukaa** (to stay) we get the following:

ni-na-po-kaa	ninapokaa	where I am staying
u-na-po-kaa	unapokaa	where you are staying
a-na-po-kaa	anapokaa	where he/she is staying
tu-na-po-kaa	tunapokaa	where we are staying
m-na-po-kaa	mnapokaa	where you (pl) are staying
wa-na-po-kaa	wanapokaa	where they are staying

With the verb **kwenda** (to go), we can have the following kind of conjugation:

ni-na-ko-enda	ninakoenda	where I am going
u-na-ko-enda	unakoenda	where you are going
a-na-ko-enda	anakoenda	where he/she is going
m-na-ko-enda	mnakoenda	where you (pl) are going
wa-na-ko-enda	wanakoenda	where they are going

Traditional grammars point out that when the reference is of direction or motion, then we use -ko- as indicated above. Similarly, with the verb **kuishi** (to live), we can have the following forms involving the relative particle **-mo-**:

ni-na-mo-ishi	ninamoishi	where I live in
u-na-mo-ishi	unamoishi	where you live in
a-na-mo-ishi	anamoishi	where he/she lives in
m-na-mo-ishi	mnamoishi	where you (p) live in
wa-na-mo-ishi	wanamoishi	where they live in

Traditional classification of particles **po, ko** and **mo** along the parameters of definite, indefinite and "inside-ness" or motion has recently come under severe criticism from some scholars. In his doctoral dissertation, *Leonard (1982)* identifies instances of Swahili writers using the particle **ko** when the location is obviously definite and **po** when the location is not necessarily definite. Findings such as these are valid. These days, native speakers do not always make a clear-cut distinction between **po**, **ko** and **mo** particles in their speech and in writing, as was done by traditional grammars. Yet, the **mo** particle, more or less, still retains its original meaning.

19 Relatives III: The Relative With the Verbs "to be" and "to have" ("KUWA")

The particle -li-, which is different in function from the past tense marker -li-, can be classified as the verb "to be" when added to a relative particle functioning as a suffix and preceded by a subject prefix. For example:

ni-li-ye	niliye	I who am
u-li-ye	uliye	you who are
a-li-ye	aliye	he/she who is
tu-li-o	tulio	we who are
m-li-o	mlio	you (pl) who are
wa-li-o	walio	they who are

M-MI class
| u-li-o | ulio | it which is |
| i-li-yo | iliyo | they which are |

JI-MA class
| li-li-lo | lililo | it which is |
| ya-li-yo | yaliyo | they which are |

KI-VI class
| ki-li-cho | kilicho | it which is |
| vi-li-vyo | vilivyo | they which are |

N-N class
| i-li-yo | iliyo | it which is |
| zi-li-zo | zilizo | they which are |

U-U class
| u-li-o | ulio | it which is |
| zi-li-zo | zilizo | they which are |

Below are examples of how the particle -li- is used:

    a.   **Mtu aliye tayari, aseme tu.**
           Whoever is ready should say so.
    b.   **Chukua mizigo iliyo myepesi.**
           Carry the loads which are light.

c. **Ondosha nguo zilizo chafu.**
Remove the clothes which are dirty.
d. **Kuta zilizo kubwa ni chache.**
Walls which are big are few.

Present negative

The negative of the verb stem -li- is -si-. This verb follows the subject prefix but precedes the relative particle. For example:

ni-si-ye	nisiye	I who am not
u-si-ye	usiye	you who are not
a-si-ye	asiye	he/she who is not
tu-si-o	tusio	we who are not
m-si-o	msio	you (pl) who are not
wa-si-o	wasio	they who are not

M-MI class

u-si-o	usio	it which is not
i-si-yo	isiyo	they which are not

JI-MA class

li-si-lo	lisilo	it which is not
ya-si-yo	yasiyo	they which are not

KI-VI class

ki-si-cho	kisicho	it which is not
vi-si-vyo	visivyo	they which are not

N-N class

i-si-yo	isiyo	it which is not
zi-si-zo	zisizo	they which are not

U-U class

u-si-o	usio	it which is not
zi-si-zo	zisizo	they which are not

The following examples explain the concept of the present negative:

a. **Kijana asiye mwanamapinduzi hatakiwi nchini.**
A youth who is not a revolutionary is not accepted in the country.

b. **Usinunue kisu kisicho kikali.**
Do not buy a knife which is not sharp.
c. **Simba wasio wakali hawatatudhuru.**
Lions which are not fierce will not harm us.

In some situations, the particle -li- co-occurs with the negative copular **si** to express non identification. For example:

Wale walio si watoto wapo hapa.
Those who are not children are here.

The verb "kuwa"

The verb **kuwa** (to be) can also co-occur with a relative particle to refer to different tenses, as shown below:

a. **Sisi tuliokuwa tayari, tuondoke sasa.**
We who were ready should leave now.
b. **Wale watakaokuwa wagonjwa, waende hospitali.**
Those who will be sick should go to hospital.
c. **Nyinyi mnaokuwa wabishi, mnaleta matatizo mengi.**
You who are argumentative create a lot of problems.

Negation

When the verb **kuwa** (to be) is used to express a negative sentence, the particle **si** functions as a free morpheme and, is thus, not attached to any grammatical element. For example:

a. **Wewe uliokuwa si tayari, inafaa usubiri.**
You who are not ready, had better wait.
b. **Yule atakayekuwa si mtiifu, atafukuzwa kutoka katika chama.**
He or she who will be disobedient, will be expelled from the party.
c. **Mtoto anayekuwa si mtiifu kwa wazee wake, hana maana kabisa.**
A child who is not obedient to his parents, is completely useless.

VOCABULARY

| leso | handkerchief | ghali | expensive |
| sahani | plate | jambia | dagger |

rungu	club	mtabiri	fortune-teller
adhabu	punishment	-tiifu	obedient
msaliti	traitor	mtende	date tree
gunia	sack	hatimaye	eventually
gudulia	pitcher	-chafu	dirty
tetesi	rumour	halisi	true
tekeleza	fulfil	jabari	bold
wasili	arrive	kivuli	shadow
tisha	frighten		

Exercise 19a

1. Translate the following sentences:
   a. The old man who is here comes from Pemba.
   b. The handkerchiefs which are small, are mine.
   c. The pens which are expensive are his.
   d. The plate which is here is dirty.
   e. The dagger which is big is yours.
   f. The loads which are not light are many.
   g. The editor who is famous has just passed.
   h. The fortune-tellers who are clever are quite few.
   i. Do not use a cup which is not clean.
   j. They who were not obedient, will now get punishment.
   k. The date trees which are tall are few.
   l. The club which is here is mine.
   m. Those who will be traitors to their countries will suffer eventually.
   n. The umbrellas which are red have just arrived.
   o. Remove a sack which is not yours.

2. Translate the following sentences:
   a. Gudulia lililo hapa ni kubwa sana.
   b. Lugha iliyo ngumu ni Kiarabu.
   c. Chukua mizigo isiyo mizito.
   d. Yeye aliyekuwa si mzalendo halisi, atapata shida maishani.
   e. Maduka yasiyo makubwa ni mengi hapa kijijini.
   f. Fimbo iliyo mbali haiuwi nyoka.
   g. Tetesi zilizo hapa zinatutisha.
   h. Nyumba iliyo yangu imeanguka leo.
   i. Mwalimu aliye jabari shuleni ni Odongo.
   j. Usitekeleze jambo lililo gumu.

> k. Vipuri vilivyo hapa vimewasili leo.
> l. Samaki aliye mbichi ameoza.
> m. Maji yaliyo matamu ni mazuri kunywa.
> n. Miti iliyo hapa inatupa kivuli.
> o. Jembe lisilo kali halifai kulimia.

The relatives with the verb "to have"

The relative particle may refer either to the subject or to the object. Moreover, in both cases, the concept of agreement is crucial. The following is a discussion on the relative with the subject.

Present tense

M-WA class

niliye na	I who has
uliye na	you who has
aliye na	he/she who has
tulio na	we who have
mlio na	you (pl) who have
walio na	they who have

M-MI class

ulio na	it which has
iliyo na	they which have

JI-MA class

lililo na	it which has
yaliyo na	they which have

KI-VI class

kilicho na	it which has
vilivyo na	they which have

N-N class

iliyo na	it which has
zilizo na	they which have

U-U class

ulio na	it which has
zilizo na	they which have

Past simple tense

niliyekuwa na	I who had
uliyekuwa na	you who had
aliyekuwa na	he/she who had
waliokuwa na	they who had

Future tense

nitakayekuwa na	I who shall have
utakayekuwa na	you who shall have
atakayekuwa na	he/she who shall have
watakaokuwa na	they who shall have

Negation

Like in other kinds of relative clauses, the particle -si- is used for negative constructions:

M-WA class

nisiye na	I who has not
usiye na	you who has not
asiye na	he/she who has not
tusio na	we who have not
msio na	you (pl) who have not
wasio na	they who have not

M-MI class

usio na	it which has not
isio na	they which have not

JI-MA class

lisilo na	it which has not
yasiyo na	they which have not

KI-VI class

kisicho na	it which has not
visivyo na	they which have not

N-N class

isiyo na	it which has not
zisizo na	they which have not

U-U class

usio na	it which has not
zisizo na	they which have not

Other tenses

nisiyekuwa na	I who did not/shall not have
usiyekuwa na	You who did not/will not have
asiyekuwa na	He/she who did not/will not have
wasiokuwa na	They who did not/will not have

The relative with the object

When the relative particle refers to the object, it is suffixed to **na**. The object noun precedes the verb and the subject follows it. Here are some examples:

Mzigo nilio nao	The load which I have
Kikombe nilicho nacho	The cup which I have
Kengele niliyo nayo	The bell which I have
Ukurasa nilio nao	The page which I have

With the particle "amba"

The word **amba** also co-occurs with the verb "to have" but, here again, the object noun comes first, as presented below:

Kikombe ambacho ninacho	The cup which I have
Mtungi ambao ninao	The water jar which I have
Kengele ambayo nilikuwa nayo	The bell which I had
Ukurasa ambao nitakuwa nao	The page which I will have

In negative constructions, the relative particle is still suffixed to the word **na**. For example:

Kikombe ambacho sinacho	The cup which I do not have
Mtungi ambao sinao	The water-jar which I do not have
Kengele ambayo sikuwa nayo	The bell which I did not have
Ukurasa ambao sitakuwa nao	The page which I will not have

"To have" in non-relative constructions

In Swahili, the verb "to have" is added to a relative particle to signal possession even though, strictly speaking, no relative meaning is implied.

Following are some examples:

a.	**Unayo mayai?**	**Ninayo.**
	Do you have eggs?	I have.
b.	**Vijana wana vikombe?**	**Wanavyo.**
	Do the youths have cups?	They have.
c.	**Tunazo barua nyingi.**	**Tunazo.**
	We have many letters.	We have

Wilson (1970) contends that in the case of the last example, it would not be considered to be a major grammatical error to omit the relative particle. This argument only holds when that sentence stands alone. But when it is linked to a preceding sentence which has a relative particle, Wilson's contention is not valid. In other words, there would be a need to use a relative particle, as shown below:

Mnazo barua nyingi?	**Tunazo.**
Do you have many letters?	We have.

Thus, it should be argued that where no object noun follows the verb "to have", an appropriate relative particle is used. But in the negative form, the relative particle is usually deleted:

Unazo pesa?	**Sina.**
Do you have money?	I don't have.

The deletion of the relative particle -**zo** only applies when the tense is in the present simple. In other tenses, the presence of the relative particle is essential:

a.	**Walikuwa na pesa?**	**Hawakuwa nazo.**
	Did they have money?	They didn't have.
b.	**Watakuwa na pesa?**	**Hawatakuwa nazo.**
	Will they have money?	They won't have.

VOCABULARY

toweka	disappear	**adabu**	manners
lulu	pearl	**-a thamani**	precious
mchawi	witch	**mfuasi**	follower
-kali	sour	**tarafa**	division
ramani	map	**parafujo**	screw
bahasha	envelope	**hakimu**	judge

madhehebu	denomination	silaha	weapon
kambi	camp	nishati	energy
milki	property	usoni	in future
fifia	decrease		

Exercise 19b

1. Translate the following sentences:
   a. We have big camps.
   b. The baskets he has are new.
   c. The pearl I have is very precious.
   d. Have you a sharp knife? I have.
   e. The lady who has six children has visited me today.
   f. The witches who have small houses are few.
   g. Juma who had good manners has left school.
   h. The followers we have are very faithful.
   i. The oranges we had were not sour.
   j. People who have no children in this division are few.
   k. The shoes they will have are old.
   l. The parrot Bakari had, has died.
   m. Has he any property? He has.
   n. The screws they had are quite big.
   o. The envelopes we have are small.

2. Translate the following sentences:
   a. Milango tuliyo nayo ni mipana.
   b. Mahakimu watakaokuwa nao ni wazuri.
   c. Madhehebu tuliyo nayo nchini ni mengi.
   d. Wanazo silaha nyingi? Hawana.
   e. Jukumu atalokuwa nalo ni zito.
   f. Yeye ambaye amekuwa tajiri siku hizi ni mtu mwema.
   g. Viongozi walio na milki kidogo katika kijiji chetu ni watano.
   h. Meza ambazo sitakuwa nazo ni kubwa tu.
   i. Wanafunzi wasiokuwa na nidhamu mashuleni wameongezeka siku hizi.
   j. Daftari alilokuwa nalo ni dogo.
   k. Nishati iliyo nayo mtambo huu ni kubwa.
   l. Bahati nitakayokuwa nayo usoni inaweza kufifia.
   m. Mbwa asiyekuwa na mkia ametoweka punde hivi.
   n. Unazo kunde? Sina.
   o. Kitu alicho nacho ni pesa tu.

20 Derivative Verbs

This chapter discusses Swahili verbs and their conjugated forms. It has been argued by some grammars that the Swahili verb root is rich enough to allow various forms of conjugations such that numerous meanings are produced with subtle differences. Table 8 gives a summary of the derivational suffixes found in **derivative verbs**, also called **extended radicals**.

We will first examine the various forms of the derivative verbs caused by the different extension due to the principle of vowel harmony. The derivatives under discussion in this chapter are the **passive**, **prepositional**, **stative**, **causative**, **reciprocal**, **conversive** and **augmentative verbs**.

Finally, we will examine reduplication in Swahili verbs.

The passive verb

The passive voice refers to a sentence clause or verb from where the grammatical subject is typically recipient or the "goal" of the action denoted by the verb.

In Swahili, the passive verb is obtained from the simple (base) form of the verb or in one or more of the derived forms. For example:

Simple form	Derived forms
funga (close)	fungwa, fungia, fungiwa, fungisha, fungishwa

There are general rules governing passivization in Swahili. Where the verb stem ends in one vowel, the passive extension is **-w-**, also called the allomorph of the morpheme [**-W-**]. For example:

piga (beat)	pigwa (beaten)
lima (cultivate)	limwa (cultivated)

Verbs ending in **-aa**, **-ia**, or **-ua** normally take the extension **-liw-**. For instance:

kataa (refuse)	kataliwa (be refused)
fagia (sweep)	fagiliwa (be swept)
fua (hammer)	fuliwa (be hammered)

Verbs ending in **-ea** or **-oa** normally carry the extension **-lew-**. For example:

lea (bring up)	lelewa (be brought up)
komboa (redeem)	kombolewa (be redeemed)

205

Simple verb root	Simple verb endings	Passive suffix	Preposi- tional suffix	Stative suffix	Causative suffix	Reciprocal suffix	Static suffix	Conversive suffix	Augmen- tative suffix
pik-, ing-, and-, nyw-, chom-, temb-, chuk-, kan-, lew-, ogop-, takat-, fany-, pend-	-a, -u, -aa, -a, -ua, -ea, -oa	-w-, -wa-, -ew-, -iw-, -lew-, -liw-	-i-, -e- -le-, -li-,	-ik-, -ek-, -lek-, -lik-	-z-, -sh-, -ish-, -esh-, -iz-, -ez- -ny-, -vy-, -s-, -y-	-n-	-m-, -man-	-u, -o-	-u-, -o-, -sh-, -z-, -le-, -li-

Table 8: Swahili derivational suffixes (extensions)

206

A few disyllabic verbs ending in two vowels have two varieties of the passive form. One is formed from the simple form and the other from the derived form:

zaa (beget)	**zawa**	**zaliwa** (be born)
tia (put)	**tiwa**	**tiliwa** (be put)
ua (kill)	**uawa**	**uliwa** (be killed)
jaa (be full)	**jawa**	**jaliwa** (be filled/be allowed by Almighty God)

Monosyllabic verbs, only four of which are capable of being passivized, take the passive extension **-iw-** and **-ew-**. For example:

la (eat)	**liwa** (be eaten or be eatable)
cha (fear)	**chewa** (be revered)
nywa (drink)	**nywewa** (be drunk or be drinkable)
pa (give)	**pewa** (given) **pawa** in old Swahili and its Northern dialects.

Verbs of non-Bantu origin ending with **-I** or **-U** carry the extension **-iw-** resulting in the passive form. For example:

tafsiri (translate)	**tafsiriwa** (be translated)
abudu (adore)	**abudiwa** (adored)

If the ending of the simple verb is **-e**, the passive extension is **-ew-**. For example:

samehe (forgive)	**samehewa** (forgiven)

Verbs of non-Bantu origin ending in **-ua** carry the extension **-liw-** resulting in the passive form. For example:

dharau (neglect)	**dharauliwa** (neglected)
sahau (forget)	**sahauliwa** (forgotten)

The grammatical particle **na** is used to introduce the personal agent with a passive verb. For example:

Mtoto alipigwa na mama.
The child was beaten by the mother.

Normally, the instrument or means is indicated by the particle **kwa**. This particle is used when the agent is mentioned in the same sentence. For example:

Nililetwa hapa kwa gari na mjomba.
I was brought here in a car by my uncle.

Sometimes, the agent is not mentioned. In this case, the particle **na** is used to indicate the instrument or means. For example:

> **Kijana aligongwa na gari.**
> The youth was hit by a car.

VOCABULARY

mimina	pour	**azimio**	resolution
chagua	select	**kikao**	session
pindua	topple	**tii**	obey
papa	shark	**chuma**	pluck
hadithi	narrate	**-kali**	strict
karibisha	welcome	**okoa**	save
rusha	throw	**jangili**	crook
burebure	without a reason	**mtemi**	chief
ogopa	fear	**tukio**	incident
azima	borrow	**shinda**	defeat
simama	stand	**tatua**	solve

Exercise 20a

1. Give the passive forms of the following verbs:
   vaa; chuma; chagua; pindua; jibu; dhani; tii; eleza; tembea; sadiki.

2. Change the following into the passive voice:
   a. Mwanafunzi mmoja alimlaani mwalimu mkali.
   b. Juma alinihadithia kisa chenyewe.
   c. Motaboti ya polisi iliwaokoa wavuvi watano baharini.
   d. Tuliwakaribisha wageni mbalimbali kwenye dhifa kubwa.
   e. Askari atamkamata yule jangili.
   f. Mtemi aliurusha mkuki kwa ujasiri mkubwa.
   g. Kila mtu ananiogopa.
   h. Mizigo yetu ataibeba mchukuzi.
   i. Atatueleza tu matukio yenyewe.
   j. Nani ameazima kitabu changu?
   k. Amina atamshinda tu Mariamu katika mashindano ya mbio.
   l. Vijana wengi wanakusifu siku hizi.
   m. Papa amemla mtoto aliyezama baharini.
   n. Baba yangu alinilea kwa upole sana.
   o. Mtumishi ameyamimina maji yote ndooni.
   p. Nini kinakukera kila siku?

q. Wazima-moto waliuzima moto mkali usiku wa manane majuzi.
r. Wanyama kadha wa kadha waliharibu mimea katika konde zetu.
s. Mimi nimempa taarifa yote.
t. Ugonjwa wa kipindupindu uliawaambukiza wanavijiji wengi katika kijiji cha Chawino.

3. Change the following sentences into the active voice:
   a. Tulisindikizwa na wenyeji wetu.
   b. Mkutano wa mwaka wa chama utafunguliwa na rais juma lijalo.
   c. Nilikirimiwa vizuri na rafiki yako.
   d. Mshtakiwa aliamrishwa na hakimu kusimama.
   e. Chakula kitapikwa na mama kesho?
   f. Machungwa yamenunuliwa na mtumishi wangu sasa hivi.
   g. Nazi zile ziliangushwa na wakwezi wa mtaani.
   h. Kazi hii itafanywa na kila mtu.
   i. Maazimio mengi yamepitishwa leo na kikao cha halmashauri.
   j. Mgomo ulitayarishwa vizuri na viongozi wa shirika la uchapishaji.
   k. Jambo hili limeteuliwa mara moja na mzee wangu.
   l. Nilishutumiwa bure na vijana wale.
   m. Kishada kilirushwa na Jecha juu kabisa.
   n. Ushahidi wote utatolewa na mashahidi watatu.
   o. Majengo kadha yalibomolewa na wahuni wale usiku.
   p. Kitambaa changu kiliraruliwa na mshoni.
   q. Wewe unaaminiwa na kila mtu.
   r. Nimekuwa nikisumbuliwa na mapenzi ya ndani kwa ndani.
   s. Chakula chake John kimewekwa mezani na mtumishi wangu.
   t. Nyumba yangu imejengwa na waashi wanaoishi hapa hapa kijijini.

The prepositional verb

The prepositional form of a verb carries this name because the corresponding form of such a verb in English would require the use of a preposition plus a verb. Some grammarians call this form of the verb the **applied form**. *Loogman (1965)* calls it the **directive verb**.

There are several uses associated with the prepositional form. For instance, utilizing the prepositional form of a verb in the first place indicates that an action is for the pleasure or benefit of someone.

Conversely, it may also mean that it is to the detriment of someone. Here are some examples:

a. **Mchungaji alinifung*ia* punda wangu.**
The herdsman tethered my donkey for me.
b. **Basi nikaml*ia* muhogo wake wote.**
So, I ate all his cassava for him.

In example a., the concept of benefit exhibits itself. In b., there is an issue of detriment.

The prepositional form also expresses the purpose of an action indicated by the instrument used. For example:

a. **Wanataka vikombe vya kunyw*ea* chai.**
They want cups for drinking tea.
b. **Huu ni mshipi wa kuvul*ia* samaki.**
This is a fishing-line for catching fish.

In some situations, the prepositional form is used to express motion towards a particular object. For example:

a. **Mzee alilikimbil*ia* basi kwenye kituo chake.**
The old man ran off to the station to catch the bus.
b. **Watoto wanamtup*ia* mawe mwenda wazimu.**
The children are hurling stones at the madman.

There are also general rules governing the prepositional form of verbs. These rules can be summarized as follows:

Non-monosyllabic Bantu verbs which have **-a, -i,** or **-u,** in their roots carry the extension **-i** or allomorph of the morpheme [-I].

pata (get)	**patia** (get for)
pima (measure)	**pimia** (measure for)
vuta (pull)	**vutia** (pull for)

Verbs carrying **-e,** or **-o,** in their roots take the extension **-e-.** For example:

jenga (build)	**jengea** (build for)
omba (beg)	**ombea** (beg for)

Verbs ending in two vowels, namely, **-aa, -ia** and **-ua,** carry the extension **-lia.** For example:

twaa (take)	**twalia** (take for)
lia (cry)	**lilia** (cry for)
nunua (buy)	**nunulia** (buy for)

Verbs ending in two vowels, namely **-ea** and **-oa**, carry the derivational suffix **-le-**. For example:

> **tembea** (visit) **tembelea** (visit for)
> **toa** (give) **tolea** (give for)

No specific rules exist for monosyllabic verbs since the choice of vowel in the prepositional verbs is unpredictable. For example:

> **la** (eat) **lia** (eat for)
> **nywa** (drink) **nywea** (drink for)
> **cha** (adore) **chea** (adore for)
> **ja** (come) **jia** (come for)

Verbs of non-Bantu origin ending in **-e** or **-i** take an **-a**. For example:

> **samehe** (forgive) **samehea** (forgive for)
> **fikiri** (think) **fikiria** (think for)

If the ending is **-u**, the **-u** is changed to **-ia**. As indicated below:

> **hudumu** (serve) **hudumia** (serve for)

Verbs of non-Bantu origin ending in **-au** take the extension **-li-**. For instance:

> **dharau** (ignore) **dharaulia** (ignore for)
> **sahau** (forget) **sahaulia** (forget for)

In some isolated instances, prepositional verbs are formed from nouns borrowed from Arabic. For example:

> **sala** (prayer) **salia** (pray for)
> **huruma** (pity) **hurumia** (have pity on)

Finally, prepositional verbs can occasionally produce a different meaning derived from the simple verb. For instance:

> **hama** (move from) **hamia** (move to)

VOCABULARY

chimba	dig	**tanua**	expand
hukumu	judge	**tabiri**	foretell
ukame	famine	**hudumu**	serve
pita	pass	**dua**	prayer
songea	come near	**jembe**	hoe
upande	side	**burebure**	without a reason
kasirika	be angry		

211

Exercise 20b

1. Give the prepositional forms of these verbs:
chimba, kaa, tanua, kimbia, funua, kubali, sema, suka, hukumu, ondoa.

2. Rewrite the following sentences by using an appropriate prepositional form of the verb given:
   a. Tajiri aliweka dhamana mahakamani kwa ajili yetu.
   b. Yule mganga mashuhuri alitabiri kwangu kutokea kwa ukame nchini.
   c. Kijana huyu alishughulika sana kwa ajili ya wageni wetu.
   d. Wewe ulidhani kuwa mimi ni mkaidi.
   e. Nilifungua mlango ili mama yangu apite.
   f. Mshoni alishona hii nguo kwa ajili yake.
   g. Amina alisogea kwangu bila ya shida.
   h. Nitaomba dua juu yako hivi leo.
   i. Mjomba alikimbia upande wa mtoto wake.
   j. Alitafuta jembe zuri kwa ajili yangu.
   k. Mwalimu alikasirika burebure juu ya wanafunzi wake.

The stative

The stative verb characteristically takes the extension **-k-** affixed to the ending vowel **-a**. The verb consequently indicates a condition or state of being without reference to the agent or actor. For example:

   a. **Kiti kimevunjika.**
   The chair is broken.
   b. **Kamba ile imekatika.**
   That rope is split.

The stative form is also used to express potentiality when it becomes associated with other tenses and verb forms.

   a. **Kazi hii inafanyika.**
   This work can be done.
   b. **Njia ile haikupitika.**
   That road could not be passed on.

In some verbs, the potentiality is expressed by the stative extension together with the **-an-** derivational suffix. For example:

a. **Nyumba ile inaonekana.**
That house is visible.
b. **Sukari inapatikana mjini.**
Sugar is obtainable in the town.

Likewise, general principles governing stative verbs exist.

Bantu verbs carrying the vowels **-a, -i,** or **-u** in the root and ending in a consonant take the stative extension **-ik-** or allomorph of the morpheme [**-IK**]:

bana (press)	**banika** (be pressed)
pima (measure)	**pimika** (be measured)
tuma (send)	**tumika** (be sent)

If the verb root has the vowel **-e** or **-o,** the extension is **-ek-**:

tenda (do)	**tendeka** (be done)
soma (read)	**someka** (be read or readable)

When the verbs end in two vowels, namely **-aa, -ia** and **-ua,** the stative extension is **-lik-**:

kataa (refuse)	**katalika** (be refused)
shambulia (assault)	**shambulika** (be vulnerable)
nunua (buy)	**nunulika** (be bought)

If the two vowels of the verbs end in **-ea** and **-oa,** the extension is **-lek-**. For example:

tembea (stroll)	**tembeleka** (be strolled)
ng'oa (uproot)	**ng'oleka** (be uprooted)

Of the monosyllabic verbs, only the three below have stative forms:

ja (come)	**jika** (be accessible)
la (eat)	**lika** (be eaten or eatable)
nywa (drink)	**nyweka** (be drinkable)

Verbs of foreign origin, mainly from Arabic, ending in **-i,** and **-u,** take the derivational suffix **-ik-**:

tafsiri (translate)	**tafsirika** (be translated)
hudumu (serve)	**hudumika** (be served)

When non-Bantu verbs end in **-e,** the extension is **-ek-**. For instance:

samehe (forgive)	**sameheka** (be forgiven or forgivable)

And if the ending is **-ua,** the stative extension becomes **-lik-**. For example:

dharau (ignore)		dharaulika (be ignored)	
sahau (forget)		sahaulika (be forgotten)	

Some stative verbs are formed from nominal, adjectival and adverbial stems. For example:

shughuli (business affairs)		shughulika (be busy)	
safi (clean)		safika (be clean)	
imara (firm)		imarika (be firm)	

VOCABULARY

tubu	regret	zoa	pick up
taarifa	report	twaa	take
tafuna	chew	zima	extinguish
kabati	cupboard	sauti	voice
hifadhi	recite	aya	paragraph
dhambi	sin		

Exercise 20c

1. Give the stative forms of these verbs:
   a. kata   f. zoa
   b. twaa   g. gawa
   c. okoa   h. tubu
   d. fikiri   i. nyanyua
   e. rarua   j. vaa

2. Describe the two main uses of a stative verb. Give three examples for each one.

3. Rewrite the following sentences by using an appropriate stative form of the given verbs:
   a. Mimi ninaweza kukubali taarifa yako.
   b. Wazimamoto wanaweza kuzima moto ule mkubwa.
   c. Mtumishi hawezi kufua nguo hizi zote.
   d. Yule mtoto anaweza kutafuna ubani huu.
   e. Kila mtu anaweza kula chakula hiki.
   f. Mpagazi huyu anaweza kula chakula hiki.
   g. Sisi tunaweza kusikia vizuri sauti yako.
   h. Mtu yeyote anaweza kufungua kabati langu.
   i. Mimi ninaweza kuhifadhi aya hii bila ya taabu yoyote.
   j. Mungu anaweza kusamehe madhambi madogo madogo.

The causative form

The causative verb generally conveys the idea of causing an action to be done. The nature of this causation is summarised by *Ashton (1982)* thus, " ... compulsive, persuasive and helpful causation as well as simple causation."

A few rules governing causative verbs are illustrated below:

Verbs whose endings are -ka and -ta frequently acquire causative extensions of -sh- or -s- or allomorphs of the morphemes [-sh] and [-s] respectively. For example:

waka (burn)	washa (light, itch)
chemka (boil)	chemsha (make boil)
takata (be clean)	takasa (make clean)
pita (pass)	pisha (allow to pass)
pata (get)	pasa (be obliged)

Where verbs end in two vowels, the extension is normally -z-. For example:

jaa (be full)	jaza (fill)
tembea (wander)	tembeza (hawk, show around)
pungua (grow less)	punguza (reduce)
kohoa (cough)	kohoza (cause to cough)

Quite often, verbs ending in -a take causative extensions of -ish- or -esh- according to the rules of vowel harmony. For instance:

apa (swear)	apisha (put under oath)
pika (cook)	pikisha (cause to cook)
funga (fasten)	fungisha (cause to fasten)
kopa (borrow)	kopesha (lead)
sema (speak)	semesha (cause to speak)

Where the verbs end in -na, the derivational suffix becomes -ny-. For instance:

ona (see)	onya (warn)
gawana (share)	gawanya (divide)
kana (deny)	kanya (forbid)

Verbs ending in -wa take the extension -vy-. For example:

lewa (be drunk)	levya (make drunk)
jua or juwa (know)	juvya (make impertinent)
nawa (wash hands)	navya (cause to wash hands)

215

In a few cases, the extension is -iz- or -ez-:

fanya (do)	**fanyiza** (cause to do)
penda (like)	**pendeza** (impress)

Some verbs have two causative forms with no distinct meanings. For instance:

ogopa (fear)	**ogofya, ogopesha** (make afraid)
pona (get cured)	**ponya, ponyesha** (cure)

However, some verbs with two causative forms have distinct meanings. For example:

lewa (be drunk)	**levya** (make drunk)
	lewesha (get [someone] drunk)
pita (pass)	**pisha** (let through)
	pitisha (cause to pass)

A few verbs are irregular in their causative forms. For instance:

lipa (pay)	**lipiza** (revenge) or
	lipisha (cause to pay)
shika (hold)	**shikisha** (cause to hold)
weka (put)	**wekesha** (cause to put)

Monosyllabic verbs take extensions -ish- or -esh-. For example:

fa (die)	**fisha** (bring to death)
la (eat)	**lisha** (feed)
nya (rain)	**nyesha** (make rain)
nywa (drink)	**nywesha** (give to drink)

Verbs of non-Bantu origin often take extensions -ish- or -esh-. For example:

hamaki (get angry)	**hamakisha** (provoke)
dhihiri (become clear)	**dhihirisha** (make clear)
karibu (be welcomed)	**karibisha** (welcome)
abudu (adore)	**abudisha** (make adore)

Some non-Bantu verbs are also irregular in the formation of their causative forms. For instance:

sahau (forget)	**sahaulisha** (make [someone] forget)
dharau (ignore)	**dharaulisha** (cause to ignore)

Causative verbs are often formed from nominal, adjectival and adverbial roots of, especially, loan words:

bahati (luck)	**bahatisha** (guess)
hima (urgency)	**himiza** (hasten)

rahisi (easy)	rahisisha (make easy)
tayari (ready)	tayarisha (make ready, prepare)
imara (firm)	imarisha (make firm)
haraka (hurriedly)	harakisha (hasten)

VOCABULARY

penya	enter	vota	win
poa	calm	panga	hire
ugua	be ill	thubutu	dare
nyooka	be straight	adhiri	discredit, demean

Exercise 20d

1. Give the causative forms of these verbs:
   a. panga   f. penya
   b. vota   g. ugua
   c. nyoka   h. ona
   d. poa   i. safiri
   e. adhiri   j. thubutu

2. Give the simple forms of the following causative verbs:
   a. angusha   f. patanisha
   b. semeza   g. gonganisha
   c. chekesha   h. linganisha
   d. kodisha   i. rudisha
   e. legeza   j. hitimisha

3. Construct sentences to show the difference in meaning of the following causative verbs:
   a. lipisha, lipiza
   b. apisha, apiza
   c. shikisha, shikiza
   d. pitisha, pisha
   e. eleza, elewesha

The reciprocal verb

This form of a verb refers to an action or state involving two or more subjects interacting mutually for their benefit or, sometimes, to their detriment. The subjects may or may not be human beings.

Verbs ending in -a have their reciprocal forms obtained by the extension -n or allomorphs of the morpheme [-A]. For example:

fuata (follow)	**fuatana** (follow one another)
penda (love)	**pendana** (love one another)
ita (call)	**itana** (call one another)

Verbs ending in **-i, -u,** or **-e** have their reciprocal forms obtained by adding the extension **-n-** to the prepositional form rather than the simple (base) verb.

rudi (return)	**rudiana** (return to one another)
tuhumu (suspect)	**tuhumiana** (suspect one another)
samehe (forgive)	**sameheana** (forgive one another)
dharau (despise)	**dharauliana** (despise one another)

A noun or pronoun which is different from its subject in a sentence and which follows a reciprocal verb is preceded by the particle **na** (with). For instance:

a. Alifuatana **na** baba yake sokoni.
    He went to the market with his father.

b. Nilikutana **naye** dukani.
    I met him at the shop.

VOCABULARY

zomea	boo	**mfanya biashara**	business-person
mtawala	ruler	**gombana**	quarrel
tenga	separate	**-kali**	severe, harsh
jirani	neighbour	**bagua**	discriminate
harusi	marriage	**shangwe**	rejoicing
takrima	reception, warm welcome		

Exercise 20e

1. Construct sentences to show the use of the following reciprocal verbs:
    a. gombana   c. karibiana   e. shirikiana
    b. amkiana   d. ibiana

2. Rewrite the following sentences by using an appropriate reciprocal form of the verb given:
    a. Wanafunzi walimwamkia mwalimu shuleni.
    b. Saida anataka kumtenga mumewe.
    c. Kijana yule atamshonea nguo Juma.
    d. Mwenye duka alimtukana mteja mmoja kwa matusi makali.
    e. Mkulima alimwiibia jirani yake matrekta ya kulimia.

---

f. Mtawala alimbagua mtawaliwa vibaya sana.

g. Mwenyeji alimkirimu mgeni wake kwa takrima kubwa.

h. Watazamaji wa mpira waliwazomea wachezaji wawili uwanjani.

i. Sisi tutawasaidia wale wafanya biashara kwa hali na mali.

j. Musa alimwuoa mchumba wake kwa shangwe kubwa.

Other derivative verbs

There are a few less significant derivative verbs in Swahili. These are **static, conversive** and **augmentative** verbs.

The static verb

The static verb signals a stationary condition or absence of an activity. The extension used for stative verbs is -m-. For example:

funga (close, tie)	**fungama** (be in a fixed position)
ficha (hide)	**fichama** (be in a hidden situation)
unga (join)	**ungama** (be joined)
lowa (be wet)	**lowama** (be in a soaked condition)

Quite frequently, the extension -man, is used to express static forms. For example:

funga (tie, bind)	**fungamana** (be interlaced, be united)
ficha (hide)	**fichamana** (be hidden)
shika (hold)	**shikamana** (hold together)
ganda (stick)	**gandamana** (be stuck together)

The conversive verb

The conversive verb, known as the **inversive verb** [*Loogman (1965)*], gives an opposite meaning to the verb expressed in the simple form. Rules governing vowel harmony operate here, as exemplified below:

Verbs containing the vowels -a, -i, -u or -e in their roots carry the extension -u-. For example:

panga (arrange)	**pangua** (disarrange)
ziba (stop up)	**zibua** (unstop)
funga (tie, bind)	**fungua** (untie, unbind)
teleka (put on fire)	**telekua** (put off the fire)

Verbs containing the vowel -o in their roots carry the extension -o-. For example:

choma (pierce)   chomoa (draw out)
oka (put in the fire)   okoa (take from the fire, save)

The augmentative verb

In many cases, verbs containing the mentioned vowels in their roots can give an extractive meaning instead of a reversive one. For example:

nya (drop like rain)	nyesha (fall in torrents)
kama (squeeze)	kamua (squeeze out)
chimba (dig)	chimbua (dig up)
songa (press)	songoa (press together)
potea (be lost)	potelea (be lost completely)
ingia (enter)	ingilia (interrupt)

In short, the augmentative verb shows thoroughness, intensiveness, depth and continuousness of an action. These ideas are mutually exclusive but are frequently complementary.

Reduplication

Reduplication is a term used in morphology to refer to a process of repetition in which the form of the prefix or suffix reflects certain phonological characteristics of the root. This process is found in a number of languages, such as Hindi, Greek and Swahili.

In this section, we shall describe the reduplication of the verbs in Swahili. *Loogman (1965)* has mentioned the term frequentative verb to describe the type of verb which has been reduplicated. For example:

chezacheza	(play persistently)
pigapiga	(strike with repeated blows)

These two verbs indicate the repetition of an action at close intervals, or that an action is continuous over a certain period of time. The verbs are formed by the reduplication of their verb stems and only operate in situations where the verb stem is non-monosyllabic.

There are many other Swahili verbs that can be reduplicated. Below are some examples:

omba (beg)	ombaomba (pester)
sema (speak)	semasema (prattle)
chelewesha (delay)	cheleweshachelewesha (delay persistently)

In some verbs, it is possible to repeat only part of a stem:

gogota	(make a continuous tapping)
pepeta	(sift)

21 The Group

In Hallidayan grammar (systemic linguistics), the term **group** is used to refer to a unit on the rankscale intermediate between clause and word. Some grammars use the word **phrase** in place of **group**. In Swahili grammar, the term **group** is also used by grammarians, such as *Maw* (1969). They classify groups as follows:

Nominal groups

The items that fall under nominal groups are as follows:

a. Single nouns or two nouns conjoined by a coordinating conjunction.

   (i) *Mary* **amewasili.**
   Mary has arrived.
   (ii) *Mkulima* **na** *mfanyakazi* **wanakula.**
   The farmer and *the worker* are eating.

b. A noun followed by an adjective functioning as a modifier. For instance:

   (i) *Wezi wawili* **wamekamatwa.**
   Two thieves have been arrested.
   (ii) *Kijana huyu* **ni mrefu.**
   This youth is tall.

c. A noun preceded by a deictic marker functioning as a modifier. For example:

   (i) *Yule mzee* **anakera sana.**
   That old man is troubling a lot.
   (ii) *Kila mtu* **atakufa tu.**
   Every person will definitely die.

d. Pronouns. Although not normally modified, they can also be items forming nominal groups. For instance:

   (i) *Sisi* **tunashirikiana sana.**
   We are co-operating a lot.
   (ii) *Kile* **kinaniumiza vibaya.**
   That is hurting me excessively.

e. Pronouns with modifiers. For instance:

   (i) *Vyenu vyote* **ni vizuri.**
   All yours is good.

(ii) *Yule mgonjwa* **anaumwa sana.**
That sick person is very ill.

f.   A noun followed by a verbal noun. For example:

(i) *Kilimo cha kufa na kupona* **kinatekelezwa vizuri katika Tanzania.**
Large-scale agricultural production is well implemented in Tanzania.
(ii) *Kazi ya kulea* **ina taabu sana.**
Bringing up a child is a difficult task.

g.   A noun preceded by a verbal noun. For example:

(i) *Kwenda kwa miguu* **kunachosha.**
Going on foot is exhausting.
(ii) *Kula kwa kijiko* **si desturi yetu.**
Eating with a spoon is not our custom.

Identification of nominal groups

There are three tests for identifying nominal groups in a Swahili sentence. The first test is to use the passive method. For example:

Mwalimu alimpiga mwanafunzi.
The teacher beat the student.

If we passivize the sentence, the result is as follows:

Mwanafunzi alipigwa na mwalimu.
The student was beaten by the teacher.

We can argue that the nouns **mwalimu** (the teacher) and **mwanafunzi** (the student) are nominal groups because the two nouns have freely exchanged positions without destroying the grammaticality of the sentences. This would not be possible for an item which is not a noun, as can be seen in the example below:

* **Alipigwa mwanafunzi mwalimu na.**

The word **alipigwa** (he was beaten) is not a nominal group because the construction above is not acceptable in Swahili.

The second test is the **interrogative transformation.** In this test, certain interrogative pronouns, namely, **nani** (who), **nini** (which) and the **-pi** enclitic, are used to identify a nominal group in instances where passivisation cannot work at all. For example:

Kariuki amekula sasa hivi.
Kariuki has just eaten.

In this sentence, Kariuki is a nominal group. But the passive test cannot identify the nominal item because of the presence of only one noun, **Kariuki.** There is no other noun which can exchange position with it. Hence, the interrogative transformation test is employed here. For instance:

Nani amekula sasa hivi?
Who has eaten just now?

If the interrogative pronoun **nani** (who) is inserted in the initial position to transform the original sentence into a question form, the answer to this question would be **Kariuki.** This word is obviously a noun and therefore it belongs to a nominal group.

The third test is the **cleft transformation**. This means that the original sentence is transformed such that a relative particle is inserted in the full verb and it is then followed by a copular verb, normally **NI**, for the affirmative form and **SI**, for the negative. For example:

Msichana amepika wali.
The girl has cooked the rice.

By employing cleft-transformation, the new sentence would be as follows:

Aliyepika wali ni msichana.
It is the girl who cooked the rice.

In this case, the nominal group items are **wali** (rice) and **msichana** (girl) for they tell us clearly what has been cooked and who did the cooking. Likewise, we can negate this cleft sentence by using the copular verb **SI**:

Aliyepika wali si msichana.
It is not the girl who cooked the rice.

Again, the nominal group items in this example are **wali** and **msichana.** In both the affirmative and negative cleft sentences, the **who** and **what** items produce the nominal groups.

Verbal groups

The basic structure of the verbal groups in Swahili is as follows:

a. Where there is a full verb alone, sometimes called the **lexical verb**. For instance:

223

(i) **Mtumishi** *alienda* **sokoni.**
The servant *went* to the market.
(ii) *Chukua* **vikombe hivi.**
Take these cups.

b.   Where there is a full verb co-occuring with one or more auxiliaries. For example:

(i) **Mtoto** *alikuwa anaenda* **shuleni.**
The child *was going* to school.
(ii) **Wajumbe** *walikuwa wakianza* **kufika kwa wingi.**
The delegates *had been arriving* in large numbers.

c.   Where there is a copular verb functioning as a full verb. For example:

(i) **Mwalimu yule** *ni* **mkali.**
The teacher *is* strict.
(ii) **Kitabu changu** *kimo* **sandukuni.**
My book *is* in the box.

Adverbial groups

Adverbial groups are almost always adjuncts in clause structure. Adjuncts may be simple or complex. For instance:

a.   **Mwanafunzi anaimba** *vizuri.*
The student is singing *well.*
b.   **Aliondoka** *kwa vishindo vikubwa.*
He left *in a rough manner.*

In sentence (a), the adverbial group is **simple**. It is made up of a single word. In (b), the group consists of three words. Hence, we refer to this structure as **complex**. *Maw (1969)* calls it a **compound**.

Position possibilities of adverbial groups

Like adverbs, adverbial groups can also fill different positions within a clause. The following four positions are quite common:

a.   They may come first, usually to give focus to the adverbial group itself:

Kwa ukarimu mkubwa, **kijana aliwaalika wageni.**
With great generosity, the youth invited the guests.

b.   They may sometimes precede the verbal group. For example:

   (i)   **Yeye** *aghalabu* **hula wali.**
         He *generally* eats rice.
   (ii) **Mimi** *kila siku* **ninalima.**
         I cultivate *every day*.

c.   They may immediately follow the verbal group when there is no complement. For instance:

   (i)   **Mhadhiri alihutubia** *ukumbini.*
         The lecturer lectured *in the hall*.
   (ii) **Mgeni alisafiri** *jana.*
         The guest travelled *yesterday*.

d.   They may occupy the last position when there is a complement. For example:

   (i)   **Mzungu alimwona mtumishi wake** *jikoni.*
         The European saw his servant *in the kitchen*.
   (ii) **Mlinzi alimkamata mwizi** *kijasiri.*
         The guard arrested the thief *valiantly*.

VOCABULARY

pora	steal	**kitisho**	intimidation
wajibika	be accountable	**tangatanga**	roam
jifunza	learn	**kijuujuu**	superficially
fika	arrive	**kapu**	big basket
mvulana	boy	**idara**	department
tangaza	announce	**ukweli**	truth
taraji	expect	**abiri**	travel
amkua	greet	**sawazisha**	equalize
unga mkono	support	**adimika**	be scarce

Exercise 21

1.   What is the structure of a nominal group in Swahili? Give four different forms of a nominal group with three examples in each case.

2.   What tests are used to identify nominal groups in Swahili?

3. Pick out adverbial groups in the following sentences:
    a. Wezi wale wamepora bidhaa kwa vitisho vikubwa.
    b. Mimi kamwe sitakubali hilo kosa.
    c. Anatangatanga hapa na pale.
    d. Tunajifunza mashairi kwa moyo.
    e. Kijuujuu mzee yule anaelewa yale mambo.
    f. Fika haraka mwanangu.
    g. Mtalii anaweza kuwasili kwa mara ya pili.
    h. Mvua inanyesha kidogokidogo.
    i. Paka amelala chini ya kapu.
    j. Mjomba hututembelea kwa nadra.
    k. Yule mvulana kila Ijumaa ndiyo husali.
    l. Mamia kwa mamia walihudhuria mazishi ya mzee wangu.
    m. Vipuri vya magari ya Toyota vinapatikana kwa wingi.
    n. Huku na huku akanipa pesa zangu zote.
    o. Idara ya kazi imetangaza nafasi nyingi za kazi mwezi huu.
    p. Ukweli utabainika tu baadaye.
    q. Hatimaye mchezaji wa timu ya "Arsenal" alisawazisha goli kwa ufundi.
    r. Kila waziri anawajibika kikazi.
    s. Tai huruka juu kuliko mwewe.
    t. Asha anataraji wakati wowote kusafiri.
    u. Ni kweli kwamba wale wageni waliabiri katika jahazi.
    v. Askari wa mgambo walijipanga safusafu kumwamkia rais.
    w. Kwa dhati yangu, mimi nakuunga mkono.
    x. Wapagazi wanafanya kazi mchana kutwa.
    y. Siku hizi sukari imeadimika.

22 The Clause

The term **clause** has been used by some models of grammar to refer to a unit of grammatical organisation smaller than the sentence, but larger than phrases, words or morphemes.

Traditionally, a clause has been classified into two: "main" or "superordinate" and "subordinate" or "dependant" clauses. This traditional classification, however, operates along finite and non-finite parameters depending on the form of the verb used, and further divisions are sometimes made.

A clause can be a sentence in its own right or a segment of a sentence. It consists of a subject and a predicate.

In systematic linguistics, a clause comprising of a simple sentence (that is a sentence made up of a single clause) consists of structures. These structures are **subject, predicator, complement** and **adjunct**, symbolized by the exponents **S, P, C** and **A** respectively.

Generally, a clause is made up of a subject and a predicator. The other elements of structure, namely, complement and adjunct, operate only as optional grammatical items. However, in some situations, as will be illustrated shortly, complement and adjunct items can become obligatory. We will now turn to the description of these four elements of structure, as they are applicable in Swahili grammar.

Subject

All items in Swahili functioning as subjects have the following characteristics:

a. They are nominal group items, whether simple or complex, as reflected in the following examples:
    (i) *Omino* **amewasili leo.**
    Omino has arrived today.
    (ii) *Wewe* **unanisumbua sana.**
    You are pestering me a lot.
    (iii) *Kijana huyu* **anatoka Nairobi.**
    This youth comes from Nairobi.
    (iv) *Mkulima na mshauri wake* **wanalima kwa pamoja.**
    The farmer and his assistant are cultivating together.

b. They are in number concord with a subject prefix in the main verb except when that verb, occurs with an auxiliary. For example:
    (i) **Rafiki yangu *amepata* kitanda hospitali.**
    My friend is admitted in hospital.

(ii) **Yeye *a*naringa sana.**
He is boasting a lot.

(iii) **Watoto *wa*litaka kwenda kulala.**
The children wanted to sleep.

c. They are verbal noun items, whether alone or modified by a noun, an adverb or by another verbal noun. For example:

(i) *Kuiba* **hakufurahishi.**
Stealing is not welcomed.

(ii) *Kutembea kwa maringo* **kunaudhi.**
Walking pompously is abominable.

(iii) *Kuimba na kucheza kwao* **kunavutia.**
Their singing and playing is fascinating.

d. They can be adverbial group items. For example:

(i) *Haraka haraka* **haina baraka.**
Hurry hurry has no blessing.

(ii) *Polepole sana* **haipendezi wakati mwingine.**
Too much wasting of time is sometimes not welcomed.

e. They can be relative clause items. For instance:

(i) **Walimu *watakaosafiri* kesho ni wawili.**
The teachers *who will travel* tomorrow are two.

(ii) **Mtu *anayenishutumu mimi kila mara* ni John tu.**
The person *who accuses me every now and then* is only John.

f. They can be relative clause items carrying an **amba** construction. For example:

(i) *Jambo ambalo silipendi* **ni kudharau watu.**
The one thing I dislike is to ignore other people.

(ii) **Watu *ambao wamefika hivi leo* ni wageni wangu.**
The people *who have arrived today* are my guests.

Predicator

In Swahili, the predicator has the following features:

a. It is represented either by a main verb alone or by its co-occurrence at the same time with an auxiliary. For example:

(i) **John *ni* mfupi.**
John *is* short.

(ii) **Watoto** *wanaimba* **ukumbini.**
The children *are singing* in the hall.

(iii) **Mpishi** *alikuwa anapika* **wali.**
The servant *was cooking* rice.

b. It is usually in number concord with the subject. For example:

(i) **Ugonjwa** *u*metapakaa nchini.
The disease has spread in the country.

(ii) **Wavulana** *wa*meondoka sasa hivi.
The boys have just left.

c. It usually follows a subject. For instance:

(i) **Mwezi** *u*meandama.
The moon has been sighted.

(ii) **Meli** *i*tawasili kesho.
The ship will arrive tomorrow.

Complement

a. The complement is usually represented by a nominal group item which is in the objective case. For example:

(i) **Maelfu walimkaribisha** *Waziri wa Elimu.*
Thousands welcomed *the Minister of Education.*

(ii) **Mwalimu amempiga** *mwanafunzi.*
The teacher has beaten *a student.*

b. It is sometimes followed by another complement. For example:

(i) **Mwalimu amempa mtoto** *zawadi.*
The teacher has given the child *a present.*

(ii) **Mwizi alimwibia mwanamke** *mkoba wake* **jana.**
A thief robbed a woman of *her purse* yesterday.

c. It usually follows immediately after a predicator:

(i) **Kijana amekopa** *pesa.*
The youth has borrowed *money.*

(ii) **Wapagazi wataibeba** *mizigo yote.*
Porters will carry *all the loads.*

229

Adjunct

The characteristics of adjuncts are:

a. They usually consist of an adverb or an adverbial group or an adverbial relative clause. For instance:

    (i) **Mimi nitakuja *kesho*.**
         I will come *tomorrow*.

    (ii) **Wanabunge walisafiri *kwa ndege*.**
         The parliamentarians travelled *by air*.

    (iii) **Alifika *wakati nilipolala*.**
         He arrived *when I was asleep*.

b. They are usually optional. For example:

    (i) **Wakulima wanalima mpunga (sasa).**
         The farmers are cultivating rice (now).

    (ii) **Mariamu ataolewa (karibu).**
         Mariamu will get married (soon).

c. They are obligatory only after a small set of verbs, usually those of copulars of place. For example:

    (i) **Mama yangu yumo *mashakani*.**
         My mother is in *problems*.

    (ii) **Sisi tupo *hapa*.**
         We are *here*.

d. They are not in number concord with the subject, predicator or complement. For example:

    (i) **Walikuja *kwa miguu*.**
         They came *on foot*.

    (ii) **Kazi yote imekwenda *upogoupogo*.**
         The whole job has gone *awry*.

e. They may occur more than once in succession in a clause. For instance:

    (i) **Njoo *hapa kwa haraka*.**
         Come *here quickly*.

    (ii) **Msichana alipita *kule kwa madaha*.**
         The girl passed *there with pomposity*.

We can now illustrate the four clause structures and their exponents by examining the following simple sentences:

a.   **Mashua imezama.**
    S   P
   The boat has sunk.

b.   **Kila mtu yumo katika chumba chake.**
    S   P   A
   Every person is in his/her room.

c.   **Mwanamke amembeba mtoto wake.**
       S   P   C
   The woman has carried her child.

d.   **Kijana alionekana mnyonge.**
    S   P   C
   The youth looked humble.

e.   **Mimi nitamnunulia mwanangu baiskeli.**
    S   P   C   C
   I will buy a bicycle for my child.

f.   **Rubani aliendesha ndege kwa utulivu.**
    S   P   C   A
   The pilot piloted the plane carefully.

g.   **Watu watafika huku mapema.**
    S   P   A   A
   The people will arrive here early.

Kinds of clauses

A clause usually has a verb; whether it has a finite or a non-finite form of that verb and regardless of whether there is a subject or not. In traditional grammar, it was considered that a clause had to have a subject. This theory no longer holds in modern grammars.

Like in English, clauses in Swahili can be classified along two divisions: **main** and **subordinate** or **dependent clauses**. We can illustrate this division graphically:

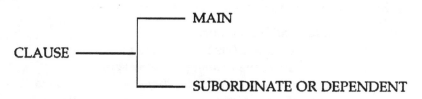

Figure 2

Subordinate clauses

Subordinate clauses possess certain properties. First of all, they do not produce an acceptable construction if a main clause is left out of a sentence. For example:

> **Mtumishi alikuwa akifyeka majani** *niliposikia kelele nyingi nje.*
> The servant was cutting grass *when I heard a lot of noise outside.*

The clause in italics is a dependent one. If it is left out, the remaining part of the sentence will still be grammatically correct because it is the main clause. Conversely, if the main clause is omitted, the remaining part of the sentence will be unacceptable.

Secondly, and this is closely associated with the first property, subordinate clauses do not convey a complete meaning if they do not co-occur with their main clause.

Thirdly, subordinate clauses are usually identified by the presence of subordinate markers, sometimes called **indicators of subordination**, such as **ingawa**, (although), **ili** (so that), **kwa vile** (because) and **kwamba** (that). A detailed description of these markers and their constraints is given in the next chapter.

Meanwhile, it is important to examine some of the examples of these dependent clauses introduced by their subordinate markers:

a. **Mkulima anasema** *kwamba* **atavuna kahawa nyingi msimu huu.**
   The farmer says *that* he will harvest a lot of coffee this season.

b. *Ingawa* **Sharifa ni hodari, lakini anaonekana mvivu sana.**
   Although Sharifa is clever, she looks very lazy.

c. **Nilikwenda mbio nyumbani** *ili* **nisije kuchelewa.**
   I ran home quite fast *so that* I would not be late.

Some of the subordinate markers are bound morphemes infixed within their verb. *Wesana-Chomi (1973)* refers to such constructions with bound morphemes as instances of **relativization**. For example:

a. **Sielewi ali*ko*tokomea.**
   I do not know *where* he has gone to.

b. **Tunamsifu sana ana*vyo*pika muhogo.**
   We admire her a lot for *the way* she cooks cassava.

c. **Seremala hatanikuta nyumbani ataka*po*fika kesho.**
   The carpenter will not find me home *when* he comes tomorrow.

Also, as will be elaborated in the next chapter, subordinate clauses can generally precede or follow their main clauses. For example:

Alipoingia chumbani, alikuta buku.
When he entered the room, he found a big rat.

The clauses of this sentence can be rearranged thus to produce an acceptable grammatical string:

Alimkuta buku alipoingia chumbani.
He found a big rat when he entered the room.

Subordinate clauses can be classified along the following divisions:

1. Embedded subordinate clauses.

The term **embedded** has been explained in the chapter on **relative clauses**. The concept of "embedded", sometimes called **rankshift**, is found in relative constructions such as the ones below:

(i) **Mpagazi [[aliyekuja jana]] anaumwa sana.**
The porter [[who came yesterday]] is very sick.
(ii) **Kikombe [[kilichovunjika sasa hivi]] ni changu.**
The cup [[which has broken just now]] is mine.

In sentence (i), the relative clause **aliyekuja jana,** (who came yesterday) is embedded in the main sentence **mpagazi anaumwa sana** (the porter is very sick). The relative pronoun marker **ye** (who) is infixed to the verb of the embedded clause and refers back to the nominal head **mpagazi** (porter). Since the embedded clause does not convey a complete meaning, we can describe that construction as a subordinate clause.

Similarly, in (ii), the construction **kilichovunjika sasa hivi** (which has broken just now) is a subordinate clause. This clause is embedded in the main sentence **kikombe ni changu** (the cup is mine). The relative particle **cho** (which) in the embedded clause refers back to the nominal head **kikombe** (cup).

In some instances, embedded clauses in Swahili are also introduced by the particles **kuwa** and **kwamba** (that). For example;

a. **Anakataa *kuwa yeye in mwongo.***
He denies *that he is a liar.*
b. **Waziri alisema *kwamba viwanda vingi vitafungwa.***
The minister said *that many factories will be closed down.*

Some grammars refer to the constructions introduced by complementisers **kuwa** and **kwamba** as **complement clauses** since they are structures which have a "completing" function for their main clauses.

Groups can also undergo rankshifts in Swahili. For example:

Kijana anayeishi [kwenye ule mlima] ni Ahmed.
The youth who lives [on that mountain] is Ahmed.

We could easily change the structure of the above sentence in the following manner:

Kijana anayekaa mlimani ni Hamisi.
The youth who lives on the mountain is Hamisi.

In this example, we find that a single word **mlimani** (on the mountain) has been used instead of the group **kwenye ule mlima** (on that mountain). Hence, we say that the group has been rankshifted.

2. Subordinate clauses of condition

Certain indicators of conditional clauses are employed in Swahili. In the affirmative sentences, the morpheme **-ki** is used. This morpheme has already been discussed at length in the previous chapters. It is, however, worth mentioning that the syntactic function of the **-ki-** marker is to signal a subordinate clause of condition. Here are some examples:

(i) *Ukienda mbio sana,* **utaanguka.**
If you run fast, you will fall down.

(ii) *Akipita muuzaji-maziwa hapa,* **nitanunua maziwa yake.**
If the milk seller passes here, I will buy his/her milk.

In some situations, a subordinate clause of condition can also be formed by using the word **kama** (if) in the initial position and infixing an appropriate tense marker in the verb. For example:

(i) *Kama atalala sasa hivi,* **basi atakosa chakula chake baadaye.**
If he sleeps now, he will miss his food later.

(ii) *Kama ulikuja jana,* **basi labda ilikuwa jioni.**
If you came yesterday, it was probably in the afternoon.

Sometimes, a subordinate clause of condition is also introduced by the word **endapo**, meaning "if", "in case of" or "when it happens":

(i) *Endapo kaondoka kesho,* **nitakuarifu haraka.**
If he leaves tomorrow, I will inform you immediately.

(ii) *Endapo rais amestaafu,* **nani atachukua nafasi yake?**
If the president retires, who will succeed him?

234

Again, conditional clauses are expressed by the grammatical particles **nge,** **ngeli** and **ngali** to introduce what some grammars call the **suppositional condition.** For example:

(i) **Ningemwambia ile habari, angefurahi sana.**
If I would have told him the news, he would have been very pleased.
(ii) **Ingelianguka theluji, tungelisikia tu.**
If it would have snowed, we would have certainly heard.

Maw (1985) regards these constructions as instances of **interdependence.** (See also Chapter 18).

In negative sentences, the subordinate clause of condition is introduced by the marker **-sipo-.** For example:

(i) *Usipolala mapema,* **nitakupiga sana.**
If you do not sleep early, I will beat you severely.
(ii) *Nisipoenda kesho,* **nitaikosa kazi.**
If I do not go tomorrow, I will miss the work.

Similarly, using the word **kama** in the initial position and prefixing an appropriate negative marker in the verb can also introduce a subordinate clause of condition. For example:

(i) *Kama haji hapa,* **nitamlaumu sana.**
If he doesn't come here, I will blame him a lot.
(ii) *Kama sisomi sana,* **sitafaulu mtihani.**
If I do not work hard, I will not pass the examination.

Alternatively, we can insert the negative morpheme **-si-** immediately after the subject prefix to express negation of suppositional condition forms, thus:

(i) **Usingekuja hapa, usingemwona shangazi yako.**
If you would not have come here, you would not have seen your aunt.
(ii) **Asingelala mapema, angechelewa kuamka.**
If she would not have slept early, she would have woken up late.

3. Subordinate clauses of cause (reason)

Subordinate clauses of cause or reason are most commonly introduced by the conjunctions **kwa sababu, kwa vile, kwani, kwa kuwa** and **kwa maana,** all of which mean "because", "for", "the reason being", "as" and "since". For example:

(i) **Alikuja hapa kwa miguu** *kwa sababu alikosa usafiri.*
He came here on foot *because he missed transport.*

(ii) **Mimi sitaweza kuja kwenye dhifa yako** *kwa vile mama ni mgonjwa nyumbani.*
I will not attend your party *as my mother is sick at home.*

(iii) **Wakulima watafika kesho hapa** *kwani wanataka kuonana na mkurugenzi wa kilimo.*
The farmers will come here tomorrow *because they want to see the director of agriculture.*

(iv) *Kwa kuwa umeanguka vibaya kwenye mtihani wako,* **itakubidi uurejee mwaka.**
Because you have failed badly in your examination, you will have to repeat the year.

(v) **Mzazi alimpiga mwanawe** *kwa maana hana adabu hata kidogo.*
The parent beat his son *because he does not have good manners at all.*

Clauses introduced by infinitive forms can also be used for cause or reason even with the absence of a conjunction. For example:

(i) *Kujiona amechoka sana,* **akaamua kulala.**
Seeing that he was tired, he decided to sleep.

ii) *Kuona hakuna mpishi yoyote jikoni,* **akaanza kupika chakula mwenyewe.**
Seeing that there was no cook in the kitchen, he began to cook the food himself.

Sometimes, clauses of reason can be in the form of a relative construction. *Wesana-Chomi (1974)* refers to such constructions as the **relative reason clause.** For example:

(i) **Vijana wengi walimstahi na kumpenda** *kwa vile alivyokuwa mzuri kwa sura.*
Many young people respected and loved her *as she was beautiful.*

(ii) **Kwa ujumla, uchunguzi huu haukuwa mrefu** *kwa vile ambavyo ushahidi uliokuwa katika kinasasauti* **ulikuwa madhubuti.**
All in all, the hearing was not long *as the evidence which was on the tape was strong.*

4. Subordinate clauses of concession

Subordinate clauses of concession are introduced mainly by expressions such as **ingawa**, **ijapokuwa**, **ingawaje**, **japo** and **hata kama** to provide contrasts in the two propositions in a sentence. All the expressions carry the equivalent meaning of "although", "though", "albeit" and "even if". For example:

(i) *Ingawa aliniita sana,* lakini sikusikia kabisa.
   Although he called me loudly, I did not hear at all.
(ii) **Msichana yule ni mkarimu sana** *ingawaje ni mvivu.*
   That girl is very generous *although she is lazy.*
(iii) *Hata kama anaumwa,* basi tuarifiwe.
   Even if he is sick, we should be informed.

Other subordinate markers of concession include phrases such as **hata ikiwa** (even if) and **wakati ambapo** (whereas). They are utilised as follows:

(i) *Hata ikiwa ni mjinga,* uaminifu lakini anao sana.
   Even if he is stupid, at least he is honest.
(ii) *Wakati ambapo Zaghlul anaonekana mzalendo halisi,* **ndugu yake ni msaliti.**
   Whereas Zaghlul seems to be a true nationalist, his brother is a traitor.

5. Subordinate clauses of purpose

Subordinate clauses of purpose are introduced by indicators such as **ili**, **kusudi** and **ili kwamba**, corresponding in meaning to English terms such as "so that", "in order that" and "so as to". For example:

(i) **Niliondoka mapema** *ili niliwahi gari la moshi.*
   I left early *so as to catch the train.*
(ii) **Askari alimjongelea mwizi** *kusudi amkamate.*
   The policeman approached the thief *so as to catch him.*

In the purpose clause, the subjunctive form of the verb can also be used as in sentence (ii) above.

Sometimes, the indicators are optionally omitted if the main clause is in the imperative form. For example:

(i) **Mwite (ili) niseme naye.**
   Call him (that) I may speak to him.
(ii) **Waite vijana (ili) wakusaidie kazi.**
   Call the youths to help you do the work.

Clauses of purpose are negated by inserting a negative copular **-si-**. For instance:

(i) **Soma kwa juhudi** *usije ukashindwa.*
Study hard *lest you fail.*
(ii) **Ondoka hapa kwa haraka** *usije ukakamatwa.*
Leave here immediately *lest you be arrested.*

6. Subordinate clauses of time (temporal clauses)

Being indicators of time, this group of subordinate clauses are introduced by terms like **mpaka** (until), **baada ya** (after), **tangu** (since) and **kabla ya** (before). For example:

(i) **Watoto watakwenda shuleni** *mpaka wakue kabisa.*
The children will go to school *until they are fully grown.*
(ii) **Alirudi nyumbani** *baada ya kumaliza kazi.*
She returned home *after finishing the work.*
(iii) *Tangu aje hapa,* **amekuwa akiudhi watu tu.**
Since he/she arrived here, he/she has only been pestering people.
(iv) *Kabla ya mgeni kuondoka,* **takriban watu wote walipeana naye mkono.**
Before the guest left, almost all the people shook hands with him.

Earlier chapters have shown that the particle **-po-** is a relative marker of time. Therefore, the syntactic function of this marker is to introduce a subordinate clause of time. This grammatical particle is inserted within the verb. For example:

(i) *Ulipoondoka,* **mvua ikaanza kunyesha.**
When you left, it started raining.
(ii) *Nilipokuwa nikisema,* **mgeni akaingia.**
When I was speaking, a guest came in.

7. Subordinate clauses of place

Subordinate clauses of place are indicated by the relative markers **-ko-**, **-po-** and **-mo-**. Each of the grammatical particles are used according to the area the speaker wishes to particularize. For example:

(i) **Hatufahamu** *alikokwenda msafiri.*
We do not know *where the traveller has gone to.*

(ii) *Alipokamatwa yule mwizi* ni mbali sana.
Where that thief has been arrested is quite far.

(iii) **Kuna kitanda kikubwa** *chumbani anamolala.*
There is a big bed *in the room he sleeps in.*

8. Subordinate clauses of manner

Again, on the chapter of relatives, it was pointed out that the particle -vyo- is used basically to indicate manner. Thus, subordinate clauses of manner are identified by the presence of this relative marker infixed within the verb. For example:

(i) **Sipendi** *anavyokula.*
I do not like *the way he eats.*

(ii) **Pika** *unavyopenda.*
Cook *as you like.*

Sometimes, subordinate clauses of manner are introduced by words such as **kama** (like) and **kadiri** (as many as) with the particle -vyo- inserted within the verb. For instance:

(i) **Sema** *kama alivyosema.*
Say *as he did.*

(ii) **Chukua mizigo hii** *kadiri uwezavyo.*
Carry these loads, *as many as you can.*

Likewise, subordinate clauses of manner are also introduced by the complementizer **ya**. For instance:

(i) **Hajui jinsi** *ya kufanya kazi yangu.*
He does not know the method of doing my work.

(ii) **Tulikuwa tunafikiri** *jinsi ya kumwongoza kijana yule.*
We were thinking the way *of guiding that youth.*

9. Subordinate clauses of result

Subordinate clauses of result are introduced by the words **hata** (so that) and **mpaka** (till). For example:

(i) **Tulipanda maua mengi mno** *hata bustani ikapendeza hatimaye.*
We planted many flowers *such that the garden ultimately looked beautiful.*

(ii) **Mwanariadha alikimbia mbio mno** *mpaka mwisho akaanguka.*
The athlete ran so fast *that he eventually fell down.*

10. Infinitive subordinate clauses

Subordinate clauses in this group are introduced by the infinitive **ku-**, thus indicating the non-finite form of a clause which is subjectless. For example:

(i) **Mtumishi ameenda sokoni *kununua samaki*.**
The servant went to the market *to buy fish*.

(ii) ***Kukaa tu*, wageni wakatokea.**
Soon after he took a seat, the guests appeared.

Main clauses

A main clause is an independent one. In other words, it can stand on its own as a sentence. It can also be argued that a main clause conveys a complete meaning even if the subordinate clause is left out. For example:

(i) ***Saida alikuwa akiimba* kabla ya sisi kufika ukumbini.**
Saida was singing before we arrived in the hall.

(ii) ***Nitakulaumu sana* kama hukuja kesho.**
I will blame you a lot if you do not come tomorrow.

In sentence (i), the main clause is **Saida alikuwa akiimba** (Saida was singing). In (ii), the main clause is **Nitakulaumu sana** (I will blame you a lot). Both these clauses have meaning even if their subordinate clauses are omitted.

Main clauses in Swahili can be subdivided into the following classes.

1. Interrogative

These clauses contain a question word or a morpheme for asking a question although this may not be necessary in some instances. For example:

(i) **Watu wangapi wamefika?**
How many people have arrived?

(ii) **Je unaipenda lugha ya Kirusi?**
Do you like the Russian language?

2. Imperative

In the following clauses, there is a verbal item which does not have a subject.

(i) **Njoo hapa upesi.**
Come here quickly.

(ii) **Tafadhali pika viazi baadaye.**
Please cook potatoes afterwards.

(iii) **Ondosheni kila kitu.**
Remove everything.

In sentence (iii), the suffix **-eni** is added to the verbal root **ondosha** (remove) to pluralize the sentence.

3. Declarative
There are three sub-classes of declarative sentences: **verbal, copular** and **zero-predicated** forms.

4. Verbal sentences
In these clauses, there are main verbs which are either subject-marked or carry a habitual marker **hu**. For example:

(i) **Mwalimu anafundisha wanafunzi.**
The teacher is teaching students.
(ii) **Huja hapa kila siku.**
He comes here every day.

5. Copular sentences
The clauses of this sub-class contain a copular which functions as a full verb in a sentence. For example:

(i) **Yeye ni kijana mrefu.**
He is a tall youth.
(ii) **Hawa si wageni kabisa.**
These are not strangers at all.

6. Zero-predicated sentences
These clauses do not carry any verbal item although they may have a subject and a complement, or even an adjunct in some cases. For example:

(i) **Mimi mpumbavu!**
I am stupid!
(ii) **Yeye mfupi sana.**
He is very short.

In some restricted conditions, it is possible to find that the subject and the verbal item are omitted in the subordinate clause. For example:

Hata kama masikini, **yeye anawaheshimu watu vizuri.**
Even if poor, he respects people well.

Here, we find that the subject **yeye** (he) and the copular verb **ni** (is) have been left out in the subordinate clause **Hata kama masikini** (although poor). Grammarians refer to this construction as a **verbless clause**.

In situations where the verbless clause has a subject, only the verb is retrieved. For example:

Kwa ujumla, watu hamsini walizama mtoni, *wengi wao wanawake.*
Altogether, fifty people were drowned in the river, *many of them women [many of whom were women].*

VOCABULARY

simama	stand	**vua**	fish
machachari	restive, restless	**wasaa**	time
thakili	cruel	**kemea**	blame
kihori	a small canoe	**fufua**	revive
kikwelikweli	genuinely	**nunda**	wild
rejesha	return	**tafuta**	seek
harufu	smell	**haribu**	spoil
tabia	custom	**jaza**	fill
kibaba	measure	**dawa**	medicine
potea	miss	**katibu-muhtasi**	private secretary
uangalifu	care		

Exercise 22

1. Differentiate between subordinate and main clauses. Give three examples of each.

2. Discuss with examples the differences and relationships between the following concepts:
   a. subject
   b. predicator
   c. nominal group
   d. verbal group

3. Analyse the following clauses by giving their elements of structure. For example:
   Kikombe changu ni kidogo.

S	P	C
My cup	is	small.

   a. Askari alisimama wima uwanjani.
   b. Pika chakula vizuri.

c. Leo asubuhi katibu-muhtasi wangu amesafiri.

d. Basi yule kijana ni machachari tu.

e. Sina wasaa hata kidogo.

f. Yule mzee ni thakili ajabu.

g. Kwa nini mzee unamkemea mwanao kila mara?

h. Kihori chetu kilitaka kuzama upande mmoja.

i. Nchi za Afrika zimeazimia kikwelikweli kufufua uchumi wao.

j. Yule bawabu anamchumia bwana wake maua.

k. Paka wako aliyekuja hapa ni nunda.

l. Pesa zako nimekurejeshea.

m. Mimi nitaitafuta elimu kila mahali.

n. Yale maua yenye harufu nzuri ni yangu.

o. Redio hii ameiharibu Tom.

p. Kula kwa kijiko si hulka yetu nyumbani.

q. Haba na haba hujaza kibaba.

r. Dawa daktari wangu alinipa majuzi.

s. Sanduku langu limepotea tangu wiki jana.

t. Wavuvi huvua samaki kwa uangalifu mkubwa.

23 The Sentence

The sentence was first described by traditional grammars as a unit with the expression of a complete thought. Later grammars qualified the traditional definition and began to think in terms of structural independence or autonomy of this unit, thus reflecting the influence of the American linguist Leonard Bloomfield, who described the sentence along the same lines. The sentence has also been described as the largest unit about which grammatical statements are made. Recent research by some scholars, however, has attempted to discover larger grammatical units such, as paragraph and discourse, but so far, little has been achieved compared to the sentence, whose constituent structures can be stated in formal and distributional terms.

Simple sentences

Sentences in Swahili (like in English) can consist of a single clause. Such units are called **simple sentences** since they are made up of only one clause. For instance:

    a.   **Kijana ameenda sokoni.**
        The youth has gone to the market.
    b.   **Mvua labda itanyesha leo jioni.**
        It will probably rain this afternoon.

Both sentences a. and b. above consist of only one verb. In a., the verb is **enda** (go) and in b., it is **nyesha** (rain).

    Simple sentences can also be described in terms of mood. They are all in active voice indicated by the suffix **-a** in the verb stems of Bantu origin. For example:

    a.   **Owuor anacheza kabumbu sasa.**
        Owuor is playing soccer now.
    b.   **Miti hii ilianguka jana.**
        These trees fell down yesterday.

In non-Bantu verbs, the last vowels, as was seen in the preceding chapters, are **i, e** and **u**. They are reflected in the following sentences:

    a.   **Mwanafunzi anadurusu masomo yake.**
        The student is revising his lessons.
    b.   **Mbona unafikiri sana siku hizi?**
        Why are you thinking a lot these days?
    c.   **Mwalimu amemsamehe mwanafunzi.**
        The teacher has forgiven the student.

   d.   **Nimesahau kalamu yangu shuleni.**
       I have forgotten my pen in school.

Complex sentences

Complex sentences consist of only one main clause and at least one subordinate clause. For example:

   a.   **Ikinyesha mvua kesho, hatutaenda shuleni.**
       If it rains tomorrow, we will not go to school.
   b.   **Ingawa Chumu ni mnene lakini anaweza kukimbia vizuri, kwa vile hufanya mazoezi ya mwili mara kwa mara.**
       Although Chumu is fat, he can run well because he frequently performs physical exercises.

Sentence (a) is made up of one main clause, the other being a subordinate one. In (b), there is also one main clause but subordinate clauses are two. Thus, constructions (a) and (b) are said to be **complex sentences**.

     The term **subordinate clause** seems to refer to the function played by an embedded sentence. In such cases, the function of such a sentence is to modify the matrix constituent in which it is specifically embedded.

Subordination

The two examples illustrated above show that clauses of unequal status have been linked together to form a complex sentence. We are arguing that the clauses are not of equal status because one is a main clause and the others are subordinate to it. This process of conjoining clauses of unequal rank to form a sentence is called **subordination**. Some grammars refer to this process as **hypotaxis** or **hypotactic** structures.

Markers of subordination

In Swahili, various exponents or markers are used to explain each concept of subordination. These markers introduce a dependent clause which can convey different meanings: reason, purpose, condition, time, result, volition, etc. We shall now examine these markers of subordination and the meanings they convey by examining the following sentences:

   a.   **Mwanafunzi alipigwa *kwa sababu* alikuwa akifanya kelele darasani.**
       The student was beaten because he was making noise in the class.
   b.   **Wakulima wanalima *ili* raia wapate chakula.**
       The farmers cultivate so that the citizens can get food.

c. *Kama* **waziri atafika kijijini kesho, wanavijiji wengi watakwenda kumpokea.**
   If the minister arrives in the village tomorrow, many villagers will go to receive him.

d. *Tangu* **kijana yule afike hapa, amekuwa akijaribu kunikera kila mara.**
   Ever since that youth arrived here, he has been trying to pester me every now and again.

e. **Mwanariadha alikimbia mbio mno** *hata* **akaanguka.**
   The athlete ran so fast that he fell down.

f. **Dawo atacheza mpira leo** *ingawa* **ni mgonjwa.**
   Dawo will play football today although he is sick.

In sentences a., the subordinate marker **kwa sababu** (because) gives the sense of reason. In b., the word **ili** (so that) shows purpose and in c., we get the sense of condition because of the word **kama** (if). In d., the subordinate marker **tangu** (ever since) conveys the notion of time dimension. The remaining subordinate markers **hata** (so that) and **ingawa** (although) in e. and f. indicate result and volition respectively.

There are other subordinate markers in Swahili, such as **kwa vile** (because), **kwamba** (that), **endapo** (if), **ijapokuwa** (although) and **madamu** (since).

In the previous chapter, it was pointed out that some instances of subordinate clauses are identified by bound morphemes infixed within their verb. These bound grammatical particles convey various meanings: time, manner and place. For instance:

a. **Kaka yangu ali***po***ingia chumbani, akamkuta mtumishi tu.**
   When my elder brother entered the room, he saw only the servant.

b. **Sipendi hata kidogo msichana yule ana***vyo***tembea.**
   I do not like at all the way that girl walks.

c. **Hatuelewi hata chembe tuna***ko***kwenda.**
   We do not know at all where we are going.

The bound morphemes **-po-**, **-vyo-** and **-ko-** in sentences a., b. and c. above indicate time, manner and place respectively.

Order of subordinate and main clauses

There is no fixed order for the position of subordinate clauses although some guidelines can be given. Generally, conditional clauses precede the main ones. For example:

a. **Kama atakuja kesho, tutampasha habari.**
If he comes tomorrow, we will inform him.

b. **Ikiwa mwezi utaandama kesho, basi Waislamu wote nchini watafunga tu.**
If the moon is sighted tomorrow, all the Muslims will definitely fast.

However, subordinate clauses of purpose, reason and volition usually follow the main verb. For example:

a. **Wananchi walipiga kura ili wapate kumchagua rais mpya.**
The people voted so that they could choose a new president.

b. **Baba alinipiga kwa kuwa nilivunja vikombe.**
My father beat me because I broke the cups.

c. **Wanafunzi walifaulu mtihani ingawa hawakufanya kazi kwa bidii.**
The students passed the examination although they did not work hard.

The order governing subordinate clauses can change if they are intended to provide topics for their sentences. Thus, we can say this for the subordinate clauses of purpose, reason and volition. For example:

a. **Ili wapate kumchagua rais mpya, wananchi walipiga kura.**
In order that they may choose a new president, the people voted.

b. **Kwa kuwa nilivunja vikombe, baba alinipiga.**
Because I broke the cups, my father beat me.

c. **Ingawa hawakufanya kazi kwa bidii, wanafunzi walifaulu mtihani.**
Although they did not work hard, the students passed the examination.

The subordinate clauses (a) to (c) above are quite acceptable in Swahili grammar although they stand in the initial position. Here, these clauses function as topics of their discourse.

Similarly, it can be argued that temporal subordinate clauses which occur in the initial position also function as topics for their sentences, as in the examples below:

a. **Alipoingia darasani tu, yule mwanafunzi akaanza kupiga kelele.**
When he had just entered the classroom, the student started making noise.

247

b. **Mvua ilipokwisha, sisi tukatoka nje.**
When it stopped raining, we went out.

Yet, in some subordinate clauses, this flexibility does not work at all. For example, in expressions with the subordinate conjunction **kuwa** and **kwamba**, both meaning "that", the main clause must come in the initial position:

a. **Kijana alisema kwamba atakuja kesho sokoni.**
The youth said that he will come to the market tomorrow.
b. **Mimi ninaamini kwa dhati kuwa timu ya Cameroon inaweza kulitwaa Kombe la Dunia siku moja.**
I sincerely believe that Cameroon can grab the World Cup one day.

It is evident from these sentences that the subordinate expressions must follow their main clauses.

Compound sentences

Compound sentences consist of at least two main clauses. For example:

a. **Nitamwita msichana yule hapa au pengine nitamweendea kule.**
I will call that girl to come here or I will probably go to see her there.
b. **Hamisi ni mwongo tena ni mwizi mkubwa.**
Hamisi is a liar and, furthermore, he is a real thief.

Both sentences a. and b. have two main clauses joined by coordinating conjunctions **au** (or) and **tena** (in addition) respectively. The clauses in each sentence are therefore of equal status. They have identical structures. Such constructions of equivalent forms are referred to in modern grammars as **paratactic structures**. In traditional grammar, they would be referred to as **compound sentences**.

Compound sentences can also exist in situations where there is a subordinate clause, besides two main clauses, as indicated in the examples below:

a. **Mkulima analima na labda atavuna karibu kwa kuwa shamba lake lina rotuba nyingi.**
The farmer is cultivating and probably he will harvest soon because he has a fertile plantation.
b. **Mpishi yule anapika chakula wakati sisi sote tumelala na anapakua chakula na kukila chote wakati sisi tunataka kuamka.**
That cook cooks the food when we are all asleep and dishes up the food and eats it all when we are about to wake up.

Similarly, in examples a. and b., there are two main clauses joined by the coordinating conjunction **na** (and) together with a subordinate clause in each sentence.

Interdependent constructions

Interdependent constructions occur in the following situations:

a. When each verb in the construction gives a complete meaning of the action taking place.
b. When each verb in the construction takes the tense markers -NGE- or -NGALI- or -NGELI-. As *Maw (1969)* has also pointed out, these tense markers function as exponents of interdependence. For example:

    (i)   **Ungekuja, ungekiona.**
        If you had come, you would have seen it.
    (ii) **Angalikuwa tajiri, angalitusaidia.**
        If he were rich, he would have helped us.
    (iii) **Ningeliondoka hapa, wanafunzi wangelipiga kelele.**
        If I had left here, the students would have made noise.

c. The use of one form of the tense marker in one construction necessitates the use of a similar or different form of the tense markers in another construction. For example:

    (i)   **Wangalilala mapema jana, wangaliamka pia mapema.**
        If they had slept early yesterday, they would have woken early.
    (ii) **Ungepika muhogo leo, mimi ningeliula wote peke yangu.**
        If you had cooked cassava today, I would have eaten all of it.

Appositional constructions

Appositional constructions are sequences of units which are constituents at the same grammatical level, and which have an identity or similarity of reference. For example:

    Ali Mzee, mchinja nyama, atawasili hapa kesho.
    Ali Mzee, the butcher, will arrive here tomorrow.

In the example above, we have two nominal groups, **Ali Mzee** and **mchinja nyama** (the butcher) all possessing an identity of reference and a similar syntactic function.

In other words, each nominal group can be used in the same sentence above without affecting the notion of acceptability. For example:

a. **Ali Mzee atawasili hapa kesho.**
Ali Mzee will arrive here tomorrow.
b. **Mchinja nyama atawasili hapa kesho.**
The butcher will arrive here tomorrow.

In the previous chapter, we described the various kinds of clauses in a sentence. In this chapter, we have described the elements of these clauses in a sentence.

First of all, it should be realized that a main clause is symbolized by Alpha (α), while the nearest dependent clause to Alpha is symbolized by Beta (β).

Another dependent clause on Beta is Gamma (G). The clause dependent upon Gamma is Delta (δ) and so on. In brief, a sentence, can have a main clause joined by dependent clauses symbolized by β, δ, δ ...

The following examples are presented below to illustrate this point:

a. **Sikufika darasani jana kwa vile nilikuwa mgonjwa.**
I did not come to class yesterday because I was sick.
b. **Rafiki yangu alipofika jana nyumbani, nilikuwa nimelala kwa sababu nilikuwa nimechoka sana.**
When my friend arrived at home yesterday, I was asleep because I was very tired.
c. **Wazee wanalima na huku watoto wanawasaidia.**
The parents are cultivating and their children are helping them.

Sentences a. and b. above are instances of subordination symbolized by β and δ. But in c., there is an instance of coordination, sometimes called **linkage** symbolized by α.

VOCABULARY

njia	road	ufokoni	to the shore
kichochoro	alley	kwa pupa	hastily
amuru	instruct	kusudia	intend
kadhia	report	maonevu	injustices
karibisha	welcome	vuta	pull
nguvu	power	rudi nyuma	retreat
-kaidi	obstinate	chukia	dislike
hatari	danger	-embamba	narrow
hama	vacate	mbeleni	ahead
nyakua	snatch	timu	team

250

Exercise 23

1. Explain and give two examples of each of the following concepts:
   a. subordinate clause
   b. compound sentence
   c. interdependent constructions
   d. appositional constructions

2. Identify the clause boundaries of the following sentences by using appropriate markers. For example:

   Sielewi hata kidogo kama mama atawasili kesho.
   I do not understand at all if my mother will arrive tomorrow.

   Sielewi hata kidogo // kama mama atawasili kesho.

   a. Nenda njia hiyohiyo wala usirudi nyuma.
   b. Akija hapa kwa pupa, atakosa kila kitu.
   c. Kichochoro kile ni chembamba sana tena ni kichafu.
   d. Ingawa umekusudia kuniadhibu lakini mimi sitakubali hata kidogo kwa sababu haya ni maonevu.
   e. Ule ni mti ambao ulianguka jana.
   f. Usiponieleza kadhia yenyewe, nitasikitika sana.
   g. Tuliteremka chini kuwakaribisha wageni.
   h. Utastaajabu ukimwona njiani anavyotembea.
   i. Fanya hilo jambo upesi wala usirudi nyuma.
   j. Alipoondoka, alikwenda zake nyumbani kuonana na wazee wake.
   k. Kwa jinsi ninavyokupenda nitakusaidia tu ingawa hutapenda mimi kufanya hivyo.
   l. Kula wanakula hata ikiwa kidogokidogo.
   m. Rudi hapa upesi kabla sijakupiga.
   n. Serikali ina nguvu kwani ikitaka kufanya jambo basi itafanya tu hata kama raia watachukia.
   o. Wewe ndiyo tu mtu mkaidi lakini ndugu yako ni mtiifu sana.
   p. Rubani aliamuru kwamba abiria katika ndege wafunge mikanda yao vitini kwa vile hatari ilikuwa mbeleni.
   q. Ukitaka usitake utaihama tu nyumba hii.
   r. Lipi linakukera mwanangu?
   s. Maelfu kwa maelfu waliisherehekea timu ya "Simba" iliponyakua "Kombe la Washindi" hivi majuzi.
   t. Wavuvi hutega nyavu zao kunapokuchwa na huzivuta ufukoni kunapokucha.

References

Abdul Aziz, M. (1971). "Tanzania's National Language Policy and the Rise of Swahili Political Culture." In *Language Use and Social Change*, edited by W. Whitely. Nairobi: Oxford University Press.

Ashton, E.O. (1982). *Swahili Grammar (Including Intonation)*. London: Longman, Green and Co. Ltd.

Berry, M. (1975). *An Introduction to Systematic Linguistics I: Structures and Systems*. New York: St. Martins Press.

Brain, J.L. (1977).*Basic Structure of Swahili*. Syracuse University.

Halliday, M.A.K. and R. Hasan (1976). *Cohesion in English*. London: Longman.

Halliday, M.A. (1985). *An Introduction to Functional Grammar*. London: Edward Arnold Publishers Ltd.

Kapinga, M.C. (1983). *Sarufi Maumbo Ya Kiswahili Sanifu*. Dar es Salaam: Institute of Kiswahili Research, University of Dar-es-salaam.

Keach, C.N. (1980). "The Syntax and Interpretation of the Relative Clause Construction in Swahili." Ph.D. Dissertation, University of Massachusetts.

Khamis, A.M. (1972). "A Consideration of Grammatical Roles in Swahili." Ph.D. Dissertation, University of York.

Leonard, R. (1982). "The Semantic System of deixis in Standard Swahili." Ph.D. Dissertation, Columbia University.

Loogman, A. (1965). *Swahili Grammar and Syntax*, Duquesne Studies - African Series Editions. Pittsburg, P.A.: Duquesne University Press.

Maw, J. (1969). *Sentences in Swahili: A Study of their Internal Relationships*. Surrey, England: The Gresham Press.

Maw, J. and J. Kelly (1975). *Intonation in Swahili*. London: University of London.

Maw, J. (1985). *Twende! A Practical Swahili Course*. New York: Oxford University Press.

Mbaabu, I. (1985). *Sarufi Ya Kiswahili*. Nairobi: Kenya Publishing & Book Marketing Co. Ltd.

Mbotela, W. (1979). *Jifunze Kiswahili*, Vol.2. Nairobi: Swahili Language Consultants & Publishers.

Mdee, J.S. (1986). *Kiswahili: Muundo na Matumizi Yake*. Nairobi: Intercontinental Publishers.

Mfaume, E.G. (1983). "A Dependency Grammar Approach to the Study of Word Order Changes in a Swahili Declarative Sentence." MA Dissertation, University of Dar-es-Saalam.

Mohamed, S.A. (1988). "The Forgotten KI- in Swahili." *Kiswahili, Journal of the Institute of Kiswahili Research* 55.

Mshindo, H.B. (1987). "The Uses of "ka" in Pemba Swahili Variety." MA Dissertation, University of Dar-es- Salaam.

Mushingi, T.S. (1989). *"Vernacular Languages as Media of Instruction: The Case of Swahili in Zaire."* Ph.D. Dissertation, George Town University.

Myachina, E.N. (1981). *The Swahili Language*. London: Routledge & Kegan Paul Ltd.

Nurse, D. and T. Spear (1985). *The Swahili: Reconstructing the History and Language of an African Society*. Philadelphia, PA: University of Pennsylvania Press.

Perrot, D. (1969). *Teach Yourself Swahili*. New York: David Mckay Company, Inc.

Polomé, E. (1967). *Swahili Language Handbook*. Washington, D.C.: The Center for Applied Linguistics.

Reynolds, K.H. (1989). "The Structure of the Kiswahili Nominal." Ph.D. Dissertation, University of Washington.

Roderick, A.J. and P. Rosenbaum (1968). *English Transformational Grammar*. Blaisdell Publishing Company.

Russel, J. (1992). "From Reanalysis to Convergence: Swahili-Amba." *Linguistics* Vol 16, pp. 121-138.

Sawie, M. (1980). "Discourse Reference and Pronominalization in Arabic." Ph.D. Dissertation, Ohio State University.

Steere, E. (1976). *Handbook of the Swahili*. London: Society for Promoting Christian Knowledge.

Telemans, G.M. (1977). "A Morphotactical Section Analysis of the Swahili Verb with Implications for the Teaching of English to Speakers of Swahili." Ph.D. Dissertation, Teachers College; Columbia University.

Vitale, A.J. (1981). *Swahili Syntax*. Dordrecht-Holland/Cinnaminson, U.S.A.: Foris Publications.

Wesana-Chomi, E. (1973). "Towards the Syntax of Complex Sentences in Swahili." *Kiswahili: Journal of the Institute of Kiswahili Research*. Vol, 43, pp. 30-51.

Wesana-Chomi, E. (1974). "Subordinate Adverbial Clauses in English and Swahili." Ph.D. Dissertation, University of New York.

Whiteley, W.H. (1969). *Swahili: The Rise of a National Language*. London: Methuen & Co. Ltd.

Wilson, P.M. (1970). *Simplified Swahili*. Hong Kong: Longman Group (FE) Ltd.

Zawawi, S. (1971). *Kiswahili Kwa Kitendo*. New York: Harper and Row.

———— (1971). *"An Appraisal of the Present Tense in Swahili and a New Formulation."* MA Dissertation, Columbia University.

———— (1974). *"Loan Words and their Effect on the Classification of the Swahili Nominals: A Morphological Treatment."* Ph.D. Dissertation, Columbia University.

Ziadeh, F, and R.B. Winder(1957). *An Introduction to Modern Arabic*. Princeton, NJ: Princeton University Press.

Vocabulary

Swahili - English

Following is a summary of vocabulary items used in this book after each exercise. The list is arranged alphabetically and contains only nouns, verbs, adjectives and a few adverbs. The listed verbs are in their stem form and are numbered in their last letter if they carry more than one meaning. Other verbs which carry more than one meaning but have not appeared in the vocabulary list of each exercise have not been listed below.

abadan	never	askari wa polisi	policeman
abiri	travel	athiri	influence
abiria	passenger	aya	paragraph
achia huru	acquit	azima	borrow
adabu	manners	azimio	resolution
adhabu	punishment	badili	change
adhibu	punish	bafu	bathroom
adhiri	discredit, demean	bagua	discriminate
		baharia	sailor
adimika	be scarce	bahasha	envelope
aghalabu	usually	bahati	luck
ajali	accident	bahati nasibu	lottery
ambia	inform, tell	bahili	miser, stingy
amini	believe, trust	bakora	stick
-aminifu	honest	bakunja	stupid person
amkia	greet	bandari	harbour
amua	decide	bashasha	humour
amuru	instruct	bashashi	humorous person
andama (1)	sight (v)		
andama (2)	chase, follow	bata mzinga	turkey
angamia	perish	bawabu	doorkeeper
anguka	fall, drop	beba	carry
anika	put out to dry	bendera	flag
anza	start	beramu	placard
ardhi	land	bidii	diligence
asali	honey	bila ya sababu	without a reason
asherati	prostitute		
asilani	never	bilauri	tumbler
askari wa		binafsi yangu	personally
mgambo	militia	birika	kettle

257

boga	pumpkin	chunguza	investigate
bohari	godown, store	daftari	book
bomba	pipe	dari	ceiling
bomoa	break, destroy	desturi	customs
bonde	valley	dhahiri	clear
boriti	pole	dhambi	sins
boya	buoy	dhifa	party, banquet
bovu	rotten	dhihaki	ridicule, mock
buibui	spider	dua	prayer
burebure	unnecessarily	dumu	last
busara	wisdom	dungu	cockpit
bweka	bark	durusu	revise
bwege	stupid person	-embamba	narrow
chafu	dirty	embe	mango
chafua	spoil, disrupt	endelea	progress
chagua	appoint, elect	endesha	operate
chamba	insult	enea	spread
chana (1)	tear	fagia	sweep
chana (2)	comb	fagio	broom
chandarua	mosquito net	fahamisha	explain
chanua	blossom	fahamu	understand
chapisha	publish	fanya (1)	do
chemka	boil	fanya (2)	hold
chapuchapu	hurriedly, quickly	farasi	horse
		fenesi	jackfruit
chimba (1)	dig	ficha	hide, conceal
chimba (2)	harm	fidia	compensation
chirizika	trickle	fifia	fade, disappear
chokoza	tease	fika	arrive
chombo	vessel	fo-fo-fo	absolutely, utterly
chomoza	appear		
chopi	lot	fuata	imitate
chukia	dislike, hate	fufua	revive
chukiza	disgust	fuga	domesticate
chukua (1)	match	fujo	chaos
chukua (2)	carry	fundibomba	plumber
chuma	pluck	funga (1)	close
chumvi	salt	funga (2)	fast
chunga	sift	fungua	release
chungu	cooking-pot	furaha	happiness
chungua	spy	gari	vehicle

ghala	store, barn	hundi	cheque
ghali	expensive	husudu	admire
ghasi	disturb	idara	department
godoro	mattress	imara	firm, steadfast
gololi	marble	ingia ndani	enter
goma	strike, refuse	ishara	signal
gonga	strike	ishi	live
gulio	market	ita	call, summon
-gumu	difficult	iva	become ripe
gunia	sack	jabari	brave
gundi	glue	jadili	discuss
gwaride	parade	jalada	cover (of a
hadhari	care, caution		book)
hadithi	narrate	jambazi	villain
hafla	reception	jambia	dagger
hajiri	emigrate	jamii	meeting
hakika	certainly	jangili	crooked person
hakimu	judge	jaribu	attempt
hakimu mkuu	senior magis-	jarida	newspaper
	trate	jasusi	spy
halmashauri	council	jaza	fill
hama	vacate, emi-	jela	prison
	grate	jembe	hoe
hamaki	get angry	jeneza	coffin
hamu	anxiety	jeshi	army
haribu	spoil, destroy	jibu	answer
harufu	smell	jificha	hide oneself
harusi	marriage	jifunza	learn
hatari	danger	jirafu	fridge
hatimaye	eventually	jirani	neighbour
hifadhi (1)	preserve	jitihadi	work hard
hifadhi (2)	read by heart	jitimai	sorrow
hitaji	require, need	jiunga	join oneself
hitimu	end, graduate	jongea	move nearer
hofu	fear	jogoo	cock
hoi	tired	juhudi	effort
hongo	bribe	jukumu	task
hotuba	speech, sermon	kaanga	fry
hudumu	serve	kabati	cupboard
hujumu	invade	kabili	face, confront
hukumu	judge	kadhalika	also

259

kadhia	report, affairs	kifungu	passage
kagua	check	kihori	a small canoe
-kaidi	obstinate	kijana	youth
-kakamizi	obstinate	kijuujuu	superficially
-kali (1)	fierce	kikwelikweli	genuinely
-kali (2)	severe, harsh	kilemba	turban
-kali (3)	sour	kima	monkey
-kali (4)	strict	kimbunga	hurricane
kama (maziwa)	milk	kina	depth
kamata	catch, arrest	kinyozi	barber
kamba	prawn	kiongozi	leader
kambi	camp	kipanga	falcon
kandanda	soccer	kipele	pimple
kanisa	church	kipupwe	cold season
kapu	big basket	kiri	confess
karafuu	cloves	kirimu	entertain
karatasi	paper	kishada	kite
karibisha	welcome	kitalu	courtyard
karibu	soon	kitambulisho	identity card
karibuni	recently	kitisho	intimidation
karimu	generous, hospitable	kito	jewel
		kivuli	shadow
kasha	chest	kiwanda	factory
kashfa	scandal	kiwanja	pitch
kasi	speed	kizibao	waistcoat
kasirika	be angry	kodi	rent
kataa	refuse	kohoa	cough
kataza	forbid	kokota	pull
katibu muhtasi	private secre-tary	kongamano	symposium
		kopesha	lend
kelele	noise	kosa	mistake
kemea	rebuke, blame	kubali	agree
kera	disturb, vex	kufuru	blasphemy
kibaba	measure of a pint or pound	kuku	hen
		kumbusha	remind
kibanda	hut	kunde	French beans
kichochoro	alley	kusudia	intend, deter-mine
kidhi	satisfy		
kifaranga	fowl	kuukuu	old
kiranja	prefect	kwa makelele	loudly
kifungo	button	kwa wingi	abundantly

kwaruza	scratch	maridadi	dandy
laani	curse	maringo	boasting, graceful gait
labda	perhaps		
ladha	taste, flavour	masaibu	hardships
laini	soft	mashariki	east
lala	sleep	masharti	terms
lalamika	complain	masihara	jokes, jest
lambo, bwawa	dam	mateka	prisoner
laumu	blame, rebuke	matumaini	spirits
legea	be loose	mawingu	clouds
leso	handkerchief	maziko	funeral
leta	bring	mazungumzo	conversation
lia	ring	mbeleni	ahead
likizo	leave	mbinguni	at the sky
lima	cultivate	mboga	vegetable
linda	guard	mbolea	fertilizer
lingana	resemble	mchana	daytime
lugha	language	mchawi	wizard
lulu	pearl	mchimba migodi	miner
maandamano	demonstrations	mchochole	poor
machachari	restive, restless	mchoraji	artist
mada	topic	mchukuzi	porter
madhehebu	denomination	mchuuzi	hawker
madhubuti	firm	mdahalo	debate
maendeleo	progress, development	mfadhili	donor
		mfanyabiashara	businessman
mahari	dowry	mfanyakazi	workman
mahuluku	human being	mfuasi	follower
maiti	corpse	mfungwa	prisoner
majinato	pomposity	mgeni	guest
majira	season	mgomo	strike
majununi	lunatic	mgogoro	deadlock
makala	article, passage	mgonjwa	patient
malighafi	raw materials	mgonjwa wa ukimwi	AIDS patient
maliza	complete		
manyoya	feathers	mhadhiri	lecturer
maonyesho	exhibitions	mhariri	editor
maonevu	injustices	mhasibu	accountant
mapema	early	mhojiwa	interviewee
mara moja	at once	mhunzi	blacksmith
mara kwa mara	frequently	milele	forever

milki	property	mvuvi	fisherman
mimina	pour on	mwaga	spill
mjeledi	whip	mwanaanga	spaceman
mjomba	uncle	mwanakijiji	villager
mkaazi	inhabitant	mwanamke	woman
mkaguzi	inspector	mwanariadha	athlete
mkalimani	interpreter	mwanasiasa	politician
mkurufunzi	tutor	mwandishi	writer
mkwasi	rich person	mwanzoni	in the begin-
mlango	door		ning
mlevi	drunkard	mwashi	mason
mlingoti	mast	mwasi	rebel
mlinzi	guard	mwembe	mango tree
mlolongo	queue	mwenda kwa	pedestrian
mmea	plant	miguu	
motoni	hell	mwewe	African kite
mpagazi	porter	mwiba	thorn
mpaka	till	mwiko	large cooking
mpango	plan		spoon
mpito	transition,	mwishoni	at the end
	interim	mwizi wa	
msafara	caravan	nyumba	burglar
msafiri	passenger	Myunani	Greek
msaliti	traitor	mzalendo	nationalist
msasi	hunter	mzigo	luggage
mshahara	salary	mzinga	cannon
mshtaki	plaintiff	Mzungu	European
mshtakiwa	accused	nasaha	advice
msiba	misfortune	ndoa	marriage
mtaalamu	scholar	ndovu	elephant
mtabiri	fortune teller	neemeka	prosper
mtama	millet	ng'ara	glitter
mtawala	ruler	nguruwe	pig
mtemi	chief	nguvu	force, power,
mtende	date tree		strength
mtihani	examination	nidhamu	discipline
mtoto mdogo	infant	nishati	energy
muogeleaji	swimmer	njia	road
muhimu	important	njiwa	pigeon
mvua nyingi	downpour	nunda	wild (cat)
mvulana	boy	nunua	buy

nyama ya		penda	like
nguruwe	pork	pendeza	impress
nyakua	snatch	penya	penetrate, enter
nyamaza	keep quiet	peperuka	fly away
nyanyua	lift, raise	piga kura	vote
nyati	buffalo	pindua	topple
nyesha	rain	pinduka	overturn
nyoa	shave	pita	pass
nyoka	snake	poa	become cool
nyota	star	pokea	receive, accept
nyumbu	mule	polisi	policeman
nzi	fly	ponya	treat
ogopa	fear	pora	steal
okoa	save	poromoka	collapse,
omba	beg		fall down
ondoka	leave, depart,	potea	get lost, miss
	take off	poteza wakati	waste time
ondosha	abolish	pumzika	rest
ongea	converse, talk	punde	soon
opoa	save	pupa	hastiness
ota	grow	puuza	ignore
oza	rot	pwani	shore
paa (1)	deer	rabsha	disorder,
paa (2)	go up		confusion
pagaa	carry	raha	happiness
palilia	cultivate	raia	citizen
pamba	cotton	rais-mteule	president-elect
panda (1)	grow	ramani	map
panda (2)	ascend, go up	ratiba	programme
pandisha	hoist	rejea, rudi	return
panga	hire	rejesha	return
papa	shark	rithi	inherit
papo hapo	immediately	riwaya	novel
parafujo	screw	riziki	necessities of
pasuka	split, burst		life
pata nafuu	recover	ropoka	prattle
patana	agree	rotuba	soil, fertility
patikana	obtainable	rudi (1)	shrink
payuka	prattle	rudi (2)	return
peleleza	investigate	rudi nyuma	retreat
pembe	horn	rufani	appeal

ruka (1)	jump	sihi	advise
ruka (2)	fly	sikia	hear
rungu	club	-sikivu	obedient
rusha	throw	silaha	weapon
rushwa	bribe, kickback	simama (1)	stop
saa	watch	simama (2)	stand
sabahi	greet	sinzia	doze
safiri	travel	siri	secret
safirisha nje	export	sita	hesitate
saga	grind	sogea	come nearer
sahani	plate	soma kwa moyo	recite
saidia	assist	staajabu	wonder, be sur-prised
salama	peace		
salimu	greet	stahili	deserve
samaki	fish	stawi	prosper, flour-ish
sana	severely, hard		
sanduku	box	subira	patience
sauti	voice	sukari	sugar
sawazisha	neutralize, equalize	sumbua	hassle, annoy
		sumu	poison
sebule	sitting room	sungura	rabbit
sega	honey comb	tabia	character, habit
shamba	plantation	tabiri	foretell
shangwe	rejoicing, demon-stration of joy	tafuna	bite
		tafuta	seek, search
		taga	lay eggs
shawishi	persuade	tajiri (1)	rich person
shehena	cargo, freight	tajiri (2)	employer
sherehe	celebrations	taka	want
sherehekea	celebrate	takrima	reception, warm wel-come
shetani	devil		
shida	problem		
shika moto	start	tamthilia	play
shinda	win, defeat	-tamu	pleasant, nice
shirika	corporation	tangatanga	wander, loiter
shiriki	participate	tangaza	announce
shirikiana	cooperate	tangazo	announcement
shona	stitch, sew	tango	cucumber
sifa	commendation, praise	tanua	expand
		tapakaa	spread
sifu	praise	tapika	vomit

tarafa	division	ubadhirifu	extravagance
taraji	expect	ubao	plank
taratibu	slowly	uchangamfu	cheerfulness
tarishi	messenger	uchumi	economy
tatua	solve	udhi	annoy
teka (1)	fetch	ufalme	kingdom
teka (2)	conquer	ugua	suffer, be ill
teketeza	destroy	ufukoni	to the shore
tekeleza	fulfil	uhamisho	transfer
teleza	slip	ujenzi wa taifa	nation building
tembelea	tour	ukame	famine
tenga	separate	ukimwi	AIDS
tengeneza	repair	ukoo	family
teremka	disembark	ukumbi	hall
teseka	suffer	ukuti	coconut leaf
tetesi	rumour	ukweli	truth
thakili	cruel	uliza	ask
thamani	value	uma	fork
theluji	snow	umoja	unity
thubutu	dare	unga mkono	support
tia	put	upande	side
tibu	cure	upelelezi	investigation
tii	obey	upepo	wind
-tiifu	obedient	upesi	quickly, easily
timu	team	ushujaa	bravery
tisha	frighten	usoni	in future
toa	extract, produce	utumwa	slavery
toboa	pierce	uwongo	lies
tokea	occur	uza	sell
toroka	escape	uzungu	European way
toweka	disappear		of life
tua	land	viazi vikuu	yams
tukana	insult	vibaya	severely
tumia (1)	exploit	vimba	swell
tumia (2)	spend, use	vipusa	spare parts
tusi	insult	vita	war
twaa	take	vizuri	well, effectively
twiga	giraffe	vota	win
ua	kill	vua	undress
uadui	enmity	vuja	ooze
uangalifu	care	vuma	blow

vunja (1)	break	zama	be drowned,
vunja (2)	dissolve, cancel		sink
vuruga	spoil, disrupt	zamani	formerly
vuta	pull	zana	implements
vutia	attract	zembe	lazy
wajibika	be accountable	ziara	visit
waka	burn	zilizala	earthquake
wanguwangu	hurriedly	zima	extinguish
wasaa	time, opportu-	zindua	awaken
	nity	zirai	faint
wasili	arrive	zoa	pick up
waza	ponder, think	zomea	boo
woga	cowardice	zulia	carpet
yai	egg	zuga	deceive
yosayosa	hurriedly	zuia	ban
zaa	bear	zungumza	converse
zagaa	prevail	zuru	visit

Index

adjective 63
Adjectives 63
adjectives, vowel stem 54, 58
adjectives:
  agreement of 63
  consonant stem 63
adverbs 93
Adverbs of place 96
Adverbs:
  of degree 97
  of frequency 97
  of manner 97
  of time 96
adverbs:
  types of 96
allomorph 22, 37
allophone 10, 11
Amba relatives 180, 186
Appositional constructions 249
articulation,
  Manner of 4, 5
articulation, places of 2, 3
aspiration,
  in Swahili 7
augmentative verb 220
auxiliary verbs 80

backward pronominalization 114

causative verb 215
class prefix 21, 26
class-prefixes,
  bantu 26
clause 227
Clauses of purpose 238
clauses:
  kinds of 231

cleft constructions 186
cleft transformation 223
complementary distribution 11
composition 35
compound nouns 35
conditional tenses:
  Recent findings on 168
Conjunctions 103
conjunctions
  subordinating 103
conjunctions:
  coordinating 103
Consonant clusters 7
consonant clusters:
  constraints governing 8
consonantal clusters vii
Consonants 3, 4
consonants:
  dental 4
Consonants:
  aspiration in 7
consonants:
  alveolar 4
  glottal 4
  labiodental 4
  Morphophonemic changes
    affecting 23
  velar 4
contraction 20
conversive verb 219
Copular sentences 241
Copular verbs:
  in Swahili 85

Demonstrative adjectives 67
Demonstratives 27
Derivation 29

Descriptive adjectives 66
Deverbatives 29
devoiced 7
diphthong 5
Double class membership 47

five cardinal vowels 2
Formation of nouns 31
forward pronominalization 115
fricative 8
fricatives 5, 24
future tense 134

general relatives
    see tenseless relatives 181
generalizing pronouns
    see quasi pronouns 113
grammatical categories 35
    causative 35
    conversive 35
    prepositional 35
    reciprocal 35
    stative 35
grammatical categories:
    passive 35

harmorganic 3
Hindi 7
homographs 13

imperative 72
Imperative, clauses 240
imperative plural 73
Indefinite markers 28
infinitive form 71
Infinitive subordinate clauses
    240
inflectional affixes 26
Interdependent constructions
    249
interjection 119

Interjections 118, 119
interjections:
    terms sometimes used as 119
Interrogative adjectives 67
Interrogative, clauses 240
Interrogatives 28
Intonation 13
intonation:
    functions of 18

JI-MA Class 30
Juncture 19

Lamu 145
lax 7
lexical units 37
linguistic unit 10

M-WA class 29
Main clauses:
    kind of 240
Medial clusters 8
monomorphemic 37
Monosyllabic verbs 128
monosyllabic verbs 73
morpheme 36
morphemes:
    Bound and free 37
morphology vii, 220
Morphophonemic change 22
Morphophonemic changes 20
Morphophonemic changes affect
    consonants 24
morphophonemic changes:
    feature of 21

Narrative use of -KA- 161
nasals 5
Negative conditional tense 156
negative future 145
negative imperative 74

negative past 148
negative present 142
negative subjunctive:
  uses of 76
NGALI Tense 166
NGE Tense 165
NGELI Tense 167
Nominal derivation 29
nominal groups:
  Identification of 222
NOUN CLASSES 40
  KI-VI class 42
  M-MI class 40
  N-N class 43
  JI-MA class 41
  KU- class 46
  M-WA class 40
  PA- class 47
  U-U class 45
Noun formation 32, 34
Numerical adjectives 67

object prefix 60
object prefixes:
  direct 60
  indirect 60

palatalization 24
passive verb 205
Past and future imperfect 156
Personal pronouns 27
phoneme 10, 11
phonetic classification 7
Phonology 1
Phonology, Swahili 1
phonotactic rules 9
Pitch 13
Possessive adjectives 66
possessives 28
Predicator, in Swahili 228
prepositional verb 209

prepositions:
  examples of 100
Present negative 197
Present participle function 155
Present perfect tense 131
pronominal forms 27
Pronominalization 114
pronominalization:
  constraints in 115
Pronouns 108
pronouns:
  Demonstrative 111
  Emphasis of 113
  Interrogative 112
  personal 108
  possessive 110
  Quasi 113
  Relative 112
  types of 108
pseudo-cleft 186
pseudo-cleft sentence 187

Quasi-adjectives 68

rankshifted clauses 184
reduced relative clauses 177
Reduplication 220
relative clause 177, 179
relative clause:
  Syntactic position of the 192
relative clauses:
  Constraints in 185
  functional definition of 182
  Multiple uses of 183
  Syntactic function of 184
Relative of place 194
Relatives of manner 191

semivowels 5
sentence, the 244
  Complex sentences 245

269

sentence, the:
Compound sentences 248
simple past tense 127
simple prepositions 100
sound,
fricative 5
lateral 5
voiced and voiceless 6
speech, the organs of 3
static verb 219
stative verbs 213
stops 5
Stress 12
stress:
In Swahili, 12
use of 12
subject prefix 58
subject prefixes 48
subjunctive forms 75
Subordinate clauses 232
Subordinate clauses of cause
(reason) 235
Subordinate clauses of
concession 237
Subordinate clauses of condition
234
Subordinate clauses of manner
239
Subordinate clauses of place 238
Subordinate clauses of purpose
237
Subordinate clauses of result 239
Subordinate clauses of time
(temporal clauses) 238
Suffix -A 34
Suffix -E 33
Suffix -I 29
Suffix -JI 30
Suffix -JI:
M-WA class 30
Suffix -O:
function 31

Suffix -U 30
Suprasegmental 12
Swahili adjectives:
types of 66
Swahili class 58, 60
Swahili consonants vii
Swahili consonants,
Articulatory systems of 6
Swahili derivational suffixes 206
Swahili phonology vii
Swahili verbs 205
Swahili:
allophones in 10
complex prepositions 102
consonant clustering, in 8
contraction in 20
five cardinal vowels 1
Forms of demonstrative
markers 175
negative tenses 141
Nominal forms 26
nominal stem 26
pitch in 13
possessive pronouns in 110
possessive stem 28
relativization in 180
secondary vowels 2
Word formation in 26
syllabic consonant 11
syllable 11
syntax vii

tense 7
tenseless relatives 181
tenses:
Combination of the 167
Negative conditional 168
Syntactic function of the 167
tone pattern 13
triphthong 5

U-U class 30
unit of grammar
  see morpheme 36
unit of pronunciation 11

Verbal derivation 35
Verbal stems 28
verbs
  varieties of 80
VERBS - 1 71
Vowel stem adjectives 54, 55
Vowels vii, 1
Vowels, production of 1

Word order 65

Zanzibar 145
Zero-predicated sentences 241

CPSIA information can be obtained
at www.ICGtesting.com
Printed in the USA
LVHW111921090822
725527LV00003B/262

9 789966 467614